Poor Britain

POOR BRITAIN

Joanna Mack and Stewart Lansley

Foreword by A.H. Halsey

London
GEORGE ALLEN & UNWIN
Boston   Sydney

George Allen & Unwin (Publishers) Ltd,
40 Museum Street, London WC1A 1LU, UK

George Allen & Unwin (Publishers) Ltd,
Park Lane, Hemel Hempstead, Herts HP2 4TE, UK

Allen & Unwin, Inc.,
Fifty Cross Street, Winchester, Mass. 01890, USA

George Allen & Unwin Australia Pty Ltd,
8 Napier Street, North Sydney, NSW 2060, Australia

First published in 1985

British Library Cataloguing in Publication Data

Mack, Joanna
  Poor Britain.
1. Poor—Great Britain
I. Title   II. Lansley, Stewart
305.5′69′0941   HC260.P6
ISBN 0-04-336082-3
ISBN 0-04-336083-1 Pbk

Library of Congress Cataloging in Publication Data

Mack , Joanna.
  Poor Britain.
Bibliography: p.
Includes index.
1. Poor—Great Britain.   2. Economic assistance,
Domestic—Great Britain—Public opinion.   3. Public
welfare—Great Britain—Public opinion.   4. Public
opinion—Great Britain. I. Lansley, Stewart.   II. Title.
HC260.P6M32   1985   305.5′69′0941   84-28305
ISBN 0-04-336082-3 (alk. paper)
ISBN 0-04-336083-1 (pbk. : alk. paper)

Set in 11 on 12 point Garamond by Mathematical Composition Setters Ltd,
7 Ivy Street, Salisbury, Wiltshire, England
and printed in Great Britain by
Hazell Watson and Viney Ltd.,
Aylesbury, Bucks.

Dr Owen: While wishing the Prime Minister a happy Christmas . . .

Mr Boyes: Humbug.

Dr Owen: . . . may I ask whether she is aware that 15 million people in Britain – that is the official figure – will be living at or below the poverty line this Christmas? . . .

The Prime Minister: I recognise the right hon. Gentleman's very studied question. Before I answer him, may I ask him which definition of poverty he is using to reach that figure?

Dr Owen: It is the official Government statistic relating to the 3 million unemployed families, the 6 million families that are living on low wages and pensioners who face high costs for rented accommodation. If she checks that total, she will find that 15 million Britons are at or below the poverty line.

The Prime Minister: There is no Government definition of poverty. There are some 7 million people who live in families that are supported by supplementary benefit. There are many other different definitions of poverty, which is why I asked the right hon. Gentleman to say which definition he was using. Many of the low-paid on supplementary benefit have incomes about 40 per cent above that level. They are wholly artificial definitions. *The fact remains that people who are living in need are fully and properly provided for.*

[The House of Commons,
22 December 1983, emphasis added]

Contents

xii *Contents*

Conclusions

List of figures

List of tables

All tables are taken from the LWT/MORI *Breadline Britain* survey (1983), unless otherwise stated.

Preface and Acknowledgements

This book is based on the London Weekend Television series *Breadline Britain*, first broadcast in the summer of 1983. The series examined the lives of the poor in Britain in the 1980s. It was based on a major survey of people's living standards, conducted by Market and Opinion Research International (MORI). The four programmes were illustrated through the eyes of seven families representative of the poor.

These two sources also provide the bulk of the material for this book, though the context in which they are used is somewhat different. While the television series aimed to provide a broad-ranging introduction to the nature of poverty and its causes, illustrated vividly through the day-to-day experiences of the poor, the book's aim is more specifically to develop a new approach to the measurement of relative deprivation and poverty and to examine public attitudes to the role of the welfare state.

Although the book provides a detailed analysis of the original data provided by the LWT/MORI survey, it assumes no prior knowledge of either the academic literature or statistical techniques. Indeed, we hope that the book is readily accessible to any person interested in the future for the poor. Throughout, the theoretical arguments are illustrated by reference to the lives of the poor today, drawn in the main from the seven families featured in the television series but also from the many other families who helped us during the making of the series.

A lot of people contributed towards the making of the television series and the writing of the book. We are indebted to them all.

The survey itself was an enterprise depending critically on the contributions of others. The conceptual framework for the survey originated in conversation with Vic George. The design of the survey was a joint effort between the *Breadline Britain* team and MORI; in particular we would like to thank Steve Schiffers of LWT who extensively researched the Social

Science Research Council's survey archives for ideas and Brian Gosschalk of MORI who directed the survey with great understanding of what was required. In devising the questionnaire, we called extensively on the advice of Peter Townsend, Richard Berthoud, David Piachaud and Peter Taylor-Gooby. We would also like to thank Keith Hughes of the TAB Shop for his efficient and speedy programming of the computer analysis of the survey data.

Many people at LWT, either currently or recently, contributed towards the making of the *Breadline Britain* series or the production of the book. We would like to thank Su Wilkins, who co-researched the series; David Tereshchuk, the initial editor of the series, and his successor Julian Norridge; Paul Coueslant of LWT's community unit; Mary Murphy and her team in the library; and Jackie Gooden who typed Part II of the book. In particular, we are grateful to Jane Hewland, head of features at LWT – without her advice and support neither the television series nor this book would have been possible.

Vic George, David Piachaud, Peter Golding, Fran Bennett and Peter Taylor-Gooby have been kind enough to plough through earlier drafts of various chapters of the book. Their comments were all extremely useful and pertinent. Liz Paton has greatly improved the style and clarity.

Many others have contributed in many other ways to the project. In particular, we would like to thank A. H. Halsey, whose comments and encouragement have been greatly valued; Meghnad Desai for the statistical analysis he carried out to test for an 'income threshold'; the staff of both the Child Poverty Action Group and the Low Pay Unit, who were always ready to help in providing information and comments; and Harold Frayman, who has had the patience to discuss the project right from its conception – regularly, in depth, in detail and as a result no doubt *ad nauseam*.

However, perhaps above all we would like to thank all the families and individuals currently suffering great hardship who nevertheless had the courage to help us in the making of *Breadline Britain*. We wish to remember Ernie Pegman who died soon after his eightieth birthday. At the age of 79, he told us:

> All I think about is when I reach the age of 80 that's me lot, I don't want to live no longer. Because I've had enough, haven't I, of worry. It's a disgrace when you get to such an age and you got to worry. It doesn't say much for the society we live in.

This book has been written with the hope that in some small way it might help promote the kinds of changes in society that would improve the lives of the millions of people now living in such desperate circumstances.

The views and opinions expressed in the book are, of course, our responsibility and ours alone.

JOANNA MACK
STEWART LANSLEY

October, 1984

Foreword

by Professor A. H. Halsey

Poverty and Plenty

Joanna Mack and Stewart Lansley have written a sober book on a sombre subject. Poverty and how it should be dealt with can never be far from the concerns of any society: for society is essentially an evolved apparatus for the protection and enrichment of life and the prevention or delay of death. Society means a shared life. If some and not others are poor, then the principles on which life is shared are at issue: society itself is in question. All societies have either solved the question or perished. In modern society, where the means of solution include an historically-unprecedented command over nature, the question, somewhat paradoxically, becomes more rather than less urgent. To the degree that mankind dominates nature, so the expectation of plenitude is raised in every group and individual within society. Governments in rich societies face sterner tests of the legitimacy of their role in distributing the fruits of a more powerful human control of the sources of plenty.

Moreover and more particularly, Britain in the mid eighties faces the poverty question in a still more difficult form. Contemporary Britain has a peculiar history. Because it was the first democracy and the first industrial nation it was the place *par excellence* in which the promise of *shared riches* was born earliest and most vigorously developed. Because it was the country in which the idea of political democracy was most securely founded it became also an island in which the idea of citizenship, which is democracy beyond the polling booth embracing ultimately all social and economic as well as political relations, could be most extensively elaborated. British governments, especially since the Second World War, have been accordingly exposed to especially strong demands for fair distribution and have been especially vulnerable to any sustainable charge of social injustice or failure of compassion.

Still more threatening to the frailty of government is that political parties in such a developed democracy are subjected to the chronic temptation, if not the virtual necessity, of bidding against each other in promises of delivery of the demanded combination of affluence with fair shares. And competitive hustings are played out on a stage with stronger illumination of the varied life and fortune of all the classes, status groups, regions, and ethnic communities which make up the society. Single-interest pressure groups add to the footlights and the chorus. On this view the part of Government in dealing with poverty is played against a background of increasing glare and noise.

At the same time some of the props which traditionally served to mute the social drama have been at least partially removed. In Victorian Britain the class structure and the status order reinforced each other to stabilize and perpetuate a society which was *both integrated and unequal*. The legitimacy of the unequal shares of wealth and income generated by a free market in capital and labour was widely accepted. Poverty was therefore accepted as an unavoidable, if regrettable, law of political economy. And the solutions lay not so much with governments as with private individuals and voluntary associations in self-help and charity. The Friendly Societies and Co-operative Societies of the urban industrial working class and the Charity Organisation Society of the middle class were energetic social responses to a class structure which some applauded, others resented, and most accepted in the hope that 'progress' would gradually mitigate and eventually abate its most tragic consequence – undeserved poverty.

The status order supported these responses. Working-class respectability disciplined the use of meagre resources among millions of families depending for their survival on manual labour. Horizons restricted by monochrome residential districts inhibited resentful comparisons. Educational and occupational opportunities widening, however slowly, held out the hope of a better future, sanctioned success, and justified failure. But the experience of the middle years of the twentieth century has weakened status support for class-based poverty. Labour governments demonstrate that the superior classes are not necessarily born to rule. They also demonstrate that a working man's party in government is no guarantee that poverty will be ablolished. Such experiences, by eroding trust in political hierarchy and political authority, further reduce more general belief and confidence in society itself.

Under these conditions the most likely victims are the poor. But even then the catalogue of British difficulties is incomplete. So far I have summarily listed only the rising popular demands and expectations of a mature democracy with a long history of economic growth. To this list of difficulties for Government must also be added the more recent history of reversal of national fortune. Britain in the twentieth century has lost its empire and its place as the leading industrial economy. Put in the terms now current in international press and television, what was once a leading if not *the* leading world power is now a declining off-shore island of Europe with a fate perhaps closer to Portugal or Greece than to the USA or the USSR. Britain of course shares with other industrial countries the series of economic recessions which began with the oil crisis of 1973. Despite becoming herself an oil producer, Britain has fared conspicuously badly as an economy in the past decade. These recent failures have reduced, or at least been perceived as reducing, our *capacity* simultaneously with the rise of more stringent demands on our performance as a country committed to protecting all citizens from poverty.

The response in the mid and late seventies seemed to have confirmed this pessimistic diagnosis. A political party was returned to power in 1979 which had in effect announced its intention to solve the problem by disavowing governmental responsibility for it. Poverty, according to the resurgent doctrine of market liberalism, was a problem for the private sector. The duty of government was to diminish itself, to release the powers of enterprise, to encourage the creation of wealth and so to reduce poverty. It is probably significant that Mrs Thatcher's government was first elected by a people which had revealed itself in international studies in 1976 as the one among all the peoples of Europe which was most inclined to blame the poor for their poverty, to see the causes of poverty in failures of individual character and exertion rather than in imperfection or incompleteness of the welfare services.

What, then, is the prospect surveyed by Joanna Mack and Stewart Lansley on the basis of the LWT/MORI poll of 1983 and their appraisal of current political and parliamentary debate? Time and opinion have moved on. Unemployment has multiplied massively since 1979 to become a national disaster. Poverty on the conventional definition of receipt of supplementary benefit has risen in melancholy harmony with the unemployment figures. Unemployment is plainly seen as a principle cause and its incidence is perceived as largely beyond the capacity of its victims to control. Public willingness to accept higher taxation so as to relieve poverty is less than either logic might decree or compassion invite: but public disapproval of the social policies of the Conservative government has become the mood of the majority and seems to be reflected in less muted, more explicit opposition on the Conservative benches of the House of Commons.

The authors of this study welcome these recent shifts of attitude towards the poor. But that is not their most important purpose, nor the signal value of their book. Their more fundamental contribution lies in defining and measuring the extent of poverty in Britain today. That contribution can be the better appreciated if the history of how the poor have been conceived and counted is briefly recalled.

A hundred years ago controversy raged in Britain over the question of what proportion of the population was in poverty. The Marxist theory of an increasing polarization of society between bourgeois rich and proletarian poor was stridently asserted by H. M. Hyndman and the Social Democratic Foundation and supported by propagandist pamphleteering of which *The Bitter Cry of Outcast London* is the best remembered. The liberal reaction, apart from Christian socialist active concern, was to attempt precise measurement. Charles Booth's and later Rowntree's surveys were landmarks of charitably inspired but rationally disciplined measurement. That Booth confounded Hyndman only to be widely misreported by radical propagandists need not concern us here. What is important is that a submerged tenth was identified and that the criteria for defining poverty were essentially absolute. The idea of poverty in the minds of the liberal social investigators was that of an income sufficient to maintain bare subsistence by an individual or family practicing rigorously ascetic rationality in the spending of meagre resources.

The approach to measuring poverty through absolute definitions has, and will always have, utility. Such a definition offers a firm base on which to gauge trends, whereas a relativist approach in its simplest form (the x per cent with the lowest incomes) guarantees that the poor are always with us. But an absolute definition passes authority to some external judge – a physiologist or economist or medical expert – and ignores the subjective state of either the advantaged or the disadvantaged members of society. The relative approach strives for internal or participative judgement recognizing that we are 'members one of another'. Its notion of poverty is cultural. The poor are poor in comparison with other members of society. They are excluded from sharing in the normal life of their country. So a relative approach must be added for a full appraisal of poverty: and the rise of citizenship, together with the increasing visibility of variation in standards of living, gives further point to relativist descriptions.

It is here that the present book makes its relevant contribution. The authors have defined poverty by asking a cross-section of British people to specify what elements of material life they regard as necessary to minimal sharing in contemporary British society. The answers would have been different in Booth's time or in Cannes or Calcutta now. They reflect current British conceptions of the indispensable decencies. And it turns out that there is a high degree of consensus as to what these decencies are. Then, given the definition, it is a relatively simple task to count and map the poor, to describe what they are denied, and to draw the correlates (of age, sex, occupation, education, and employment) which are associated with poverty. Finally, the authors use the survey to assess the attitudes of the nation to its poor and the willingness of the fortunate to relieve the unfortunate.

The book deserves wide attention. A minority believes that the Thatcher administration already has affected policies for a rich future in which the halt, the sick, and the lame will be properly cared for. Another minority seeks destruction of the social order followed by a new regime in which the welfare of all will be ensured. The majority is neither impressed by the Thatcher performance nor persuaded by the promise of revolution. On either path they fear the threat of a new polarization – a society divided between those who are and those who are not securely employed in a 'high tech' economy. Poverty always threatens the social order. The political challenge, now more urgent than ever, is to devise fair ways of distributing new plenitude from a new industrial revolution. Neither market liberalism nor Marxist revolution has plausible answers. The plight of the new poor needs patient democratic government for its relief. Joanna Mack and Stewart Lansley offer one simple tool in the service of a complex machinery of social reintegration. Their yardstick of poverty makes sense of the way we now live. It constitutes a powerful indictment of present policy and offers a clear guide to the action required in a responsible democracy.

A. H. Halsey
Oxford
December 1984

Introduction

1

Going Down

The growing ranks of the poor

When you're in work, you just think to yourself, oh, I've got a job, tell the truth you think I'm alright Jack. You don't worry about things like unemployment until it happens to you – and then it hits you like a bomb. Your standard goes down and it just keeps going down, and it's difficult to get back up again. You're going down and down and you're trying to get yourself up and you just seem to go down more. [Unemployed father of three]

For most of the postwar period, poverty has been largely a forgotten problem. The early successes of the postwar economic and social policies lulled people into believing that deprivation and hardship belonged to the past. Throughout the 1950s, unemployment remained comparatively low, welfare spending steadily grew, modest economic growth was sustained. This prosperity contrasted sharply with what had gone before.

During the mass unemployment of the 1930s, hunger and hardship were an all too common experience. The war itself required sacrifices from the mass of people. For some their lives were devastated as their homes and possessions were all destroyed. For many there were material hardships never previously experienced. But after the war, as rationing faded out, living standards improved – and not just to what had once been known but, for the majority of people, to new heights. By the end of the 1950s the Prime Minister, Harold Macmillan, could proclaim that people had never had it so good. The poor could be forgotten.

In the 1960s, Britain's economy began to falter. Poverty

was 'rediscovered' by academic researchers. New pressure groups were founded to promote the cause of the poor. The impact on the public consciousness was small, however. To the extent that the 'rediscovery' of poverty was more widely accepted, the poor themselves were often seen to be to blame.

In the 1970s, the poor came to be blamed not just for their own problems, but also for the nation's. Britain was increasingly seen to be in a rapid decline. In the desperate search for explanations, the poor became scapegoats. Welfare spending, it was claimed, was too high. Money was being 'diverted' away from the 'real' economy. The incentive to work hard had, it was said, been taken away by the 'generosity' of public 'handouts'. The poor were scroungers; their plight unrecognised.

In the 1980s, all this began to change. As Professor A. H. Halsey has observed, the problems of the poor have returned to the nation's agenda:

> With more people unemployed even than in the depths of the depression of the 1930s, it is not surprising that there is widespread interest in and anxiety about poverty. At a time when state intervention as a means of government is being questioned and public expenditure reduced, the old questions of who are the poor, what causes poverty and how it can be cured, are all raised afresh. (LWT, 1983)

The growth of 'poverty'

The impact of the recession and the impact of the government's social policies are the two key reasons for the renewed concern about 'poverty'. While these two factors are, of course, intertwined, both are of critical importance.

Unemployment has more than doubled since 1979. Most of those who join the ranks of the unemployed experience a sharp drop in living standards and, for those who have been unemployed for any length of time, the consequent hardship is intense. In the mid-1980s, over 1 million people had been unemployed for over a year.

The recession has also affected the labour market in other ways that have been detrimental to the poor. Pay differentials have widened sharply since 1979. Those low-paid manual workers who have managed to stay in work have suffered a deterioration in their relative pay: in 1978, the lowest-paid 10 per cent of male workers earned 66.8 per cent of the national average; in 1983, their earnings had fallen to 64.1 per cent of the average. At the same time, the highest-paid 10 per cent saw their earnings rise from 157.9 per cent of the average to 169.7 per cent. It is the poor who have born the brunt of the recession.

The government has done little to mitigate these trends. Indeed, when Mrs Thatcher came to power in May 1979, she was committed to a radical change in the role of government. All previous postwar governments had acted to offset the increases in inequality that had resulted from the changes in the distribution of income through the labour market by increasing welfare spending. The Thatcher administration was committed to 'rolling back' the frontiers of the state. Although the consequent changes have been less radical than heralded, they have nevertheless fuelled the trend towards a more unequal society. The latest official figures on the distribution of income only go up to 1981/2 (Central Statistical Office, 1984), but the mark of the new Conservative government is clear. The share of after-tax income received by the bottom 10 per cent declined from 2.9 per cent in 1978/9 to 2.4 per cent in 1981/2, while the share of the top 10 per cent increased from 23.4 per cent to 25.6 per cent. The share of the super-rich (the top 1 per cent) also rose: from 3.9 per cent to 4.6 per cent, marking the first increase in the share taken by the super-rich since 1949.

There have been many government policies that have contributed to these trends, the most important being the changes in taxation and social security. Since 1979, the national level of taxes on incomes (income tax and national insurance contributions) has risen. However, while the low-paid have had to hand over an increased proportion of their wages to the state, the burden of tax on those on the highest incomes has, by contrast, fallen. Overall, the well-off and the rich have gained about £2,600 million between 1979 and 1984 from tax concessions. At the same time, there have been several changes in social security that have made those dependent on benefits poorer. Earnings-related supplements for all short-term benefits – unemployment and sickness benefit, and maternity and widow's allowance – were abolished from April 1981. This hit, in particular, the rising number of people unemployed for less than six months, who were as a consequence forced on to supplementary benefit. In addition, the statutory link between long-term benefits, such as pensions, and earnings was repealed and these benefits were increased in line with inflation only. Housing benefit has also been sharply cut. All in all, benefit cuts over the life of Mrs Thatcher's first term in office amounted to some £1,600 million, most of which represented a cut in the incomes of the poorest sections of the community.

Finally, changes in housing policy have also served to reinforce social and economic inequalities. In particular, subsidies for local authority housing have been cut substantially. From 1978/9 to 1983/4, housing subsidies to council tenants were reduced by 60 per cent, and as a consequence rents rose over that period at double the rate of inflation. Council house rents are now higher in relation to earnings than at any time since the war. At the same time, the cuts in housing benefit mean that many tenants are receiving less help in paying these ever-increasing rents. By contrast, the tax concessions enjoyed by those buying their own home through a mortgage have been protected. Indeed, the upper limit on tax relief on mortgage interest payments was raised from £25,000 to £30,000 in April 1983. Given the sharp polarisation of society by income and class between owner-occupation and local authority housing, these changes have sharply exacerbated inequalities. The result of all these trends has been that the living conditions of many of the poor have declined.

On top of this, there has been an increase in the numbers of people living on low incomes. This trend is clearly shown by looking at the numbers living on or around the supplementary benefit level. The aim of supplementary benefit is to ensure that all those who are not in full-time work do not fall below a set income level. The minimum income level provided by supplementary benefit is sometimes called the 'state's poverty line'. From 1960 to 1977, the estimated number of people living *below* the supplementary benefit level remained roughly constant at around 2 million. From 1977 to 1979, the number rose slightly to around 2.13 million. In the next two years this number rose by nearly a quarter to reach 2.64 million (DHSS, 1983). Since then, the government has stopped publishing the figures on an annual basis, and now publishes them every two years. The number of households with incomes *equal* to supplementary benefit has also risen. In 1983, over 7 million people were dependent on supplementary benefit, a rise of 16 per cent since December 1981 and of 60 per cent since December 1979. If we assume that the number below supplementary benefit has risen since 1981 at the same rate as in the previous two years, then the numbers of people living *on or below* the supplementary benefit level stood at 8.6 million people in 1983. This compares with just over 6 million in 1979.

Researchers have, however, often used another measure for estimating the numbers on or below the 'state's poverty line'. Instead of taking the supplementary benefit scale rates on their own, a level of 140 per cent of the supplementary benefit rate is taken. This is to allow for the fact that most claimants have incomes that are higher than the basic rates. This results from the extra 'special needs' allowances that many claimants receive and the fact that claimants are allowed to keep a small amount of income from earnings and savings on top of their state benefit. If this level is used, some 15 million people – more than a quarter of the population – were in 'poverty' in 1981.

The debate about 'poverty'

These measures of 'poverty' are by no means universally accepted, however. The Prime Minister herself has described them as 'wholly artificial definitions' – and, indeed, they are precisely that. Although the supplementary benefit rates are approved by parliament each year, they are not based on any assessment of what people need.

The level of supplementary benefit is, in many ways, an historical accident. Based on its predecessor, national assistance, the rates stem from the level laid down by the 1945 Labour government when it set up the modern social security system. This, in turn, was the result of various compromises made when translating the recommendations of the Beveridge Report, *Social Insurance and Allied Services* (Beveridge, 1942), into law. The levels set down in the Beveridge Report, while stemming from the research work of Seebohm Rowntree, were in turn essentially arbitrary. All that has happened in the intervening years is that national assistance and then supplementary benefit have been uprated, generally, either in line with inflation or with earnings. But there has never been any overall assessment of why one particular level of supplementary benefit should be chosen rather than another.

Although the numbers on or around the supplementary benefit level provide useful information on the distribution of income in society and although the numbers below the supplementary benefit level provide an assessment of the failures of the system on its own terms, neither measure provides an agreed estimate of the extent of 'poverty'.

The problems with using the supplementary benefit level to define the numbers in poverty have long been recognised. For example, J. C. Kincaid argued in the early 1970s:

> There is no good reason why official definitions of financial poverty should be accepted as having any special validity. Government policy is based on what it thinks can be afforded at any particular time rather than on judgements about the income people need to maintain any kind of decent existence... Since the Second World War, no British Government has ever carried out an inquiry to establish the minimum amount of income which people *need*. (Kincaid, 1973, p.179)

This gap remains as true now as in the early 1970s. Governments have sponsored studies into how supplementary benefit claimants cope (see, most recently, Berthoud, 1984), but there has never been an assessment of what people need. The most important postwar attempt to fill this gap was a pioneering and original survey by Professor Peter Townsend (1979), but the fieldwork was done in 1968-9 – it is now fifteen years out of date.

The *Breadline Britain* survey

The main purpose of the *Breadline Britain* survey was to try, in a modest way, to update the work of Townsend. This book is largely a report of these findings. Though our approach differs from that adopted by Townsend in a number of significant respects, the study belongs firmly to the same tradition. In particular, the study attempts to measure the extent of poverty not in terms of some arbitrary income level but in terms of the extent to which the poor are excluded from the way of living that is expected and customary in society today. This requires a survey not just of the poor but of the rest of society as well.

The main aim of the survey was, then, to provide an assessment of what it is that people need for living in Britain in the 1980s and in what ways people fail to meet these standards. The central idea of the study is that poverty can be defined in terms of 'an enforced lack of socially perceived necessities'. To pursue this theme, the survey had to gain information in two main areas. First, and for the first time ever, the public's view on what constitutes a minimum living standard was tapped. Second, a complementary set of information on people's actual living standards had to be established; a comprehensive look at people's 'ways of living' had not been attempted since Townsend's survey.

On the basis of these data, a new approach to the measurement of the extent of poverty is developed. In turn, this provides a new basis from which to evaluate the effectiveness of the welfare state.

The survey had, however, one further important aim: to examine attitudes towards the role of the welfare state, in particular in relation to the poor. In the context of the debate in recent years about the role of the welfare state and of the government's current review of social security spending, the public's views on these questions are of interest. The survey set out to identify public attitudes to state provision for the poor, to inequality and to specific anti-poverty measures.

To investigate these questions, London Weekend Television commissioned Market and Opinion Research International (MORI), a company specialising in political and social opinion polls and survey research, to design and conduct the *Breadline Britain* survey. The fieldwork was carried out in February 1983 with a quota sample of 1,174 people from throughout Britain. The sampling method is discussed in Appendix A, pp. 287–290, but as the book relies heavily on the opinions of this sample it is worth drawing out some general points.

The sample was designed, first, to enable a view representative of the population as a whole to be gained and, second, to ensure that the sub-group of the poor was large enough to enable their living standards to be examined. The first of these aims has been achieved. The checkbacks made on the weighted sample as a whole – whether on, for example, age of the respondents or housing tenure – show that the sample is in line with Britain's population profile. The survey's findings that refer to the sample as a whole can be taken to be representative of the adult population of Britain.

The second aim was more difficult to achieve within the cost constraints of the survey. The sample was designed to ensure a high representation of poor households and, in general, the analysis of the living standards of the poor is based on a sub-group of about 200 households. This means that when the figures refer specifically to this group they are somewhat less precise than those for the whole sample (for statistical detail see Appendix A). Clearly, a larger sample would have been desirable but, in general, the findings give a good guide to the scale of deprivation suffered by the poor

The *Breadline Britain* survey does, then, provide up-to

date information on the comparative living standards of the poor and attitudes to the poor. Although the picture is at times painted with broad strokes, it does throw light on the overall situation of the poor today. It is a light that is much needed for there is a great sparsity of other information. While the official national surveys of income and living conditions, in particular, the Family Expenditure Survey and the General Household Survey, provide a wide range of important information, none of them offer a comparative picture of people's 'ways of living' or, more importantly, any assessment of need. Further, the government's analysis of these surveys in terms of the poor is limited. It produces only a handful of tables, and recently this has been cut back to just every other year.

There is, moreover, some concern that information about the hardship suffered by the poor is 'suppressed'. For example, on 16 June 1984, *The Economist* reported in a short article headed *Print no Evil*:

> Whitehall is using its muscle to suppress an international report on the poverty created by long-term unemployment in Britain and other industrialised countries . . .. The subject is a sensitive one.

Poor Britain

This book tackles these politically sensitive areas. At its core there is one fundamental question: are the poor in Britain in the 1980s too poor? The answer affects all the other questions on the future for the poor.

In the House of Commons on 22 December 1983, Mrs Thatcher stated boldly:

> . . . people who are living in need are fully and properly provided for.

Part I of this book sets out to establish whether or not this is the case. With more and more people living on low incomes, the question of whether their consequent living standards are adequate is of considerable political significance. We also hope that in answering this question we have contributed to the academic debate on the definition and measurement of poverty.

In Part II of the book, we turn to public attitudes to the poor and to welfare spending. It provides an indication of the impact of the recession and soaring unemployment on such attitudes. In addition, with a government committed to 'rolling back the frontiers of the state', it throws light on the scope for this kind of action within welfare policy. Finally, and perhaps most importantly, this study provides some indication of whether the kinds of action needed to improve the lot of the poor would gain public support.

PART I

Poverty in Britain in the 1980s

2

How Poor is too Poor?

Defining poverty

> Because I'm on sup. ben. my kids don't get what other kids get. It's just as simple as that. They just don't. They miss out on a lot of things. I consider I'm poor and if you look at other people, working people, you're at the bottom. [A single parent living on supplementary benefit]

The poor in Britain may be much better off than in the past, but they remain excluded from the way of life that most people take for granted. In comparison with the standard of living of others around them, it seems to the poor that they and their children miss out. Mary is a single parent with a 5-year-old son:

> Now he is at school, and tells me about other children's bikes, and the toys they take, and holidays, and days out with parents, and it breaks my heart for there is nothing for him; if he has food and clothes he can have nothing else.

Mary feels that her situation is not just unsatisfactory but unjust. However, while the feelings of the poor are important, they do not provide an adequate answer to the question: how poor is too poor? Perhaps this single parent is simply being unreasonable in wanting toys, or even more so holidays, for her child.

This chapter examines the problem of determining how poor is too poor. How do we decide whether children today should be entitled to toys and holidays; or whether food and clothes are enough; or even what sorts of food and what quality of clothes? On what terms are such decisions made?

There have been many approaches over the years to tackling these questions. This chapter will develop a new approach to the concept of poverty based on the views of society generally. Before we examine this idea, however, we look back at earlier attempts to define poverty, for the approach of this study is based on the lessons learnt.

The search for an 'absolute' poverty line

Throughout this century there have been proponents of the idea that it is possible to draw up an absolute minimum standard of living on the basis of what is required for physical health or fitness. It is this kind of concept that lies behind the view that there is no real poverty in Britain today. Although this view would have few adherents in academic circles, it is none the less highly influential, being a popular notion and more specifically carrying weight among the present Conservative party leadership. For example, Sir Keith Joseph, Secretary of State for Education and one of the leading figures on the 'New Right', has argued:

> An absolute standard means one defined by reference to the actual needs of the poor and not by reference to the expenditure of those who are not poor. A family is poor if it cannot afford to eat. (Joseph and Sumption, 1979, pp. 27–8)

While the political right is on its own in tending to view 'poverty' exclusively in these 'absolute' terms, others, too, have found the concept of 'absolute' poverty useful. For example, Tony Crosland argued in *The Future of Socialism*:

> Primary poverty has been largely eliminated; the Beveridge revolution has been carried through.... It is true that considerable areas of social distress, not mainly due to primary poverty and of a character not always

foreseen by pre-war socialists, still remain. But that is a new and different question. (Crosland, 1964, p. 59)

The concept of 'absolute' or 'primary' poverty was developed during the last century. Though it is now associated with attempts to limit the needs of the poor, at the time it was seen as a way of drawing attention to the plight of the poor. Seebohm Rowntree, in his classic study of poverty in York in 1899, defined 'primary poverty' as an income 'insufficient to obtain the minimum necessaries for the maintenance of merely physical efficiency'. He ruled out spending on 'the maintenance of mental, moral or social sides of human nature'. Spending on food, clothing and shelter was all that he allowed:

A family living upon the scale allowed for must never spend a penny on railway fare or omnibus. They must never go into the country unless they walk. They must never purchase a halfpenny newspaper or spend a penny to buy a ticket for a popular concert. They must write no letters to absent children, for they cannot afford to pay the postage. They must never contribute anything to their church or chapel, or give any help to a neighbour which costs them money. They cannot save nor can they join a sick club or trade union, because they cannot pay the necessary subscriptions. The children must have no pocket money for dolls, marbles or sweets. The father must smoke no tobacco and drink no beer. The mother must never buy any pretty clothes for herself or her children, the character of the family wardrobe as for the family diet being governed by the regulation 'nothing must be bought but that which is absolutely necessary for the maintenance of physical health and what is bought must be of the plainest and most economical description'. (Rowntree, 1922, p. 167)

Rowntree's aim in adopting such a stringent definition was to demolish the view that poverty was due to fecklessness and not to low wages. He felt he had established his case when he found that 15 per cent of the working-class population of York were, in 1899, living in 'primary poverty'. However, his findings in themselves posed contradictions and problems. Clearly the 15 per cent in 'primary poverty' were surviving. They may have been hungry, they may have faced ill-health, they may even have suffered a relatively high death rate, but none of these concepts provides a clear-cut line on which to base an absolute minimum living standard. Throughout the nineteenth century, some did die directly from poverty through starvation, but in general the results were less dramatic. Friedrich Engels, writing about a harsher period some fifty years earlier, describes the effect of poverty on those at the bottom of the pile:

> To what extent want and suffering prevail among the unemployed during such a crisis, I need not describe. The poor rates are insufficient, vastly insufficient; the philanthropy of the rich is a raindrop in the ocean, lost in the moment of falling; beggary can support but few among the crowds. If the small dealers did not sell to the working people on credit at such times as long as possible – paying themselves liberally afterwards, it must be confessed – and if the working people did not help each other, every crisis would remove a multitude of surplus through death by starvation. Since, however, the most depressed period is brief, lasting, at worst, but one, two, or two and a half years, most of them emerge from it with their lives after dire privations. But indirectly by disease, etc., every crisis finds a multitude of victims. (Engels, 1969, p. 121)

This poses an intractable problem for Rowntree's concept of 'primary' poverty. There is no doubt that poor health stems from low living standards and that this makes a person susceptible to dying from disease, but others too die from disease. The susceptibility to disease and the level of life expectancy that are acceptable depend not on some absolute criterion but on the standards and expectations of the day. If this is true of Rowntree's aim of the 'maintenance of physical health' in relation to the simple question of survival, it is even more so of his aim of 'physical efficiency'. Concepts such as 'good' health' and 'fitness' are nebulous. Although Rowntree followed closely the contemporary developments in dietetic science, his nutrition levels remain not the absolute scientific statement he presumed but a level determined by the assumptions and judgements of the day. Professor A. H. Halsey summarised the unsolvable problem of the search for an absolute poverty line for the *Breadline Britain* series:

> There are some people who would want to make poverty entirely objective by seeking a measure of it outside people's heads and outside people's expectations and outside society's norms. And they sometimes think that death might do the trick for them. But it is not like that. Because of course the expectation that people have of how long they will live will always depend upon their expectations of others. It will depend on a socially created idea of life and death. And so even the use of mortality statistics is itself an essentially relative approach to poverty.

To argue that even mortality is relative is not to deny the importance of the fact that there are still in the world today many people who die of starvation, for whom poverty is an immediate cause of death. A. K. Sen has powerfully argued that for this reason there remains an important role for the concept of 'absolute' poverty:

> While it can hardly be denied that malnutrition captures only one aspect of our idea of poverty, it is an important aspect, and one that is particularly important for many developing countries. It seems clear that malnutrition must have a central place in the conception of poverty. (Sen, 1982, p. 14)

Sen's detailed studies of famine and starvation in the world today have led him to conclude:

> There is an irreducible core of absolute deprivation in

our idea of poverty which translates reports of starvation, malnutrition and visible hardship into a diagnosis of poverty without having to ascertain first the relative picture. The approach of relative deprivation supplements rather than competes with this concern with absolute dispossession. (Sen, 1978).

Although it is possible to draw up a minimum food level below which people die of starvation, and although such a concept still has widespread applicability in parts of the world, nevertheless even in many of the poorest of the Third World countries there would generally be a life expectancy greater than that of simply staving off immediate death. Living standards may be unquestionably low and life expectancy well below that of the industrialised world (and at times below that of earlier generations); even so, much of the deprivation suffered is not, strictly speaking, 'absolute' poverty.

Neither does this emphasis on the relativity of mortality deny the importance of improvements in life expectancy during this century. The poor of today – like everyone else – are likely to live considerably longer than their counterparts a hundred years ago. That of itself is of considerable significance. We can say that the poor of the nineteenth century were worse off than the poor of today, but this does not necessarily mean that the poor of the nineteenth century endured some kind of 'primary' or 'real' poverty with a living standard below an 'absolute' minimum required for health. If the standards of living of the poor of the nineteenth century are to be judged in terms of the effect on their health and life expectancy, then these judgements have to be based on the standards prevalent at that time and not on some 'absolute' criterion or on the standards of today. By the standards of the nineteenth century, the poor of the day may well be judged to have been unacceptably deprived. But that is a different judgement from that entailed in claiming that they lived in 'absolute' poverty.

This means that, while the search for a universally applicable 'absolute' poverty line above that of staving off starvation is in vain, there may still be poverty lines that can be drawn on the basis of life expectancy, or some kind of concept of good health. These 'poverty lines' would be specific to each society and to each generation. A poverty line for the 1980s would have to be drawn by today's standards.

The use of relative health standards to define poverty

For health standards to be of any possible use in defining a poverty line, it must first be established, as a precondition, that the poor in the 1980s still suffer from worse health than others.

Pamela and her 9-month-old baby live in a tiny, one-roomed attic flat in inner London:

> The rain starts falling in from the window; it's going to fall in before long because the sides are falling off. And the beasties start coming up through the floorboard; slugs, beetles, the lot. They start from behind the cooker at first and they start working their way in here. Beasties go all over the bed, the cot and all over the floor. I've been bitten more than once and Emma often gets bitten by them. They go in my food and everything and I can't eat the food at all; I have to throw everything away.

The danger of disease and infection from lack of hygiene is ever present. The health of both Pamela and her baby has suffered, but it is the baby who is most at risk. While these conditions are among the worst, it remains the case that the poor generally, and their children in particular, face greater risk of ill-health and, as a consequence, of death than others.

In 1980 the most comprehensive postwar government inquiry into the health of the nation, headed by Sir Douglas Black, completed its work. (The government severely restricted the circulation of this report but a comprehensive account can be found in Townsend and Davidson, 1982.) Looking at the mortality rates of the different social classes in terms of occupational groupings, the Black Report found that, at all stages of life, those in households where the head is an unskilled manual worker are disadvantaged compared to others. Men and women in unskilled households have a two-and-a-half times greater chance of dying before reaching retirement age than their professional counterparts. The peak of disadvantage is in infancy: the mortality rate for those born into unskilled families is some three-and-a-half times that of those born to professional families. Being poor in Britain today *is* still a matter of life and death.

What is more, the Black Report found that this gap between the chances of the poor and others dying has not changed since the turn of the century. Indeed, more recent evidence suggests that the gap may now be widening. For example, an all-party parliamentary report, drawn up by the House of Commons Social Services Committee and published in July 1984, showed that between 1978 and 1982 the class gap in perinatal deaths had widened (House of Commons, 1984).

Health and poverty remain deeply interlinked. It is not just that the poor are likely to have worse health than others, but also that ill-health is itself a *cause* of poverty. And, in turn, as those suffering from ill-health become poorer so the risks to their health become greater.

Mavis is blind, partially deaf and diabetic. Once, many years back before she lost her sight, she worked. Then, she coped. But now, at the age of 59, she has no chance of any work and depends on supplementary benefit. As a result of her consequent low living standards, her health is at risk; indeed, at times, even her life. She often runs out of money and ends up relying on whatever food happens to be around. She describes here the problems she faced one morning:

> I got some rice crispies somewhere in there and I had some sugar. I put some sugar on the rice crispies which is really supposed to be taboo, but it carries you through. The DHSS have got my life in their hands. And what can you do about it? You take insulin, and go into insulin reaction because you haven't got any

food, or go without your insulin. What happens then?
I think the diabetic specialists could tell you all about
that.

The reasons why the poor run greater risks of death and ill-
health than others are complex and varied. The problems
that Mavis faces, for example, are specific to her disabilities.
In general terms, however, it is possible to identify a person's
standard of living in areas such as housing, diet and heating
as important in determining health and life expectancy. This
was a principal theme of the Black Report and has been
unquestionably established in many other studies (see, for a
recent example, Townsend, Simpson and Tibbs, 1984).

It is because of this link between living standards and
health that there remains a widespread feeling that health
could provide the basis for a 'relative' poverty line, even if it
cannot provide the basis for an 'absolute' poverty line. The
maintenance of life itself is, after all, the most basic and fundamental requirement of a standard of living. However,
without questioning the importance of good health and a
long life expectancy, there remain many basic problems in
using these criteria to establish a poverty line.

Even the most measurable of health criteria – the mortality
rate – does not provide a cut-off point between the poor and
the rest. The poor are more likely to die than the well-off,
but so are those on middle incomes. Going from social class
I to social class V there is a gradual and continuous deterioration in life expectancy. If there was something like an
absolute minimum standard that could be identified on the
grounds of health, one would expect at some point between
the poorest and the richest a sharp deterioration in life expectancy. That does not happen. It is not possible therefore to
identify a mortality rate that indicates where a poverty line
should be drawn. What is or is not an acceptable mortality
rate remains a matter of judgement.

Using a concept of 'good health' is even more problematic,
as has been seen in relation to Rowntree's search for a standard of health sufficient for 'physical efficiency'. Some people
can be identified as fit and in good health, others as unfit and

in poor health; but there will also be many other people in between. Sir Douglas Black summarises the problem this creates:

> The difficulties in using health to set a minimum standard are quite insurmountable because of the nature of the case. It is not as if there was one thing called good health and another thing called bad health. What you actually have is a whole range from people who are desperately ill, right up to people who are running marathon races and so on. There is every grade in between those two, so you could not really select a cut-off point and say 'above that there is good health and below that there is bad health'.

Even if it were possible to identify such a thing as 'good health', the problems in relating this to living standards remain great. For example, bad housing, poor diet and lack of heating affect a person's health, but it is difficult to be more precise. In housing, while dampness is generally perceived to be unhealthy, the extent to which this is, on its own, important remains debatable. Often it is the cumulative effect of many disadvantages that is important. So far as it is possible to be more precise, it is still difficult to identify a minimum level. For example, although there is little doubt that overcrowding favours the spread of infection, this cannot readily be translated into a measure of the minimum number of square metres a person needs to occupy.

Finally, even if such minima can be identified on health grounds, they may bear little relationship to people's actual spending patterns and lifestyles. This is to imply not that people's choices are wrong but that they are based on considerations and influences apart from those of health.

Even Rowntree found, when trying to draw up a poverty line based on the sole criterion of 'physical health', that it was impossible to exclude the influence of society's norms and customs. Having identified a set of dietary minima in terms of calories and proteins, Rowntree had the problem of translating these into actual food purchases. He found, of course, that people's actual food purchases were based not simply on what they needed for health and survival but also on what he called 'national customs'. Rowntree felt that he had to make concessions to this:

> Even the poorest try to get a certain amount of meat; and though undoubtedly health can be maintained without it, we cannot, in selecting a dietary, ignore the fact that meat-eating is an almost universal custom. So is the drinking of tea and coffee, and though these do not actually supply any nutriment, a certain amount must be included in the dietary. (Rowntree, 1937, p. 78)

In doing this, Rowntree undermines the whole concept of setting a poverty line based on the criterion of health. Once tea and coffee have been allowed, why not toys and new clothes, or the many other items and activities that are consumed or desired because of wider social expectations and norms?

Tricia is a single parent with two school-aged children. At Christmas, she gave her son a bicycle worth around £30. This was his only present of the year and to afford this Tricia had saved all year, putting aside a small sum each week. To do this, she cuts back on food for herself: she usually misses breakfast; at lunchtime she just has a cup of coffee; in the evenings, she has a small meal with the children, something like eggs on toast or beans on toast. Recently, her health has been bad:

> Just these last few months, I keep having these dizzy spells and I get a lot of colds. I wouldn't say I feel fit at all. I mean a lot of people go mad at me, and say that I should at least have a dinner and a tea. They say it's not good for you. But I have got used to living the way I am, because you are only limited to what you can buy, and what you can spend, and you get into that way of life, and it's hard to get out of it.

Tricia chooses to make personal sacrifices, even to the detriment of her own health, so that her children do not miss out. If calculations on life expectancy guided people's decisions, then clearly Tricia would choose to eat properly and would anyway not give her child a bicycle, with the risks it brings of road accidents. But people simply do no behave in this way. For a wide variety of reasons, people choose to spend their money on goods and activities totally unconnected with health or even at a cost to it. It may well be that Tricia's friends are right to chide her for not eating properly, but judgements about that cannot be made in isolation from the other social customs and expectations that determine other aspects of one's standard of living.

Even taking a relative view of health or, more specifically, life expectancy does not enable a minimum standard of living to be identified. The question of how poor is too poor needs to be answered in broader terms. This will lead us right back to the way the poor themselves have been seen to judge their situation – in comparison with the living standards of others.

Viewing necessities as socially determined

There has been a long tradition that has tried to define poverty narrowly in terms of health, aiming either for a universal standard or for a standard relative to a particular moment in time. There has been an equally long tradition that has seen a person's needs as being culturally and socially, as well as physically, determined. It is a view that recognises that there is more to life than just existing. Two hundred years ago the economist Adam Smith wrote:

> By necessaries, I understand not only commodities which are indispensably necessary for the support of life but whatever the custom of the country renders it indecent for creditable people, even of the lowest order, to be without. A linen shirt, for example, is strictly speaking not a necessity of life. The Greeks and Romans lived, I suppose, very comfortably though they had no

linen. But in the present time . . . a creditable day-labourer would be ashamed to appear in public without a linen shirt, the want of which would be supposed to denote that disgraceful state of poverty. (Smith, 1812, p. 693)

This theme was adopted and first used for a more practical purpose by Charles Booth in his pioneering surveys of poverty in London from the late 1880s to the turn of the century. He defined the very poor as those whose means were insufficient 'according to the normal standards of life in this country' (Booth, 1888).

Even Seebohm Rowntree, the man who had developed the idea of 'primary' poverty, had, by the time of his second survey of York in 1936, incorporated into his definition of poverty some needs that were not related in any way to the maintenance of physical health. His 1936 definition allowed for items such as a radio, books, newspapers, beer, tobacco, presents and holidays. Although the amounts allowed were small – and largely arbitrary – Rowntree had conceded the importance of a wide range of aspects of a person's standard of living – from consumer durables to leisure activities and social participation.

The essentially relative nature of poverty is immediately obvious when viewing people's standards of living in these broader terms. Purchases of consumer durables are specific to each generation, or even each decade, and activities involving social participation have no meaning outside the society in which people live. This has long been recognised; Karl Marx wrote in 1849:

Our needs and enjoyments spring from society; we measure them, therefore, by society and not by the objects of their satisfaction. Because they are of a social nature, they are of a relative nature. (Marx, 1946, p. 269)

To view necessities as socially determined is explicitly to view poverty as relative. For this reason this concept is often called 'relative poverty'. In practice, there has been a great deal of confusion about the concepts of 'absolute' and 'relative' poverty. In part this stems from a recognition that the living standards of the poor have risen considerably during this century and that it is important not simply to dismiss this. It also stems, however, from a failure to come to terms with the fact that, above starvation level, an 'absolute' definition of poverty cannot be sustained; that, for example, Rowntree's definition of 'primary' poverty was in fact a rather narrow definition of 'relative' poverty at the turn of the century.

The upshot has been that a body of opinion has persisted that places emphasis only on 'absolute' poverty. The fact that the poor in Britain today are better off than the poor of the past, and than the poor of other countries today, is seen to devalue their problems. Dr Rhodes Boyson, as Minister for Social Security, gave his view of 'relative' poverty to the House of Commons in a debate on the rich and the poor called by the opposition:

> Those on the poverty line in the United States earn more than 50 times the average income of someone in India. That is what relative poverty is all about. . . . Apparently, the more people earn, the more they believe poverty exists, presumably so that they can be pleased about the fact that it is not themselves who are poor. (*Hansard*, 28 June 1984)

Others, in contrast, have argued that the facts of starvation in the poorest countries of the world and the intense deprivations suffered by the poor of the past are not relevant to the problems of the poor of the industrialised world today. Tony Crosland, for example, argued not just for the importance of a concept of 'primary' poverty but also that:

> Poverty is not, after all, an absolute, but a social or cultural concept. . . . This demands a relative, subjective view of poverty, since the unhappiness and injustice it creates, even when ill-health and malnutrition are

avoided, lies in the enforced deprivation not of luxuries indeed, but of small comforts which others have and are seen to have, and which in the light of prevailing cultural standards are really 'conventional necessities'. (Crosland, 1964, p. 89)

During the 1960s this view became widely accepted, as a result – at least in part – of the work of Professor Peter Townsend. For the last thirty years, Townsend has argued that poverty can only be viewed in terms of the concept of 'relative deprivation'. In his studies of poverty he has refined this concept, culminating in his 1969 survey of living standards. In his report of this comprehensive and influential study, Townsend defined poverty as follows:

> Individuals, families and groups in the population can be said to be in poverty when they lack the resources to obtain the types of diet, participate in the activities and have the living conditions and amenities which are customary, or are at least widely encouraged or approved, in the societies to which they belong. (Townsend, 1979, p. 31)

Although something like this definition of poverty would now be widely accepted, there remains immense room for debate about what exactly it means.

Can poverty be measured objectively?

Townsend's definition of poverty begs many questions: lack of which living conditions and amenities constitutes poverty? what types of diet are we talking about? lack of participation in which activities distinguishes the poor from the non-poor? Behind these questions lies a more fundamental question: on what basis should such decisions be made? The definition in itself provides little guidance. Are activities that are 'customary' those carried out by, say, 51 per cent of the population or 90 per cent? Are those that are customary the same as those that are 'widely encouraged or approved'?

Townsend contends – and it is hotly disputed – that such questions can be answered 'objectively' – independently of the value judgements not only of individuals but more significantly of society collectively. The ultimate aim of his study, *Poverty in the United Kingdom,* was no less than 'the objectification of the measurement of poverty' (1979, p. 60).

Townsend had set himself a Herculian task. He was out of line with wider opinion, which argued that the interpretation of relative poverty required value judgements. For example, the influential American poverty researcher, Mollie Orshansky, states that:

> Poverty, like beauty, lies in the eye of the beholder. Poverty is a value judgement; it is not something one can verify or demonstrate, except by inference or suggestion, even with a measure of error. To say who is poor is to use all sorts of value judgements. (Orshansky, 1969, p. 37)

For Townsend, such an approach is 'scarcely reassuring'. While he acknowledges the difficulties in eliminating all values from social research, his aim is to develop a methodology that would put the measurement of poverty on to a 'scientific footing':

> In the final analysis, a definition of poverty may have to rest on value judgements. But this does not mean that a definition cannot be objective and that it cannot be distinguished from social or individual opinion. (Townsend, 1979, p. 38)

In Townsend's view, an examination of socio-economic conditions – in particular, the distribution of resources between individuals and the differences in their styles of living – will in itself enable those who are in poverty to be identified. In this approach there are no questions to be answered either by the researcher or, more importantly, by society at large about what people 'should' have or what they 'should' be entitled to. It is only a matter of examining real social conditions. To make this work, Townsend needed to refine his definition of poverty; the notion of 'customary' is vague and the idea of a living style that is 'widely encouraged or approved' appears, moreover, to entail some kind of collective value judgement. So Townsend goes on to state that people can be said to be in poverty when 'their resources are so seriously below those commanded by the average individual or family that they are, in effect, excluded from ordinary living patterns, customs and activities' (Townsend, 1979, p. 31). This provides the conceptual basis for the whole of Townsend's study.

Even at this stage, however, Townsend's definition, far from bringing agreement on the basis on which poverty can be measured scientifically, has been fundamentally criticised. It has been argued, most forcefully by Piachaud (1981a), that implicit in such an approach is a view that society should be uniform:

> As patterns of living become more diverse, it becomes steadily harder and less useful to think in terms of 'ordinary membership of society,' ... The reason for tackling poverty is not to create uniformity, but to push back the constraints and increase choice and freedom. (Piachaud, 1981a)

To explore these criticisms, it is necessary to look briefly at how Townsend translated his general theoretical definition into a practical measure of poverty. It is in making this transition that the problems of establishing a scientifically 'objective' measure of poverty are highlighted most sharply.

The Townsend poverty study

Townsend's study, *Poverty in the United Kingdom* (1979), is based on a major survey that he carried out in 1968–9. This is one of the most ambitious and far-reaching surveys of poverty attempted in Britain and ranks alongside the pioneering work of Booth and Rowntree. Questioning a sample of 2,000 households throughout Britain, he aimed to discover whether,

> as resources for any individual or family diminish, there is a point at which there occurs a sudden withdrawal from participation in the customs and activities sanctioned by the culture. The point at which withdrawal 'escalates' disproportionately to falling resources could be defined as the poverty line. (Townsend, 1979, p. 57)

To do this, Townsend collected, first, a comprehensive range of data on each individual's resources. He included not just cash incomes (earned and unearned) but also capital assets, the values of employment benefits in kind, the value of public social services in kind (such as subsidies to housing) and the value of private income in kind (such as gifts). This attempt to build a more comprehensive definition of income and resources is a particularly important element of the Townsend survey.

Second, Townsend collected information on 'styles of living'. This, too, represents an important development. Townsend replaced the rather narrow concept of 'consumption', which had dominated previous poverty surveys, with an approach that encompassed all aspects of a person's life. This was done by selecting sixty indicators from all the common activities in society: diet, clothing, fuel and light, home amenities, housing, the immediate environment of the home, general conditions and welfare benefits at work, family support, recreation, education, health and social relations. From this, he compiled a 'deprivation index' based on twelve of the items (see Table 2.1).

Townsend went on to identify a poverty line – and hence the numbers in poverty – by a statistical exercise relating household incomes (adjusted for household size) to the degree to which households lacked the items listed in this deprivation index. This method is discussed in greater technical detail in Chapter 6. Whatever the technical merits of the exercise, the basic assumption is that lack of these

Table 2.1 *Townsend's deprivation index*

Characteristic	% of population going without	Correlation coefficient (Pearson) (net disposable income last year)
1 Has not had a week's holiday away from home in last twelve months.	53.6	0.1892 (S = 0.001)
2 Adults only. Has not had a relative or friend to the home for a meal or snack in in the last 4 weeks.	33.4	0.0493 (S = 0.001)
3 Adults only. Has not been out in the last 4 weeks to a relative or friend for a meal or snack.	45.1	0.0515 (S = 0.001)
4 Children only (under 15). Has not had a friend to play or to tea in the last 4 weeks.	36.3	0.0643 (S = 0.020)
5 Children only. Did not have party on last birthday.	56.6	0.0660 (S = 0.016)
6 Has not had an afternoon or evening out for entertainment in the last two weeks.	47.0	0.1088 (S = 0.001)
7 Does not have fresh meat (including meals out) as many as four days a week.	19.3	0.1821 (S = 0.001)
8 Has gone through one or more days in the past fortnight without a cooked meal.	7.0	0.0684 (S = 0.001)
9 Has not had a cooked breakfast most days of the week.	67.3	0.0559 (S = 0.001)
10 Household does not have a refrigerator.	45.1	0.2419 (S = 0.001)
11 Household does not usually have a Sunday joint (3 in 4 times).	25.9	0.1734 (S = 0.001)
12 Household does not have sole use of four amenities indoors (flush WC; sink or washbasin and cold-water tap; fixed bath or shower; and gas or electric cooker).	21.4	0.1671 (S = 0.001)

Source: Townsend (1979), p. 250.

twelve items provides a measure of poverty. It is this assumption that Piachaud (1981a) and others (for example: Wedderburn, 1981; Sen, 1982; and Hemming, 1984) are disputing.

Consider, first, the situation of those who lack items from this 'deprivation index'. Piachaud argues that Townsend has left out a vital factor – choice:

> To choose not to go on holiday or eat meat is one thing: it may interest sociologists, but is of no interest to those concerned with poverty. To have little or no opportunity to take a holiday or buy meat is entirely different. (Piachaud, 1981a)

The alternative view is that a person who has never had a holiday, for example, may not miss it and so may feel that they 'choose' to go without, but nevertheless 'objectively' they remain deprived. In other words, the concept of 'choice' is, on this interpretation, misplaced, because an individual's perception of whether or not they are exercising choice will itself depend on the extent to which they are deprived. The *Breadline Britain* survey was designed to throw light on the extent to which an individual's perception of choice is determined by their income level and this debate will be discussed in greater detail later (see Chapter 4). It is worth noting here, however, that the high proportion of the population lacking certain of these items – for example the two-thirds of the population not having a cooked breakfast most days of the week (see Table 2.1) – suggests that, at least for some people for some of the items, the lack is based on a choice that has not been determined by income.

The second criticism of Townsend's deprivation index is more fundamental: why should the lack of *these* items – even if it was limited to those who do not possess them through lack of choice – be taken as a measure of poverty? Townsend puts forward one principle for the selection of an item: namely, that only a minority of the population should lack it. However, as Townsend notes, this principle has not been kept to in practice: three items are lacked by over 50 per cent of the population. The principle itself is in keeping with

Townsend's concept of poverty as exclusion from 'ordinary' styles of living. That said, it is still not clear why these twelve items have been chosen. They are all negatively correlated with income (see Table 2.1) – in other words, the poor are significantly less likely to have them than others. But there are other items from the sixty included in the survey that the poor are less likely to be able to do or possess than others and that a majority of the population have: for example, the purchase of new clothes. Why is it, then, that not having a cooked breakfast, an activity that most people do not partake in, is included in the deprivation index but not being able to buy new clothes, which by contrast only 10 per cent of the population are forced into, is not taken as a measure of poverty? To many it may seem that not being able to buy new clothes is a better indication of deprivation than not having a cooked breakfast.

Townsend argues that he compiled other indices with other combinations of items and the results produced were similar. The people who lack any particular range of items are likely also to lack other specific ranges of items. The fact that the specific items selected for the deprivation index are arbitrary or random could, then, be seen to be unimportant.

A major problem still remains: why are *any* of these items so important that to go without is to be deprived? On what basis can it be said that the items are indicators of poverty? For Townsend it is sufficient that the items represent common activities, widely practised. That said, however, what does lack of these items really measure?

Clearly, a high score on Townsend's deprivation index gives some indication of the numbers and types of people who are not participating in 'ordinary living patterns'. This in itself does not necessarily imply 'poverty'; to a greater or lesser extent, all those in the bottom half are not fully participating in society. Indeed, Townsend recognises this problem. He equates this lack of participation in ordinary living patterns with poverty only when there is 'a level of deprivation disproportionate to resources'.

As such, it is central to Townsend's identification of poverty that there is an income 'threshold' below which people disproportionately withdraw from participation in these 'ordinary living patterns'. The question of whether there is such a 'threshold' will be considered in Chapter 6. It is worth noting here, however, that even if such a threshold exists it seems conceptually an unsatisfactory way of defining poverty. If there was no threshold and instead what was observed was a steady decline in people's living standards as they become poorer, then it may still be the case that the people at the bottom end are in poverty. Indeed, the living standards of the people at the bottom end under these circumstances might be little different from those of the poor if an income threshold did exist. The existence or otherwise of a threshold has little to do with the standard of living of the poor but is dependent on the distribution of resources and living standards throughout society. This is not to challenge the concept of an income threshold – and in Chapter 6 its use will be explored – but to argue that such a threshold does not provide a *prima facie* measure of poverty.

The basic problem stems, in our view, from the distinction Townsend draws between an 'objective' and a 'socially perceived' measure of need:

> A fundamental distinction has to be made between actual and perceived need, and therefore between actual and socially perceived poverty – or more strictly, between objective and conventionally acknowledged poverty. (Townsend, 1979, p. 46)

In aiming to exclude value judgements from the assessment of 'need', Townsend inevitably comes up with indicators of 'need' that are difficult to interpret. The items in his 'deprivation index' have *not* been chosen because they fit in with a generally accepted view of need. The result of taking a concept of 'need' that is outside people's feelings and experiences is that the consequent 'deprivation' suffered from these unmet 'needs' is outside people's comprehension.

In short, observation of facts about the distribution of resources and the distribution of standards of living tells us a great deal about inequality and about the social structure of society, and as such is extremely important. But it tells us nothing about poverty. This, in essence, is at the heart of Piachaud's criticisms of Townsend's work:

> The term, 'poverty', carries with it an implication and a moral imperative that something should be done about it. The definition by an individual, or by society collectively, of what level represents 'poverty', will always be a value-judgment. Social scientists have no business trying to preempt such judgements with 'scientific' prescriptions. (Piachaud, 1981a)

A new approach to poverty

While generally accepting this statement about the nature of poverty, it is worth clarifying what we understand to be implied. We are not arguing that poverty is, in the words of Orshansky, merely 'in the eye of the beholder', that it is purely a subjective phenomenon. Nor are we arguing against pursuing a rigorous interpretation, putting aside as far as is possible our own personal value judgements. Instead we are arguing for a measure of poverty based on the social perception of needs. A. K. Sen, while arguing for the use of a concept of 'absolute' poverty, has also argued that there is an important role for a relative view of poverty. He has lucidly distinguished between the different ways in which the role of morals can be accommodated in poverty measurement:

> There is a difference between saying the exercise *is itself* a prescriptive one and saying that the exercise must *take note* of the prescriptions made by members of the community. . . . For the person studying and measuring poverty, the conventions of society are matters of fact (what *are* the contemporary standards?), and not issues of morality or of subjective search (what *should be* the contemporary standards? what *should be* my values? how do I *feel* about all this?). (Sen, 1982, p. 17)

By examining society's 'prescriptions', it is possible to move towards a definition of poverty that is not merely subjective. Townsend, in contrasting the 'social perception' of need with 'actual' need, has, in our view, obscured the search for an 'objective' measure of poverty. Indeed, it seems to us that there is no such thing as an 'objective' as opposed to a 'socially perceived' measure: items become 'necessities' only when they are *socially* perceived to be so. The term 'need' has, therefore, no meaning outside that of the perceptions of people. Again, this is an argument lucidly advanced by Sen:

> The choice of *'conditions* of deprivation' can not be independent of *'feelings* of deprivation'. Material objects cannot be evaluated in this context without reference to how people view them, and even if 'feelings' are not brought in explicitly, they must have an implicit role in the selection of 'attributes'. Townsend has rightly emphasized the importance of 'the endeavour to define the style of living which is generally shared or approved in each society'. . . . One must, however, look also at the feelings of deprivation in deciding on the style of living the failure to share which is regarded as important. (Sen, 1982, p. 16)

These social perceptions of need are themselves determined by social conditions, in particular by the distribution of resources and of living standards, but also by other factors such as the distribution of power. To put the emphasis on the 'meaning' attributed to social conditions is not to deny that these meanings are themselves socially constructed (this is argued theoretically by, among others, Berger and Luckmann, 1967). The reason why the possession of certain goods and participation in certain activities are seen as 'necessities' is, of course, a legitimate subject for study (and is pursued in Chapter 3). However, the fact that society's perceptions can be questioned and analysed does not, in our view, undermine an approach to poverty based on these perceptions. For, to reiterate, these perceptions determine the importance and significance that can be attached to the various aspects of our living standards.

The social perception of need both stems from the judgements of individuals collectively and, in turn, affects each individual's perception. Individuals sharing the social perception will feel deprived when they lack the items defined by society generally as 'necessities'. While most people will, by definition, share the judgements of society collectively, it is possible that someone who is relatively well-off may feel deprived or that someone who is poor may not feel deprived. These individual feelings are of interest but do not determine whether the person is 'too poor'. Using the concept of the 'social perception' of need, it is possible to step outside the individual's feelings to the judgement of society collectively. This becomes important when poverty is related to policy.

To argue for the importance of the social perception of need is not, however, to argue that the only poverty that can be recognised is 'conventionally acknowledged poverty'. Indeed, there seems to be no reason to assume that these two concepts are the same. There is evidence that the word 'poverty' conjures up different meanings for different people (see, for example, Townsend, 1979, and EEC, 1977), whereas the concept of 'necessities' is by no means so embedded in semantic confusions and political connotations. It seems perfectly possible that there will be people who see 'poverty' as simply about starvation but who take a broader view about what constitutes necessities in society today.

This study defines 'poverty' in terms of an enforced lack of socially perceived necessities. This should be contrasted with Townsend's approach and returns to an earlier, though still dominant, tradition. In Townsend's study, poverty is defined with reference to exclusion from the 'norm', or to the 'customary', or to 'ordinary' living patterns. Reference to a minimum, rather than the norm, is implicit in the definition of poverty as lack of necessities. It is what Townsend classes as 'minimum rights for the many' rather than 'distributional justice for all'. It is argued that the concept of a minimum separates the poor from the rest of society and labels them second-class citizens. For the poor, a 'minimum' living standard is good enough but the rest of us expect far more and may indeed feel we are entitled to far more.

This question of 'distributional justice' is extremely important, but it is a question about the degree of inequality that
should be tolerated in society and not a question about
poverty. Tackling poverty does have implications for the
degree of inequality in society, as is seen in Chapter 6, but,
in principle, the motivation for doing something about
poverty can be quite separate from that of doing something
about inequality. Two people may share the same view about
the generosity of benefits for the poor but hold contrasting
views about the extent to which the rich should be 'entitled'
to personal gain. It is likely that those who are most eager to
tackle poverty will also favour a narrowing of inequality. It is
also possible, however, that some people may regard the
greater equality implicit in tackling poverty as an unfortunate
side-effect.

Although the concept of poverty is distinct from that of
'unacceptable inequality', it is worth noting that it would be
possible to attempt to answer the broader question of 'how
poor is too poor' in terms of the extent of inequality in society. This would require turning from a *description* of the
distribution of resources to judgements about the *fairness*
of this distribution. Many people would argue that extreme
inequality is morally unacceptable. We have not attempted
to pursue this in this study – to ask, for example, whether
people feel that everyone should be entitled to a decent
home if the rich can afford two or more. Though we think
such an approach would be legitimate and valuable, it was
outside our scope.

Our aim was more restricted: to measure 'poverty'. This
too requires value judgements – but these judgements are
about *minima*, about people's *needs*. Although these
judgements will reflect society's prevalent norms, they are
about everyone's *entitlement*, not about the distribution of
resources in society.

There are dangers, for the poor, in the concept of poverty
or in any categorisation that separates poor from non-poor.
Indeed, some policies specifically directed at the relief of
poverty have done as much, and more, harm than good. The
concept of a minimum is not immune from these dangers,

but, in our view, these dangers are far outweighed by the potential advantages for the poor of policies based on minimum standards.

In seeing poverty in terms of 'minimum rights for all', we are in agreement with the Council of Europe, which in 1975 adopted the following definition:

> Persons beset by poverty: individuals or families whose resources are so small as to exclude them from the minimum acceptable way of life of the Member State in which they live. (EEC, 1981)

This adds an important dimension to the definition of poverty based on 'the enforced lack of socially perceived necessities': namely, that poverty affects a person's *way of life*. There are many aspects to our 'way of life' and some people may fall below an acceptable minimum in some aspects but not in others. Deprivation among the poor surfaces in different ways according to particular circumstances. In addition, there are different degrees of deprivation: for some people, the deprivations they face will be relatively marginal; for others, it will affect their whole way of life. In this study, we shall term the enforced lack of any particular necessity as a *deprivation*. These deprivations will only be termed *poverty* when they affect a person's way of life (see Chapter 6).

This is not to imply that there is necessarily going to be a sharp division between those in poverty and others. Indeed, it is likely that there is a continuum of living standards from the poor to the rich, which will make any cut-off point somewhat arbitrary. That said, it is useful, with reference in particular to public policy, to try to distinguish those who can be said, to a greater or lesser degree, to fall below the minimum standards of society from the people who can afford to maintain these standards.

The aim of identifying 'minimum standards' has dominated studies of poverty. Our procedure is, however, distinct. Past studies of poverty – from Rowntree onwards – have in the main attempted to identify 'minimum standards' by a combination of an 'expert' analysis of 'needs' and an examination of actual expenditure patterns. So, for example, people's minimum nutritional requirements are 'identified' by 'experts'; these are translated into minimum 'costs'; which are then converted into a minimum 'income' by reference to the proportion of people's income actually spent on food. These approaches have many problems, of which two, in our view, are critical. First, 'experts' are being asked to define a level for which their 'expertise' does not particularly qualify them. For example, a nutritionist can identify minimum levels of calories and vitamins, but this is not the same as a minimum level of food, which is influenced not only by 'scientific' assessments, but also by customs, traditions and, more generally, a sense of what is right and proper. The second problem concerns the use of people's *actual* expenditure patterns. While measures of poverty must take into account people's actual behaviour rather than just idealise what it should be, using current spending patterns to identify a minimum level is fundamentally unsatisfactory: people's actual expenditure may reflect financial circumstances rather than need.

This study takes a completely different approach. It aims to identify a minimum acceptable way of life not by reference to the views of 'experts', nor by reference to observed patterns of expenditure or observed living standards, but by reference to *the views of society as a whole*. This is, in essence, a *consensual* approach to defining minimum standards.

This is not the first time that an approach based on 'public opinion' has been adopted. Indeed, Rowntree included elements of this in identifying clothing needs. More recently, the EEC has commissioned studies based on this approach in an attempt to identify a minimum acceptable way of life. In two separate studies, one carried out in 1976 by Helene Riffault (EEC, 1977) and the other in 1979 by Professor Bernard van Praag (van Praag *et al.*, 1980; van Praag *et al.*, 1981; summarised in EEC, 1981), the EEC has tried to establish for the different member countries what level of *income* is needed to attain these minimum standards. The 1976 study asked: 'In your opinion, what is the real minimum income on which a family of four persons – a man, woman and two children between 10–15 years – in this area can make ends meet?'; and the 1979 study: 'What do you consider as the absolute minimum income for a household such as yours – an income below which you won't be able to make ends meet?'.

Though these EEC studies are important for their emphasis on the views of people themselves rather than experts, the attempt to establish a minimum standard through the concept of a minimum income causes problems. First, the questions require not only value judgements but also a *factual* knowledge of conditions in society. A person may have in mind a certain standard of living but, because they lack the experience of living at that standard, wrongly estimate the income needed. The second major problem stems from the relationship between income level and standard of living. As many studies have shown (for example, Townsend, 1979; Fiegehen, Lansley and Smith, 1977), there can be considerable variations in the standards of living of people on the same income level. This is discussed further in Chapter 4; the point in this context is that different individuals may have in mind the same minimum standard of living but, because of different responsibilities, estimate different minimum income levels. For example, parents who have to spend £10 a week on child care are likely to say that their net income to make ends meet is £10 more than others who have relatives who look after the children. Such costs are likely to be important factors in people's judgement about what is a minimum net income.

Such factors are, of course, also important in practice in determining the variations in the income people need to maintain a minimum standard of living. It may be that a simple 'minimum income' line that will ensure a 'minimum acceptable way of life' cannot be identified. This question is of considerable importance because the state's approach to poverty is dominated by the maintenance of minimum income levels. However, in our view it is a question that can be answered only after having first established minimum standards of living.

This study proceeds, therefore, by attempting to identify a minimum standard of living *directly*. We asked a representative sample of people to judge the *necessities* for living in Britain in the 1980s. To our knowledge, this approach is original. It should be stressed, at this point, that an important component of any definition of poverty is that the deprivations suffered spring from lack of resources. We accept the need, in principle, to distinguish between, say, those who are vegetarians and those who cannot afford to eat meat. Only those who face what we have termed 'an *enforced* lack of necessities' are classed as living in poverty (see Chapter 4).

The critical role of lack of resources to the concept of poverty also has wider implications, because it determines which aspects of our way of life should be included in a minimum standard of living aimed at measuring poverty. We decided that only those aspects of life facilitated by access to money should be tested in the *Breadline Britain* survey. The method adopted was to select a range of items indicative of various aspects of our way of living and to ask people whether these items were necessities. The survey concentrated on individual or personal aspects of behaviour, which were seen not only in terms of personal 'consumption' but also, following Townsend, in terms of *social* activities. The areas covered were food, heating, clothing, consumer durables, entertainment, leisure activities, holidays, and social occasions and activities. Two services that are provided at least in part by the public sector were also included: housing and public transport. Most housing is provided through the market, but even where it is provided through public services it is paid for directly. While the use of public transport is affected by the degree of subsidy, it remains a service that is primarily paid for.

Other public services were excluded – most significantly, health care and education. Such services are an important influence on each individual's quality of life, but they are not in the main paid for. Of course, the divisions are not clear-cut: a few do pay directly for health care and education and for the rest who use the public services there are often hidden costs. But in general, where such services are facilitated by access to money, it is on the margins or indirectly. Nor did it seem appropriate to include conditions at work. While we recognise that poor working conditions are concentrated among the low-paid, it is not an aspect of life that could readily be improved by higher pay. Similarly, various environmental factors, such as safety on the streets, were excluded, although again these aspects of life are generally worse for the poor than for others.

We accept that each individual's quality of life is affected by a whole range of public services, from sports centres to health care, from an emptied dustbin to education. However, the criticism, made among others by Cyril Shaw (in the letters pages of *The Sunday Times*, 28 August 1983), that the survey ignores 'Galbraith's strictures on public poverty [sic] in the midst of private affluence' is misplaced. As Galbraith himself recognised, while public squalor diminishes the lives of everyone in a community, poverty affects the individual and stems from that individual's lack of resources:

> People are poverty-stricken when their income, even if adequate for survival, falls markedly behind that of the community. Then they cannot have what the larger community regards as the minimum necessary for decency. (Galbraith, 1970, p. 259)

It is precisely this that the *Breadline Britain* survey examined.

Defining poverty in terms of a consensual view of need

In summary, this study tackles the questions 'how poor is too poor?' by identifying the minimum acceptable way of life for Britain in the 1980s. Those who have no choice but to fall below this minimum level can be said to be 'in poverty'. This concept is developed in terms of those who have an enforced lack of *socially perceived* necessities. This means that the 'necessities' of life are identified by public opinion and not by, on the one hand, the views of experts or, on the other hand, the norms of behaviour *per se*.

We have not investigated how far our definition of 'poverty' coincides with the popular definition; nor do we consider it crucial that it should do so. Critics are free to argue with our view that we are measuring 'poverty', but that would be a diversion from the central point, which is that we have established, we believe, an acceptable measurement of a minimum standard of living that everyone is entitled to enjoy. In our view, it is reasonable to equate this with the measurement of poverty. But it would not alter the implications of our findings if the people we refer to throughout as 'in poverty' were simply described as 'falling below a society-approved minimum'.

In establishing this minimum standard, we have aimed to exclude our own personal value judgements by taking the consensual judgement of society at large about people's needs. We hope to have moved towards what Sen describes as 'an objective diagnosis of conditions' based on 'an objective understanding of "feelings" ' (1982, p. 16), although some judgement is still required in interpreting the data (see Chapter 6).

There has been a tendency in discussions on poverty to imply that the research methodology one uses has strong implications for the standard of poverty one adopts. This is not necessarily the case. Rowntree adopted a very basic standard of poverty but he used three different methodologies to estimate its extent: he used the expert approach in relation to food; the public opinion approach in relation to clothing; and the actual expenditure approach in relation to housing. In adopting the 'public opinion' approach, we make no prior judgement about the level at which a minimum standard of living should be drawn.

It is worth noting in this context that the level of poverty identified using this method may fluctuate for reasons that have little to do with the poor's actual standards of living. It is possible, for example, to envisage circumstances where the number of people with a low standard of living increases but poverty as measured by this consensual definition decreases because the public's reaction to the spread of hardship is to be less generous in their view of minimum entitlements.

Generally, views that are deeply held do not fluctuate rapidly, and it seems likely that this applies to people's views on necessities (see Chapter 3). Nevertheless, even the possibility that people's perceptions of necessities may fluctuate rapidly draws attention to the importance of viewing the 'public opinion' approach to poverty alongside other information. In particular, absolute and relative changes in the distribution of income and living standards are an important backdrop for any measure of poverty.

Some people will make a fundamental criticism of this 'consensual' approach: namely, that it confuses the search for a definition of poverty by failing to take on board what Townsend describes as 'the indoctrinated quality of our social perceptions' (Townsend, 1981). As such, it risks merely reflecting the dominant interests in society, interests whose advantages are built at the expense of the poor. While accepting that this is a risk, our view is that this approach removes the concept of poverty from the arbitrary exercise of judgement by 'experts', politicians and governments, where up to now it has remained firmly entrenched, and opens it up to a more democratic representation of interests.

It has been argued in this chapter that although it is, of course, true that a collective view of what constitutes necessities is socially conditioned, this is in fact a key advantage of this approach. For the concept of poverty is trying to tap exactly the question of what it is that we as a society have come to accept as necessities – the aspects of our way of life that are so important that when people are forced to go without they are regarded as deprived and feel deprived. The very fact that people are culturally conditioned makes them the best judge of what it is that people have been culturally conditioned to expect as a minimum entitlement. Professor A. H. Halsey summed up this advantage for the *Breadline Britain* series:

> The definition of what it is to be poor is something which comes out of the relations between people. If you take a country like ours which is a democratic country, what in effect you're doing in this kind of approach is

to say let's vote all together on what we think constitutes poverty. If you get some kind of social consensus
about that definition, then that actually fits the reality
of what people experience.

It is a definition based in the reality of the commonplace
and as such has meaning for both the poor and others. In
doing this, it throws light on two of the main purposes of
studying poverty. First, it helps towards an understanding of
what it is like to be poor in Britain today. To the extent that
the poor share the same aspirations as others (and this is
examined in the next chapter), then this consensual definition has real meaning to the poor themselves. Finally, and
perhaps most importantly, this approach makes some contribution to the question of tackling poverty. In establishing
a minimum standard of living on the basis of what is to most
people unacceptable, it establishes a politically credible level.
The people who fall below this minimum level are in most
people's opinion entitled to more. In a democratic society
like Britain, this is an important criterion on which to base
policies to help the poor.

3

To Live or to Exist?
The survey's findings on today's necessities

A standard of living surely should give you the benefit of making a choice of whether you have a piece of beef or a small chop. A piece of beef would last you two or three days where a chop would last you one. Surely living standards should be able to give you the choice of being able to buy a small joint? [A disabled woman, living on supplementary benefit]

The *Breadline Britain* survey set out to discover, for the first time ever, what standard of living is considered unacceptable by society as a whole. The first task was to establish whether there is, in fact, a public consensus on what minimum standard people living in Britain in the 1980s should be entitled to.

In the last chapter, we argued that poverty can be seen in terms of an enforced lack of socially perceived necessities. People's perceptions of necessities will vary from generation to generation and from society to society. As such, poverty is relative. However, this approach makes no prior judgement about whether necessities should be confined to what are sometimes classed as subsistence items (food, clothing and heating) or whether they reflect the wide range of social activities that make up a person's standard of living. Nor does it make any prior judgement about the quality of life that constitutes this minimum. It seeks instead to find out what people themselves think.

The survey's design

The central brief given to MORI, the survey specialists commissioned by London Weekend Television to design and conduct the *Breadline Britain* survey, was as follows:

> The survey's first, and most important, aim is to try to discover whether there is a public consensus on what is an unacceptable standard of living for Britain in 1983 and, if there is a consensus, who, if anyone, falls below that standard.
>
> The idea underlying this is that a person is in 'poverty' when their standard of living falls below the minimum deemed necessary by current public opinion. This minimum may cover not only the basic essentials for survival (such as food) but also access, or otherwise, to participating in society and being able to play a social role.

The survey design was carried out in two stages. The first, qualitative, stage tapped the views of groups of different types of people across Britain: people broadly representative of the poor themselves (the low-paid, the unemployed and the elderly) and of middle-income earners. The aim was to ensure that the survey was based firmly on the reality of the lives of the poor and was generally in tune with the perceptions of a broader range of people. This was complemented by discussions with academic specialists and by an examination, with the help of the Social Science Research Council's data archive, of other surveys in the field. Trial versions of the questionnaire were tested in pilot runs.

Several questions arose in the course of the survey's design. The first was the identification of a range of goods and activities that were indicative of a minimum standard of living. Clearly, it was not possible to produce a comprehensive list of the purchases that might constitute part of this minimum standard. The items chosen had, on the one hand, to distinguish between the poor and others and, on the other hand, to be of some significance to many people. A final list of thirty-five items was chosen (see Table 3.1 below). It covers a cross-section of a household's social and personal life, including food, heating, household durables, clothing, housing conditions, transport and leisure and social activities.

The items representing each of these areas do not include things like salt, which almost everyone has, or things such as pocket calculators, which few people would miss.

Having decided what items to include, the question arose of whether or not to specify a quality for these items. For example, having decided to include possession of carpets, should we specify that they should not be 'threadbare' or that they should 'be in adequate condition'? In the end, we decided that these kinds of judgements were too subjective and, moreover, depended on one's own standard of living. We therefore confined the items to simple possession described in concrete and measurable terms. In this way, a minimum level could be identified because what became important was whether or not people could afford these goods, even if what they could afford was only the very cheapest. It did mean, however, that the comparisons that could be made between the poor and others were limited.

The next issue was to decide whether it was going to be possible to identify just one set of minima. People might, for example, feel that the needs of a single young person are very different from those of an elderly person or from those of a couple with children. Our preliminary soundings suggested that the main differences would lie between the elderly and others and so in the trial run we asked people to distinguish between the elderly and others with reference to each of the items. However, it appeared that, with the exception of a telephone, which people felt was particularly important for the elderly, people's views of what was important at this minimal level differed little between different groups. There did seem to be a standard of living to which people felt everyone was entitled. In a larger survey it would have been interesting to explore the extent to which certain groups are felt to be entitled to more than this universal minimum, but for the purposes of this study it was decided to search for a minimum that applied to all adults with, in addition, a number of items relating specifically to families (see questions 9 and 10 in the questionnaire, Appendix B, pp. 394–5).

Finally, the question had to be phrased in such a way that

it was clear that what was being asked for was the identification of a *minimum* standard of living. People's views on different aspects of one's standard of living would be expected to cover a complete range from essential to unimportant, with many shades in between. It may well be an interesting exercise to tap this range but, for the purposes of this study, it was decided to have a simple binary distinction between items that were 'necessities' and those that might be 'desirable' but were not necessary. It was important that people understood that some people would manage without these 'necessities', some even from choice, but that what they were being asked to identify were things that people should not have to do without. Different versions of questions designed to tap this concept were tried during the pilot; the final version, using a shuffle board and cards, states:

> On these cards are a number of different items which relate to our standard of living. Please would you indicate by placing in the appropriate box the living standards you feel all adults should have in Britain today. This box is for items which you think are necessary, and which all adults should be able to afford and which they should not have to do without; this box is for items which may be desirable, but are not necessary.

In addition, to find out how strongly people felt about the importance of what they had classified as necessities, we asked:

> If the Government proposed to increase income tax by one penny (1p) in the pound to enable everyone to afford the items you have said are necessities, on balance would you support or oppose this policy?

In these ways the survey aimed to identify the necessities that everyone should be entitled to. The next stage was to find out who went without each of these items, and why. The survey asked people to distinguish, for each item, those they had and could not do without; those they had and could do without; those they did not have but did not want; and those they did not have and could not afford (question 15 of the questionnaire, Appendix B, p. 397). The picture of people's actual living standards is examined in Chapters 4 and 5. This chapter looks only at the extent to which possession of goods affects people's attitudes to the definition of necessities.

These two sides to the survey – identifying the necessities and identifying those who went without them – formed its core. To analyse these data, a range of standard background variables were included: age, sex, social class, employment status, trade union membership, housing tenure, education level, marital status, health and party political leanings. Efforts were also made to identify the net disposable income of the household to which the respondent belonged (see questions 27–32 of the questionnaire, Appendix B, pp. 304–6; for details of the income measure used, see Appendix C, pp. 308–9).

The public's perception of necessities

The survey established, for the first time ever, that a majority of people see the necessities of life in Britain in the 1980s as covering a wide range of goods and activities, and that people judge a minimum standard of living on socially established criteria and not just the criteria of survival or subsistence.

Table 3.1 lists the thirty-five items that were tested, ranked by the proportion of respondents identifying each item as a 'necessity'. This ranking shows that there is a considerable degree of social consensus. Over nine in ten people are agreed about the importance of the following basic living conditions in the home:

- heating,
- an indoor toilet (not shared),
- a damp-free home,
- a bath (not shared), and
- beds for everyone.

Table 3.1 *The public's perception of necessities*

Standard-of-living items in rank order	% classing item as necessity	Standard-of-living items in rank order	% classing item as necessity
1. Heating to warm living areas of the home if it's cold	97	19. A hobby or leisure activity	64
2. Indoor toilet (not shared with another household)	96	20. Two hot meals a day (for adults)	64
3. Damp-free home	96	21. Meat or fish every other day	63
4. Bath (not shared with another household)	94	22. Presents for friends or family once a year	63
5. Beds for everyone in the household	94	23. A holiday away from home for one week a year, not with relatives	63
6. Public transport for one's needs	88	24. Leisure equipment for children e.g. sports equipment or a bicycle[a]	57
7. A warm water-proof coat	87	25. A garden	55
8. Three meals a day for children[a]	82	26. A television	51
9. Self-contained accommodation	79	27. A 'best outfit' for special occasions	48
10. Two pairs of all-weather shoes	78	28. A telephone	43
11. Enough bedrooms for every child over 10 of different sex to have his/her own[a]	77	29. An outing for children once a week[a]	40
12. Refrigerator	77	30. A dressing gown	38
13. Toys for children[a]	71	31. Children's friends round for tea/a snack once a fortnight[a]	37
14. Carpets in living rooms and bedrooms	70	32. A night out once a fortnight (adults)	36
15. Celebrations on special occasions such as Christmas	69	33. Friends/family round for a meal once a month	32
16. A roast meat joint or its equivalent once a week	67	34. A car	22
17. A washing machine	67	35. A packet of cigarettes every other day	14
18. New, not second-hand, clothes	64		

Average of all 35 items = 64.1

[a]For families with children only.

The right of everyone, regardless of income, to exactly these sorts of basic minima was a key objective of postwar housing policy until the recent sharp cutbacks in public sector housing investment.

The survey also found a considerable degree of consensus about the importance of a wide range of other goods and activities. More than two-thirds of the respondents classed the following items as necessities:

- enough money for public transport,
- a warm water-proof coat,
- three meals a day for children,
- self-contained accommodation,
- two pairs of all-weather shoes,
- a bedroom for every child over 10 of different sex,
- a refrigerator,
- toys for children,
- carpets,
- celebrations on special occasions such as Christmas,
- a roast joint or its equivalent once a week, and
- a washing machine.

This widespread consensus on what are necessities clearly reflects the standards of today and not those of the past. In Rowntree's study of poverty in York in 1899, for a family to be classed as poor 'they must never spend a penny on railway fare or omnibus'. In Britain in the 1980s, nearly nine in ten people think that such spending is not only justified but a necessity for living today.

The importance of viewing minimum standards in terms of contemporary living conditions is highlighted most forcefully by the impact of labour-saving household goods. A large majority of people think that a refrigerator and a washing machine are necessities – items that were unknown to the Victorians and even twenty years ago would have been seen as a luxury. In part, this reflects shifting standards and expectations; but it also reflects the fact that, in a practical sense, items that become customary also become necessary because other aspects of life are planned and built on the very fact that these items are customary. For example, many single elderly people have commented to us that, whereas once they could manage without a fridge, it is now so difficult to buy perishable food in small quantities that they find they need one. Professor David Donnison, ex-chairman of the now defunct Supplementary Benefits Commission, has elaborated this argument:

> The poor too often find they have to use the most expensive forms of heating and cooking (for that's all that their all-electric flats provide); they really need a refrigerator because shops are distant and their flats no longer have a ventilated larder; . . . life is difficult without a washing machine and clothes drier because there's no launderette nearby and no private open space where they can hang out the laundry – and so on. (Donnison, 1981, p. 184).

While these trends are of great importance, the survey also shows that people do not judge necessities, directly or indirectly, simply on the criterion of subsistence. It is not just that a new range of goods have become critical to coping; people also classed as necessities items that solely add to the quality of life. Included in the items that over two-thirds of people class as necessities are goods that add to one's comfort (such as carpets) and those that add to one's enjoyment (celebrations or a roast joint).

The rejection of an 'absolute' or 'subsistence-based' approach to determining necessities is seen more clearly in the items that over half of the respondents, but under two-thirds, viewed as necessities:

- new, not second-hand, clothes,
- a hobby or leisure activity,
- two hot meals a day (for adults),
- meat or fish every other day,
- presents for friends or family once a year,
- a holiday away from home for one week a year,

- leisure equipment for children
- a garden, and
- a television

All these items are primarily to do with the quality of life, with enjoyment and with joining in social activities. While these items do not have such overwhelming support as those related to coping with the more basic aspects of day-to-day living, they are nevertheless supported by a majority of people. This has been taken as the cut-off point to distinguish between items that are necessities and those that are not. While there is inevitably an element of arbitrariness at the margins for any cut-off point, a straight majority seems as fair an interpretation of a consensual view as any.

There is more disagreement about what specific 'quality of life' items are of importance than there is over, say, what constitutes basic housing conditions, but a large majority of people regard one or other of these items as necessities. There is virtually no disagreement that there should be more to life than just existing.

This finding may seem obvious, if only because it is a view that the vast majority of readers will share. It is nevertheless of considerable significance. There has long been a strand of opinion that has tried to define the needs of the poor simply in terms of subsistence items, a view reflected today by Sir Keith Joseph when he states that 'a family is poor if it cannot afford to eat' (see Chapter 2). While no doubt virtually everyone would agree that those who cannot afford to eat are poor, the *Breadline Britain* survey shows that the corollary – that only those who cannot afford to eat are poor – is widely disputed. The great majority of people think that everyone is entitled not just to eat but to eat at a certain quality (meat or fish every other day), with regularity (two hot meals a day), and in accordance with traditional customs (a roast joint once a week). The majority also think that people are entitled to clothing not only for protection (a warm water-proof coat or two pairs of all-weather shoes) but also for dignity (new, not second-hand, clothes). While Adam Smith accepted this two hundred years ago, there has nevertheless been a persistent

failure to recognise the importance of such socially determined necessities. For example, in a vitriolic attack on the
proposition that poverty in the 1980s means shopping for
clothes in second-hand shops, Auberon Waugh writes in the
The Spectator:

> But what on earth are second-hand shops for – Hooray
> Henrys and Henriettas to rig themselves out in fancy
> dress? In fact the clothes at Oxfam are generally better
> made and sometimes more fashionable than anything to
> be found in any but the most expensive new clothes
> shops. It would never occur to me to buy a new coat
> when so many dead men's overcoats are available at a
> tenth of the price for twice the quality. Once again one
> is tempted to ask what the 'breadliners' are blubbing on
> about. (Waugh, 1983)

In most people's eyes, it is Mr Waugh who is 'blubbing'.
He is, of course, entitled to the view that new clothes are not
necessary, but he is in a minority. To those who have the
luxury of popping into the Oxfam shop to buy an overcoat,
there may well be a pride in getting good value for money.
For those dependent for most of their clothes on other
people's cast-offs, the situation can look very different.
Anne's husband Roy is unemployed and they and their three
children, Michelle, Leslie and Tony, rely on second-hand
clothes:

> It's very expensive to go normal shopping these days.
> I'm not so worried about myself so much, or even Roy,
> but it would be nice to buy the kids some new clothes
> now and again. If only we could, but who can afford it?
> I know Michelle would like to be in the fashion, but I
> think she understands that we can't afford to buy new
> clothes for her.

To go without the necessities of life is not just to suffer
hunger or to risk ill-health or even death but also to be
demeaned and degraded. J. K. Galbraith describes the

situation of those who are poverty-stricken as lacking what is required for decency:

> They cannot wholly escape, therefore, the judgement of the larger community that they are indecent. They are degraded for, in the literal sense, they live outside the grades or categories which the community regards as acceptable. (Galbraith, 1970, p. 259)

In summary, the survey's findings give strong backing to a 'relative' view of deprivation. This view has been most forcefully advocated over recent years by Professor Peter Townsend. Although certain aspects of his approach have been criticised in Chapter 2, the survey does establish the relevance of the concept of 'relative poverty'. It is of interest that the recently established survey of 'British Social Attitudes' found, when explicitly asking about 'poverty', that the level of assent to the *relative* definition of poverty is now 'remarkably high' (Bosanquet, 1984, p. 94). The *Breadline Britain* findings clearly show that people make their judgements about the necessities for living on the basis of today's standards and not by some historical yardstick. Their definition of necessity goes wider than subsistence.

Finally, the survey's finding that there is a widespread social consensus about what constitute the necessities of life is in itself important. For all the differences in people's styles of living, the concept of 'socially established' necessities does in practice have meaning.

The homogeneity of views throughout society

Although by definition, all the necessities are seen as such by the majority of people, for every item there is some disagreement. When all the necessities are considered together, the majority of people will find that among the items there are one or two that they themselves do not regard as a necessity. This, in itself, is of no particular significance and is indeed implicit in the approach. What is important is that most people will agree with the classification of a large majority of the items. In other words, the list is generally indicative of the kind of minimum standard of living envisaged by the large majority of people.

However, if differences between individuals fell into patterns among groups in society then the variations would be of greater significance. It may be that certain minority groups in society hold distinctly different views on what is important. There is, in particular, plenty of evidence that styles of living are not uniform throughout society but differ between men and women, between social classes and between ethnic groups. If these differences affected the basic levels of living underlying the concept of a minimum, then it would not be particularly meaningful to talk about a universal minimum.

The survey's sample size was not large enough for any distinction to be made between different ethnic groups. The survey did, however, collect data on sex and social class. The survey found that men and women shared very similar perceptions of necessities. Social class, as is standard in surveys, was defined in relation to occupational groups, although we accept that social class is, in fact, more complex than the classification of occupational group. In this context, social class AB are those in professional and managerial occupations, social class C1 are other non-manual workers, social class C2 are skilled manual workers, social class D are semi-skilled and unskilled manual workers, and social class E are social security recipients.

Table 3.2 shows the relationship between social class and the perception of necessities. Given that, in general, people's attitudes are strongly influenced by the social class to which they belong, the survey's findings show a remarkable degree of agreement about the necessities for living in Britain in the 1980s. Only three of the twenty-six items classed as necessities by the majority of people are not also classed as a necessity by every social class: a television is seen as a necessity by those in social classes C2, D and E, but not by those in social classes AB and C1; two hot meals a day for adults are seen as a necessity by a majority of those in all the social

Table 3.2 *Social class and the perception of necessities*

Standard-of-living items in rank order for sample as a whole	AB	C1	C2	D	E
	% classing item as necessity				
Heating	96	99	99	95	95
Indoor toilet	98	95	97	95	95
Damp-free home	96	95	97	98	94
Bath	96	93	95	92	93
Beds for everyone	94	98	94	92	91
Public transport	88	91	91	87	85
Warm water-proof coat	95	88	86	84	84
Three meals a day for children	89	80	83	78	81
Self-contained accommodation	78	76	82	78	80
Two pairs of all-weather shoes	85	77	73	78	80
Sufficient bedrooms for children	74	76	81	69	81
Refrigerator	77	78	76	83	73
Toys for children	81	72	72	64	70
Carpets	59	60	75	77	77
Celebrations on special occasions	67	68	69	72	67
Roast joint once a week	61	61	69	74	68
Washing machine	60	62	72	75	64
New, not second-hand, clothes	53	64	60	79	64
Hobby or leisure activity	71	69	60	56	63
Two hot meals a day (adults)	46	65	69	69	65
Meat/fish every other day	64	61	69	61	60
Presents once a year	66	64	59	62	64
Holiday	74	63	61	63	57
Leisure equipment for children	64	55	52	55	59
Garden	41	56	59	61	53
Television	38	37	53	64	61
Best outfit	47	42	47	52	53
Telephone	46	49	34	45	45
Outing for children once a week	35	38	40	41	45
Dressing gown	36	37	35	33	49
Children's friends round once a fortnight	46	36	33	34	38
Night out once a fortnight	28	33	34	41	45
Friends/family round once a month	38	31	30	27	34
Car	22	24	28	23	11
Packet of cigarettes	12	7	14	18	19
Average of all items	63.5	62.9	64.2	65.0	64.7

classes except AB; and a garden is also seen as a necessity by
all but the ABs. Further, there is only one item classed as a
necessity by certain of the social classes but not by the
majority of society as a whole: namely a 'best outfit' for
special occasions, which is classed as a necessity by social
classes D and E but not by social classes AB, C1 and C2.

The rank order of the necessities is very similar for all the
different groups. The top five necessities are the same for all
social classes, and the items that form the top ten necessities
for the population as a whole are within the top twelve for
each of the social class groups.

There are, however, some differences. In general, the
middle classes put less emphasis on household items than the
working classes. For example, carpets were thought to be a
necessity by 59 per cent of social class AB and 60 per cent of
social class C1, but by 75 per cent of social class C2 and 77
per cent of both social classes D and E. There are two possible
explanations for these differences.

First, it could be that those who take for granted a range
of goods place less importance on their possession than those
who have had to struggle and save, or even have to go
without. The influence of possession of a good on its classification as a necessity will be examined below (pp. 65–8).

The second area of explanation relates more directly to the
question of cultural homogeneity. It could be that such
differences reflect different lifestyles or at least different
aspirations; those who desire parquet flooring and rugs may
be less inclined to regard the carpets in their rooms as necessities. The differences between the different social classes
suggest that this may, to some extent, be the case. In the case
of food, for example, those from professional and managerial
backgrounds place less emphasis than others on what have
traditionally been regarded as part of the working man's diet:
two hot meals a day and a roast on a Sunday. It seems
unlikely that professional and managerial workers attach less
importance to good food – all the other evidence suggests
quite the reverse – and there is no reason to presume that
they would place less importance on good food as part of a
minimum. What seems more likely is that styles of living

among professional and managerial groups are less likely to conform to traditional patterns.

That differences in lifestyles have some bearing on perceptions of necessities is further suggested by the items primarily concerned with enjoyment or relaxation, where the differences between the occupational groups are greatest. People from professional and managerial backgrounds (social class AB) tend to put more emphasis on leisure pursuits of a more individualistic, or even 'educational', nature. For adults, a hobby or leisure activity and a holiday are both regarded as necessities by a somewhat higher proportion of people in social class AB than in any of the other social classes; the same is true for toys and leisure equipment for children. Holidays show the most marked differences, with three-quarters of professional and managerial workers counting this as a necessity but only 57 per cent of social security recipients (social class E). By contrast, those from social class AB put less emphasis on what could be seen to be a more social form of leisure activity: a night out once a fortnight, which traditionally for many people would be the trip to the pub or club – this is seen as a necessity by only 28 per cent of social class AB compared to 45 per cent of social class E.

Out of all the thirty-five items, the greatest difference comes, however, in attitudes towards the television: this is regarded as a necessity by only 38 per cent of those in social class AB and 37 per cent in social class C1, but by 64 per cent of those in social class D and 61 per cent of those in social class E. For the poor, the television provides a cheap and ever-available form of entertainment, a distraction from the pressing problems at hand. Pamela, an unmarried mother, struggles on supplementary benefit to bring up her 9-month-old child in a decaying and decrepit attic flat:

> I watch TV from first thing in the morning till last thing at night, till the television goes off. I sit and watch it all day. That's all I've got: to watch television. I can't afford to do other things at all. The only thing I can do is sit and watch television. I can't go anywhere, I can't go out

and enjoy myself or nothing. I should be able to take my daughter out somewhere. I would take her to the zoo and things like that. Places she's never been, or seen, and half the places I haven't seen in London myself. Things that I can't afford to do.

To the middle classes, the television, though it firmly occupies a corner of all their homes, is often regarded with disdain. Such attitudes are of importance because they go hand in hand with a view among the better-off that the poor are poor because of fecklessness. S. Turner of Wolverhampton, for example, wrote to *The Sunday Times* refuting the report of the *Breadline Britain* survey that millions live in poverty:

> Anyone who visits low-income families has experience of homes which are lacking in carpets, furniture, or decent clothing for children, but contain a large colour TV...
> (*The Sunday Times*, 28 August 1983)

The survey suggests that such comments might strike a chord with the middle-class readership of *The Sunday Times* – but other groups in society view the matter very differently. Although such differences in attitudes towards necessities are relatively few, they are of importance because of the power that those in social class AB exercise over the poor. Historically, assessments of minimum needs have been made by the 'experts', by the professionals, indeed by those who have much to lose from any redistribution of resources in society. The more democratic approach taken by this survey invites the thought that the judgements being made by the professionals reflect their own interests rather than those of society generally.

Overall however, there is a high degree of homogeneity in perceptions of necessities. There are, of course, many forces in modern society that promote uniformity of aspiration and expectation. In particular, mass communications encourage a common view of desirable styles of living, both directly through advertising and indirectly through a widening of people's knowledge of standards in society outside their own immediate experience. On the other hand, there is a strong academic tradition that has shown that people make their judgements about their position in society with reference not to society as a whole but to the particular social group of which they are members (see, in particular, Runciman, 1972). As far as people's judgements about minimum standards are concerned, the *Breadline Britain* survey suggests either that people take as their 'normative' reference group (that is, the group by which they set their standards) society as a whole and not their specific group; or that at this minimal level the differences between the social groups are so marginal that, even if people take as their reference point their own social group, the final judgements remain very similar.

Either way, the degree of homogeneity found between different groups in society adds weight to the concept of 'socially perceived necessities', and provides a set of nationally sanctioned standards that override class differences. It seems that it is indeed possible to identify a form of deprivation that has a meaning shared between both those who are likely to experience such deprivation (in the classification used here, those in social class E in particular) and others.

Necessities and norms of behaviour

It is likely that these shared judgements stem, at least in part, from shared experiences. The mass of people in past generations may have lived in badly heated, uncarpeted homes, washing their clothes in the sink, but the vast majority of people today experience a pleasanter life. As a consequence, this has come to be seen as a right for all. It is in this sense that poverty is relative.

However, the relationship between the degree to which an experience or activity is widespread and the degree to which it is seen as a necessity is complex. Table 3.3 shows the proportion of the population possessing each of the items.

Table 3.3   *The relationship between the perception of necessities and the extent of possession of items*

Standard-of-living items in rank order for sample as a whole	% classing item as necessity	% of population having item[a]
Heating	97	92
Indoor toilet	96	98
Damp-free home	96	85
Bath	94	97
Beds for everyone	94	97
Public transport	88	87
Warm water-proof coat	87	88
Three meals a day for children[b]	82	90
Self-contained accommodation	79	93
Two pairs of all-weather shoes	78	84
Sufficient bedrooms for children[b]	77	76
Refrigerator	77	96
Toys for children[b]	71	92
Carpets	70	97
Celebrations on special occasions	69	93
Roast joint once a week	67	87
Washing machine	67	89
New, not second-hand, clothes	64	85
Hobby or leisure activity	64	77
Two hot meals a day (adults)	64	81
Meat/fish every other day	63	81
Presents once a year	63	90
Holiday	63	68
Leisure equipment for children[b]	57	79
Garden	55	88
Television	51	98
'Best outfit'	48	78
Telephone	43	82
Outing for children once a week[b]	40	58
Dressing gown	38	84
Children's friends round once a fortnight[b]	37	60
Night out once a fortnight	36	57
Friends/family round once a month	32	64
Car	22	61
Packet of cigarettes	14	39

[a]The responses have been weighted by numbers in household to give the % of the population.
[b]Families with children under 16 only.

For all the items classed as necessities by the majority of the population, possession is widespread: at least two-thirds of the population have them and for most items the proportion is over 80 per cent. In an affluent society like Britain, this is to be expected but it is not implicit in the approach. It is possible to imagine a society in which the majority of people do not have access to a standard of living that is generally judged to be a minimum. Indeed, many 'Third World' countries may fall into this category. Arguably, this ability to cope theoretically with very differing degrees of poverty is an advantage of this methodology over one that defines poverty with reference to the norm.

In the British context, however, necessities are not seen to be items to which only a minority of the population have access. The commonsense understanding of the word precludes even the possibility. There was no point in the survey testing whether people saw a trip to Europe once a year or a second car for the family as necessities because, although they may represent a standard of living to which most people aspire and that would not be given up willingly by those who do possess it, such items remain luxuries. Despite the fact that the survey included only items that the majority of people either possessed or could afford if they so chose and as such was not set up to test this point, the findings nevertheless indicate that widespread ownership is a prerequisite of an item being seen as a necessity. In general, the items that are not classed by a majority of the population as necessities are possessed by a smaller proportion of the population than are the items that are classed as necessities (see Table 3.3).

This comes as no surprise; it is the assumption on which most poverty studies have been based: namely, that those styles of living that are widespread are equivalent to those that are socially approved, encouraged or expected. What is of more interest, therefore, is that the relationship is not clear-cut. There are three items (a 'best outfit', a telephone and a dressing gown) regarded by the majority of the population as being merely desirable that are in fact possessed by a larger proportion of the population than are three items classed as necessities (sufficient bedrooms for children, a hobby or leisure activity, and a holiday). Thus, although widespread ownership may be a prerequisite in the British context of an item being seen as a necessity, it is not the only factor of importance. Other judgements come into play.

People set their perceptions of necessities by the concept of a minimum not by the average; the concept of a minimum depends on what is average but it nevertheless remains separate. It is worth noting in passing that this means that it is possible to imagine a society in which there is a degree of inequality but virtually no poverty. While the standard of living of those at the bottom would remain below the average, it would not be so far below that it fell below the current expectations of decency. We hasten to add that this is not a description of Britain in the 1980s.

The fact that people's judgements about necessities are not exclusively dependent on shared experience is perhaps of more immediate significance when this consensual approach is compared with the definition of poverty by reference to a norm. In Britain, the concept of poverty as exclusion from ordinary living patterns has been advanced most vigorously by Townsend. In translating this from a theoretical plane to a practical measure, he identified twelve aspects of a person's standard of living to form a 'deprivation index'. It is from this deprivation index that he identifies a poverty line (see Chapter 2 for further details of the Townsend study).

To highlight the difference between the consensual and norm-reference approach, it is worth comparing Townsend's deprivation index (Table 2.1) with the public's perceptions of necessities found in the *Breadline Britain* survey (Table 3.1). The exercise should be treated with some caution as the studies were conducted fifteen years apart. Moreover, there are two items in Townsend's index (3 and 9) that have no equivalents in the *Breadline Britain* survey and the precise wording of most of the items is not the same. Nevertheless, the comparison indicates some interesting differences. Of the ten items in Townsend's index that are loosely comparable with items in the *Breadline Britain* survey, three are not classified by the population as a whole as necessities: namely, friends round for a meal once a month, children's friends round for a tea/snack once a fortnight, and a night out once a fortnight (items 2, 4 and 6 of the Townsend index). These items relate to people's ability to partake in a social role. A central criticism Townsend makes of earlier poverty studies is that such items are not included 'because of strong social values in favour of "privacy" and the opportunity to lead a "private life"' (1983, p. 69). That the majority of people do not perceive these items to be necessities no doubt also reflects these 'strong social values'. Indeed, this is the basis on which this study has been set up; as has been argued in Chapter 2, the concept of poverty should incorporate not sidestep such social values.

This is not to argue that these indicators of participation in social roles are unimportant. A person who cannot afford to go out once a fortnight may well be more socially isolated than those who go out regularly. But so, too, is the family with one car compared to the family with two cars. The wife may well be at home all day with young children and, if the public transport in the area is poor, she will be unable to play as full a social role as the mother with access to a car. These differences between people provide measures of the effects of inequality but they can, in our view, be classed as poverty only when they are of such a degree or type as to be considered unacceptable by society as a whole.

The influences on people's perceptions of necessities

Just as the extent of ownership in society generally is not a particularly accurate guide to society's overall perception of necessities, neither is an individual's possession or otherwise of an item a particularly good guide to their perception of whether that item is a necessity. While there is a strong tendency for those who possess an item to be more likely to classify it as a necessity, possession on its own does not explain why some people classify an item as a necessity and some do not.

To investigate this further, the *Breadline Britain* survey asked people about their attitudes towards their personal possession, or lack, of each item. People who had an item were asked whether they could or could not do without it; and people who did not have an item were asked whether it was because they did not want it or because they could not afford it. Table 3.4 shows the proportions of these four categories classifying each item as a necessity.

Table 3.4   *The personal possession of items and the perception of necessities*

| | Possession of items | | | |
Standard-of-living items in rank order for sample as a whole	Have/ could not do without	Have/ could do without	Don't have/ don't want	Don't have/ can't afford
	% classing item as necessity			
Heating	98	80[a]	(—)[b]	98
Indoor toilet	99	46[a]	20[a]	75[a]
Damp-free home	98	89[a]	(—)[b]	88[a]
Bath	96	50[a]	48[a]	53[a]
Beds for everyone	95	88[a]	20[a]	77[a]
Public transport	96	78	70	70[a]
Warm water-proof coat	93	58	49[a]	73
Three meals a day for children	93	74	55[a]	76[a]
Self-contained accommodation	85	37	38[a]	62[a]
Two pairs of all-weather shoes	91	51	17[a]	71
Sufficient bedrooms for children	87	42	60	68
Refrigerator	89	38	2[a]	30[a]
Toys for children	87	56	76	74[a]
Carpets	83	40	(—)[b]	51[a]
Celebrations on special occasions	83	50	13[a]	46[a]
Roast joint once a week	89	51	19	56
Washing machine	82	37	20[a]	43
New, not second-hand, clothes	80	33	52	66
Hobby or leisure activity	82	52	32	45
Two hot meals a day (adults)	85	48	25	63[a]
Meat/fish every other day	84	50	15	61
Presents once a year	80	38	19[a]	53
Holiday	89	50	22	52
Leisure equipment for children	78	43	39	61
Garden	76	35	18	46[a]
Television	78	23	8[a]	(—)[b]

Table continued

Table 3.4 *Continued*

	Possession of items			
	Have/ could not do without	*Have/ could do without*	*Don't have/ don't want*	*Don't have/ can't afford*
Standard-of-living items in rank order for sample as a whole				
	% *classing item as necessity*			
'Best outfit'	73	34	16	40
Telephone	65	21	7	22
Outing for children once a week	61	31	20	43
Dressing gown	72	23	8	32
Children's friends round once a fortnight	64	37	15	25
Night out once a fortnight	70	33	21	30
Friends/family round once a month	59	30	11	21
Car	39	15	8	14
Packet of cigarettes	56	16	3	6
Average of all items	81	45	26	53

[a]These figures are likely to be subject to errors of around 10% as they are based on less than 5% of the sample.
[b]No figures available as numbers in group are too small.

There are both differences and similarities between the groups that are of interest. Looking at all the groups, although some groups have much lower proportions of people classifying items as necessities, there is nevertheless roughly the same ranking of the items. This suggests that, whatever judgements people make about what they personally need, they are also influenced by a general set of moral judgements about anyone's basic rights and needs.

None the less, the influence of a person's judgements about their own personal situation is very significant. When people regard an aspect of their standard of living as being of importance to themselves, they also tend to identify this as being a right for others. Those respondents having an item and feeling that they are unable to do without it are very likely to classify it as a necessity for everyone; only one item (a car) is not classified by a majority of this group as being a necessity for everyone. That said, a significant minority of this group feel that, though they cannot do without the item themselves, it is not a right for everyone. While this attitude may indicate a degree of selfishness, it is perfectly consistent with making a judgement on minimum rights for all. Such a minimum does not imply that all people should have the same or, indeed, that those who do have more will feel that they have no right to it. In general, however, people's perceptions of necessities for themselves and others are the same: for every item, this group (and it should be remembered that the 'group' for every item will to a greater or lesser extent consist of different respondents) is significantly more likely than any other group to classify it as a necessity.

Those who do not have an item but want it are the next most likely to classify that item as a necessity. The fact that they do not have an item does lessen the degree to which they think that the item is a necessity compared to those who possess the item; out of the thirty-five items, fourteen are not classified as necessities by a majority of this group. Interestingly, however, the items that this group classify as necessities mirror closely the population as a whole: only five of the twenty-six items classed as necessities by people in general are not also classified by this group as necessities.

At the other end of the scale, those who do not have an item because they do not want it are generally unlikely to regard it as a necessity for others: only five items (public transport, three meals a day for children, sufficient bedrooms for children, toys for children, and new, not second-hand, clothes) are seen by this group as being necessities. This result is hardly surprising. If individuals do not want an item they are unlikely to recognise the general social pressures that make others see it as a necessity.

The final group is, perhaps, of most interest: those who have an item but feel they can manage without it. First, their attitudes show the most divergence. There are many items where this group is fairly evenly split: for fourteen of the thirty-five items the proportions classifying it as a necessity are within the 40–60 per cent range. This in itself makes their judgements difficult to interpret. To some extent, people appear to be making some kind of moral judgement about the things one should not have to go without even if one could. On the other hand, there appears to be some kind of practical judgement going on: if you can manage without something (or at least think you can, for, of course, none of this group actually manage without) then you cannot really need it. On balance, it is this latter view that seems to win the day: more items are not classed as necessities than are.

This means that, in general, the judgements of those who have an item but feel they could manage without are sharply distinguished from those who have an item but feel they could not manage without: on average they are half as likely to classify items as necessities. As a large majority of people have all the items, this in turn means that this distinction between feeling one could or could not do without an item is critical in determining the items that, on average, across society as a whole, are classed as necessities. The more people who feel that they personally could manage without an item, the more likely it is that that item will not be classed by a majority of the population as a necessity.

There are a number of factors that might influence these perceptions. The first and most obvious possibility is that, although most people possess these items in today's society, their experiences in the past will have been very different. What the influence of these different past experiences might be is not, however, so obvious. It could be that managing without in the past leads to a perception that others can manage without today. On the other hand, experience of the difficulties entailed in managing without could lead to an appreciation of the benefits of this newly acquired way of living that leads to it being seen as a right; those who have never had to go without may not realise the deprivations involved.

The survey did not ask respondents whether there was a time in the past when they lacked these items. However, some indication of whether past experiences are a salient factor is given by looking at whether people's perceptions vary greatly by age. The elderly will have been brought up in an era when many of the items now classed as necessities were not widely available.

The relationship with age is given in Table 3.5. In general, the differences between the age groups are relatively small. All the items chosen as necessities by a majority of the sample are also considered necessities by a majority of those aged 65 or more. Further, older respondents are noticeably more likely than younger respondents to identify a number of items as necessities that were not around for much of their lives (notably the television, classed as a necessity by 63 per cent of the over 65s but only 46 per cent of 15–24 year olds) or were by no means so widespread (for example, a holiday away from home for one week a year, classed as a necessity by 68 per cent of the elderly compared to 51 per cent of the youngest age group).

Table 3.5   *Age and the perception of necessities*

Standard-of-living items in rank order for sample as a whole	Age groups					
	15–24	25–34	35–44	45–54	55–64	65+
	% classing item as necessity					
Heating	98	98	97	98	95	96
Indoor toilet	96	96	99	96	98	93
Damp-free home	96	97	97	97	98	91
Bath	94	94	98	93	96	90
Beds for everyone	93	98	94	95	96	86
Public transport	91	89	87	87	88	89
Warm water-proof coat	78	92	86	91	90	85
Three meals a day for children	82	87	84	80	82	76
Self-contained accommodation	67	76	81	84	88	79
Two pairs of all-weather shoes	65	79	74	78	90	82
Sufficient bedrooms for children	67	78	82	71	83	77
Refrigerator	75	78	84	78	74	73
Toys for children	74	78	69	71	72	64
Carpets	81	70	72	58	72	70
Celebrations on special occasions	75	78	64	65	60	67
Roast joint once a week	57	64	66	75	67	74
Washing machine	59	74	76	66	69	58

Table continued

Table 3.5 *Continued*

Standard-of-livng items in rank order for sample as a whole	15–24	25–34	35–44	45–54	55–64	65+
			% classing item as necessity			
New, not second-hand, clothes	66	59	59	65	70	67
Hobby or leisure activity	62	61	66	65	67	61
Two hot meals a day (adults)	74	65	64	63	62	58
Meat/fish every other day	56	61	70	68	65	59
Presents once a year	63	57	61	64	67	65
Holiday	51	60	64	69	67	68
Leisure equipment for children	64	55	60	52	58	51
Garden	47	65	59	53	55	49
Television	46	49	44	49	54	63
'Best outfit'	53	46	40	53	45	52
Telephone	32	35	41	41	47	60
Outing for children once a week	46	36	38	36	49	36
Dressing gown	15	35	34	40	48	53
Children's friends round once a fortnight	34	35	42	34	45	32
Night out once a fortnight	51	40	32	28	37	32
Friends/family round once a month	32	22	26	36	37	39
Car	28	20	26	29	20	13
Packet of cigarettes	12	16	13	18	10	13
Average of all items	62	64	64	64	66	64

Indeed, the differences between the age groups demonstrate the importance of present rather than past experience. For example, younger people attach more importance to a night out than others, whereas the elderly attach greater importance to a telephone, a television and a dressing gown – all differences that reflect the known fact that the young are more likely to go out to enjoy themselves while the elderly are more likely to be home-bound.

The importance of a person's immediate circumstances in determining their view of necessities is confirmed by looking at how family and household circumstances affect these perceptions (Table 3.6). Again, there is considerable homogeneity between the different groups. Where there are differences they tend to reflect what could be regarded as different degrees of 'need' or different lifestyles. So, for example, a washing machine, a garden and two hot meals a day are more likely to be seen as necessities by those with children than others. Similarly, households with children are more likely to see the items specifically for children as essential than are those who do not have the responsibility of children: for example, 78 per cent of single-parent families and 76 per cent of other families see toys for children as a necessity compared with only 65 per cent of pensioners, 65 per cent of single people and 66 per cent of other households without children.

Table 3.6   *Household type and the perception of necessities*

	Household type				
		Non-pensioners			
Standard-of-living items in rank order for sample as a whole	Pensioners All groups	Families with children[a]		Households without children	
		Single parent	All others	All	Single People
	% classing item as necessity				
Heating	96	95	98	97	93
Indoor toilet	95	99	97	94	93
Damp-free home	92	98	97	96	92
Bath	92	96	96	91	94
Beds for everyone	89	95	95	94	96
Public transport	88	91	89	88	77
Warm water-proof coat	86	92	87	87	85
Three meals a day for children[b]	76	86	87	76	79
Self-contained accommodation	79	83	76	84	78
Two pairs of all-weather shoes	83	77	74	84	63
Sufficient bedrooms for children[b]	79	86	76	75	80

Table continued

Table 3.6 *Continued*

		Household type			
		Non-pensioners			
		Families with children[a]		Households without children	
Standard-of-living items in rank order for sample as a whole	Pensioners All groups	Single parent	All others	All	Single People
		% classing item as necessity			
Refrigerator	73	67	81	76	70
Toys for children[b]	65	78	76	66	65
Carpets	72	71	71	69	70
Celebrations on special occasions	66	70	72	64	63
Roast joint once a week	72	67	67	67	48
Washing machine	55	71	71	69	50
New, not second-hand, clothes	66	68	59	70	75
Hobby or leisure activity	65	77	59	70	54
Two hot meals a day (adults)	56	76	68	60	58
Meat/fish every other day	60	63	64	65	56
Presents once a year	67	57	60	66	64
Holiday	65	60	61	67	60
Leisure equipment for children[b]	51	63	60	53	48
Garden	41	57	60	55	42
Television	60	62	45	54	59
'Best outfit'	49	50	47	46	60
Telephone	54	42	38	46	37
Outing for children once a week[b]	38	55	39	40	38
Dressing gown	57	43	29	42	46
Children's friends round once a fortnight[b]	35	37	35	40	42
Night out once a fortnight	33	52	36	35	45
Friends/family round once a month	40	36	27	34	36
Car	12	9	26	25	18
Packet of cigarettes	16	14	13	13	24
Average of all items	63.5	67.2	63.9	64.5	61.7

[a]Children over 16 at home are counted as children.
[b]Families with children only.

Other differences also reflect the effect of individual social circumstances on the importance placed on various activities. For example, single parents place greater emphasis on outings for their children: 55 per cent see this as a necessity compared to 39 per cent of other families with children and around the same proportion of all the other groups. This is probably indicative of the social isolation of many single-parent families – a fact that is also reflected in other ways. For example, 52 per cent of single parents see a night out once a fortnight as a necessity compared to around 36 per cent of other families.

In summary, people's views on what is a necessity do to some extent reflect their own personal circumstances. What is important is not so much whether they do or do not possess a particular item but more the extent to which that item is central to their particular lifestyle. Overall, however, although people's lifestyles differ, the impact these differences have on their perceptions of necessities are small. What people regard as important to themselves influences what they regard as necessities, but it is not the overriding determinant. People are, after all, being asked to answer a different and more general question.

The role of moral judgements

A person's judgement about what is a necessity, while based in part on what is important to them personally, remains a judgement about what everyone in society today should be entitled to. Consider the example of mobility. Most would agree that the ownership of a car enhances the quality of life: it provides a freedom of movement that is not otherwise accessible. Even if some would also argue that the car is environmentally damaging, for the individual at least it is desirable. However, the car remains only that: even among the people who feel that they personally could not manage without a car, only 39 per cent feel that it is a necessity for living in Britain today. Public transport, by contrast, is felt to be a right: even among those who could personally manage without public transport, 78 per cent think everyone should be able to afford public transport if they want (see Table 3.4).

These judgements are, in essence, moral. They are about rights. This is explicit in the question asked: respondents were asked to identify aspects of our way of life that everyone '*should* be able to afford and *should* not have to go without' (our emphasis).

To see how strongly people felt about these 'rights', the *Breadline Britain* survey asked if people would support increasing income tax by 1p in the pound to enable everyone to afford the items they described as necessities. Though this question moves into the political sphere, in that it is a question about practical policies, its aim was to measure not just people's commitment to tackling poverty, but their commitment to the necessities they had identified. Respondents had just identified items that they felt everyone should have, 'rights' to which everyone was entitled, but without also accepting the converse – a 'duty' to assist – their commitment to these 'rights' could be seen to be thin.

The survey's findings suggest that people do take these 'rights' seriously. When asked whether they would support or oppose an increase in income tax of 1p:

> 74 per cent supported the increase,
> 23 per cent opposed it, and
> 4 per cent didn't know.

This reinforces the view that the minimum standard of living identified in the survey represents a strong moral statement about the kind of standard of living that no one should fall below. This standard of living is one to which, in principle, all adults are entitled regardless of the particular reasons why they might not attain it. Other studies have suggested that there is more public sympathy for the old and the disabled than for the unemployed or, to a lesser extent, the low-paid (see Chapter 7). This may mean that, when practical policies are examined (see Chapter 9), there is less support for policies that would help some groups rather than others. Our findings, however establish an entitlement, in principle, for people from all backgrounds. There is only one condition: that their lack of this minimum standard of living stems from lack of resources. This question is examined in Chapter 4.

These moral views are, of course, influenced by many factors. Most obviously, there is a complex relationship between people's moral and political judgements. People's views about what kind of society they would like reflect moral judgements that can either cut across political boundaries or be primarily determined by these boundaries. So how do people's moral judgements about necessities relate to their political outlook?

The survey collected data on respondents' underlying political affiliations. During the last few years, people's voting habits have fluctuated considerably; so, to gain an insight into people's political outlook, respondents were asked which party they identified with rather than their current voting intention (see Appendix B, question 26, p. 303). Though polls of voting intention at that time indicated that Alliance support was particularly high and Labour's particularly low, this is not reflected in people's underlying attitudes. The survey found that 30 per cent of the respondents were Conservatives, 29 per cent Labour and 16 per cent Alliance, figures that are consistent with other research.

The influence of people's political outlook on their perception of necessities was found to be small (see Table 3.7). In general, people name the same items as necessities and put them in a similar order of priority, whatever their political inclination. The main difference is that Conservative supporters are somewhat less likely than others to name the quality of life items as universal rights. Overall, however, the differences are statistically insignificant.

Moreover, Conservative supporters show strong commitment to the necessities they name. Table 3.8 shows that 79 per cent of Conservatives would support a policy of raising taxes by 1p in the pound to help others have the items they had identified as necessities, a slightly higher degree of support than that found among the Labour and Alliance

Table 3.7 *Political views and the perception of necessities*

Standard-of-living items in rank order for sample as a whole	People identifying with		
	Con.	Lab.	Lib/SDP
	% classing item as necessity		
Heating	97	98	98
Indoor toilet	98	96	97
Damp-free home	96	96	98
Bath	95	94	97
Beds for everyone	94	94	96
Public transport	88	91	85
Warm water-proof coat	90	84	82
Three meals a day for children	86	80	89
Self-contained accommodation	80	81	85
Two pairs of all-weather shoes	81	77	81
Sufficient bedrooms for children	77	80	78
Refrigerator	76	80	82
Toys for children	68	73	74
Carpets	67	74	73
Celebrations on special occasions	69	70	70
Roast joint once a week	65	69	71
Washing machine	61	72	73
New, not second-hand, clothes	61	69	67
Hobby or leisure activity	67	63	67
Two hot meals a day (adults)	59	70	69
Meat/fish every other day	64	58	78
Presents once a year	65	58	67
Holiday	66	64	67
Leisure equipment for children	57	56	59
Garden	49	59	59
Television	44	58	55
'Best outfit'	46	59	47
Telephone	42	42	46
Outing for children once a week	36	47	39
Dressing gown	41	38	40
Children's friends round once a fortnight	37	38	41
Night out once a fortnight	32	44	34
Friends/family round once a month	30	36	35
Car	26	19	19
Packet of cigarettes	10	15	15
Average of all items	63.4	65.8	66.7

Table 3.8   *Political views and commitment to the necessities*

'If the Government proposed to increase income tax by one penny (1p) in the pound to enable everyone to afford the items you have said are necessities, on balance would you support or oppose this policy?'

		People identifying with:		
	All	*Con.*	*Lab.*	*Lib/SDP*
	%	%	%	%
Support	74	79	73	77
Oppose	23	16	21	19
Don't know	4	5	6	3

groups. This is particularly significant since Conservatives are generally less likely to support policies involving higher taxation. It suggests that the views of Conservative voters on this issue are at odds with the strand of thinking at present dominating the Conservative party, which emphasises an 'absolute' rather than a 'relative' view of need (see, for example, the House of Commons debate on 'The Rich and the Poor', 28 June 1984 – *Hansard*, Vol. 62, No. 181, HMSO). Although this strand of thinking accepts that the state has a responsibility to ensure a minimum level of living for everyone, the level itself is judged on the basis of a narrow interpretation of need. This is in keeping with a strong faith in the fairness of the market system – people's material entitlements should be determined in the main by the free market and not by the state. Interventions in the free market are seen as largely unnecessary and even damaging (see, for example, Joseph and Sumption, 1979; Boyson, 1971). This attitude is also in line with a primary emphasis on individual achievement: people should be given the opportunity to 'earn' a decent living but their 'rights' are more limited.

The present Conservative government is thus out of line not only with the public's perception of needs but also with that of Conservative voters. There has, of course, been a strong tradition in the Conservative party that has taken a more generous view of the needs of the poor (see, for a contemporary example, Gilmour, 1983). The views exhibited by

Conservatives in this survey could be seen to be more in line with this tradition.

Overall, the most striking finding is the high degree of consensus among people of all political persuasions about a minimum standard for the poor. There may well be considerable disagreement about means (see Chapters 7 and 9), but at least people concur about ends. In other words, there is a moral consensus about people's entitlements.

A culturally specific view of poverty

The homogeneity of views shown by people both from very different personal circumstances and also holding very different political ideologies suggests that judgements are being made on the basis of a cohesive view of the kind of society we ought to live in. There is, it seems, a general cultural ethos about what is sufficient and proper.

Interestingly, selected items from the *Breadline Britain* questionnaire have been used in a recent survey in Denmark, which provides some opportunity for cultural comparisons (see Table 3.9). While the evidence is, it should be stressed, limited, it does suggest that general cultural attitudes are important and that, although the classification of necessities is influenced by the extent of ownership, it is not directly dependent upon it.

Consider the roast joint. In Britain this is part of traditional custom: the family lunch on a Sunday is the one time in the week when, even if money is short, every effort will be made to serve a 'decent' meal. In Denmark while a large majority of the Danes will in fact eat a roast joint once a week (75 per cent), it is not vested with the same status: only 50 per cent of Danes regard this as a necessity compared to 67 per cent of the British. What is regarded as a mark of minimum respectability appears to be influenced not just by the extent of practice but also by such factors as tradition.

People's views about what constitutes a 'decent' living gradually change as general living standards change. For example, 92 per cent of the Danish sample had a telephone

Table 3.9 *The Danish view of necessities*

Selected standard-of-living items ranked by % of British sample classifying each item as necessary	*% of Danish sample*[a] *ranking item as necessity*	*% of Danish sample having item*[b]
Heating	97	98
Indoor toilet	94	96
Damp-free home	90	88
Bath	89	93
Warm water-proof coat	89	93
Three meals a day for children	91	(—)[c]
Two pairs of all-weather shoes	64	82
Sufficient bedrooms for children	66	(—)[c]
Refrigerator	94	98
Roast joint once a week	50	75
Meat/fish every other day	69	90
Holiday	47	58
Leisure equipment for children	67	(—)[c]
Television	55	93
Telephone	71	92
Friends/family round once a month	26	48
Car	35	69

[a]Quota sample of 938 persons, surveyed 19–30 November 1983.

[b]These figures are not strictly comparable with those for Britain in Table 3.3 as they give simply the percentage of the sample and have not been adjusted by household size to show the percentage of the population.

[c]The percentage of families with children, rather than the sample, having an item cannot be calculated from the information available.

Source: AIM, Copenhagen.

compared to around 80 per cent of the British sample, and interestingly the Danes are strikingly more likely to see this as a necessity than the British (71 per cent compared to 47 per cent). Both the Danish survey and *Breadline Britain* itself suggest that, when a large majority of people (say, 85 per cent or more) have a good or activity, it is very likely to be seen as a necessity.

The establishment of this general cultural ethos is, of course, extremely complex and its examination is beyond the scope of this study. It will vary from country to country, although the evidence of this study suggests that, in Britain at least, it does not vary greatly from community to community. What is regarded as a necessity in one country will not necessarily be regarded as such in another. This means that someone who is poor in one country may well not be considered poor in another. It also means that when two countries (say, A and B) are being compared it is possible that there will be *less* poverty in country A than in country B in terms of a common standard, but *more* poverty in country A than in B in terms of the internal standards of each country. There is nothing contradictory in this and it does not undermine the reality of the deprivations experienced by the poor in country A. There is no one correct answer to the question of which country has the greatest degree of poverty. In some circumstances, it is appropriate to make comparisons on the basis of a common standard; in others, on the basis of the respective standards of each country.

As far as the experiences and feelings of people in Britain are concerned, it is the cultural standards of this country that are important. And, as far as policies to tackle poverty within Britain are concerned, it is measures based on these internal standards that are important. It is of little relevance to an unemployed family in Birmingham that they are better off than an agricultural worker in India.

Although this study is concerned exclusively with poverty in Britain, it is worth mentioning in passing that the standards set by this survey for people in Britain do not preclude or prejudice the setting of other standards on which to base international comparisons or even policy. People in Britain may well accept that there are fundamental rights that any citizen anywhere should be entitled to. If this was the case, however, it would be a different kind of judgement from those exercised in drawing up minimum standards for Britain. Saying that no one should die of starvation, for example, is a political and ethical judgement based not on personal experience but exclusively on concepts of morality. It has been argued that moral judgements are involved in drawing up minimum living standards in Britain, but they are based on people's day-to-day experiences and reflect those. It is this that gives strength to this approach to poverty.

A minimum standard of living for Britain in the 1980s

In establishing a minimum standard of living, it is not possible to come up with a detailed description of every single aspect of life that should be included. Instead, a range of items has to be selected that is indicative of these minimum standards. This means that some ambiguity inevitably surrounds the minimum standards described. In addition, the items in the *Breadline Britain* survey were open to some interpretation as regards quality and cheapness. The items are nevertheless sufficiently representative and sufficiently precise to give a general picture of a minimum standard of living for Britain in the 1980s.

The survey found widespread agreement between all groups in society about the items that are classified as necessities. The homogeneity of views is striking. People from all walks of life, from across the generations, from widely varying family circumstances, and with fundamentally opposed political beliefs, share the same view of the kind of society Britain should be in terms of the minimum standards of living to which all citizens should be entitled. Their views are based, it seems, on a general cultural ethos of what is decent and proper. This suggests that these views are deeply held. They are unlikely to fluctuate rapidly or to be affected by the kinds of changes in political climate that influence the public's views on policies (see Chapters 7 and 9). This is an advantage when using the measure of poverty developed here to determine and assess policy.

Perhaps most importantly, the survey's findings show that people see the necessities for living in Britain today not in terms of subsistence, nor in terms of some historical yardstick – but in terms of a *relative* view of needs based on the standards of today. The minimum standard of living established reflects people's feelings about what is so essential that to go without would be a deprivation. It is also based on a judgement about people's rights. Virtually everyone thinks that everyone in Britain today should be entitled to a life that is more than just a struggle for existence. The next chapter shows whether the poor in Britain today can choose to live or are forced just to exist.

4

The Other Britain
The extent of deprivation

> There are some times I think to myself it's my fault and that's when I start getting niggly and take it out on the family, which I shouldn't do but the pressure just builds up inside you and you just explode and that's it. But then I'm not the only one. There's three million more who go through the same things and it's just part of life. [An unemployed father]

In recent years there has been growing concern about the increase in the numbers of people living on low incomes. This increase has stemmed from two factors: first, the recession, which has led to a sharp rise in the numbers of unemployed; and, second, the social welfare and taxation policies of the government, which have tended to benefit the rich at the expense of the poor.

However, an increase in the numbers on low incomes does not automatically mean that there has been a rise in the numbers in *poverty*. It may be that this group, although worse off than others, are nevertheless managing adequately. They may not, in other words, be deprived. These questions can only be answered in terms of people's living standards.

The minimum standard of living established by the *Breadline Britain* survey provides a benchmark for judging whether the minimum income provided by the state – supplementary benefit – is adequate. To pursue this question requires a detailed examination of the standard of living of supplementary benefit claimants. Are those on the lowest incomes forced to go without the socially established necessities for living in Britain in the 1980s?

On its own, this will not provide a complete measure of the extent of poverty in Britain today. There are reasons to expect that there will be some who are not on the very lowest incomes who nevertheless have among the lowest living standards. The living standards of other households must also be examined to see whose are so low that they fall below the minimum standards of society today. This also throws some light on whether the tax and benefit system is working effectively to alleviate poverty: in this context, whether the wider range of benefits – in particular, child benefit – are sufficient.

In the remaining three chapters in Part I, the minimum standards laid down in Chapter 3 will be used to develop a measure of poverty. First, those who are deprived need to be identified. In this study, we have defined deprivation in terms of an enforced lack of socially perceived necessities. The extent and distribution of deprivation is examined in this chapter. In Chapter 5, the effect of these deprivations on people's lives is examined. Whether a person who is deprived is also in poverty will depend on the impact of deprivation on their way of life. In Chapter 6, these two strands are pulled together to distinguish between those 'in poverty' and those who are managing. It is, in our view, important to establish some kind of indication of the extent of poverty in Britain today so as to assess the size of the problem and the implications of this for policy.

The lack of socially perceived necessities

The *Breadline Britain* survey asked respondents which of the thirty-five standard-of-living items they had and which they did not have. For those items that they did not have, they were also asked whether this was by choice or because they could not afford it. This led to two measures of the extent to which people lack the twenty-six items classed by the majority of the population as necessities. First, there are the total numbers of people lacking a necessity for whatever reason, and second there is a smaller group who lack a necessity because they cannot afford it. These two measures are given in Table 4.1. (The picture presented holds for both

Table 4.1 *The lack of socially perceived necessities*

The 26 standard-of-living 'necessities' in rank order	% of population[a] not having item[b]	% of population unable to afford item	% of population not wanting item
Heating	6	6	0
Indoor toilet	1	1	0
Damp-free home	10	8	2
Bath	2	2	0
Beds for everyone	2	1	1
Public transport	9	3	6
Warm water-proof coat	10	7	3
Three meals a day for children[c]	7	4	3
Self-contained accommodation	6	3	3
Two pairs of all-weather shoes	15	11	4
Sufficient bedrooms for children[c]	17	10	7
Refrigerator	2	1	1
Toys for children[c]	5	3	2
Carpets	3	2	1
Celebrations on special occasions	6	4	2
Roast joint once a week	12	7	5
Washing machine	9	5	4
New, not second-hand, clothes	13	8	5
Hobby or leisure activity	21	9	12
Two hot meals a day (adults)	18	4	14
Meat/fish every other day	17	9	8
Presents once a year	8	5	3
Holiday	30	23	7
Leisure equipment for children[c]	17	13	4
Garden	10	5	5
Television	1	—[d]	1

[a]The responses have been weighted by numbers in household to give the percentage of the population.

[b]This includes both those who do not have an item because they say they do not want it and those who do not have an item because they say they cannot afford it.

[c]Families with children under 16 only.

[d]Less than 0.5%.

men and women. There were only two items for which there was a statistically significant difference between the sexes: a holiday, which more women went without because they could not afford it, and a hobby, which more women went without because they did not want it.)

Whichever measure is taken, the number of people lacking each of the necessities is substantial. Consider, at this stage, only those who lack a necessity because they cannot afford it and take for the moment, people's evaluation of this as being correct. Applying the survey's findings to the population as a whole, and grouping the necessities together into specific aspects of life, shows that:

- approximately 3 million people in Britain today cannot afford to heat the living areas of their home
- around 6 million go without some essential aspect of clothing – such as a warm waterproof coat – because of lack of money
- some 1.5 million children go without toys or, for older children, leisure and sports equipment because their parents do not have enough money
- nearly 3.5 million people do not have consumer durables such as carpets, a washing machine or a fridge because of lack of money
- around 3 million people cannot afford celebrations at Christmas or presents for the family once a year.
- at least 5.5 million people cannot afford basic items of food such as meat or fish every other day, a roast joint once a week or two hot meals a day.
- nearly half a million children do not have three meals a day because their parents are so short of money.

These figures present a stark picture of the extent to which people cannot afford necessities. Many questions remain, however. Is this use of those who say they cannot afford a necessity an accurate measure of an 'enforced' lack of necessities – or at least the best available? Is it right to exclude those who do not have an item because they do not want it? Townsend, in his pioneering study of poverty in Britain, included all those who did not have one of his standard-of-living items in his measures of poverty and did not 'control' for 'taste' in this way. The argument behind this alternative approach is that people's feelings of 'choice' are themselves determined by their economic situation, so the feeling that one does not want an item becomes a rationalisation for the fact that one cannot afford it.

Table 4.1 shows that for about one-third of the items it does not matter much which measure is taken – the difference between the two being 1 percentage point or less. For most of the items, however, it makes a significant difference. In general, the difference is greatest for items in the bottom half of the rank order of necessities. That in itself does not tip the balance either for or against excluding those who feel they do not want an item. It is likely that there will be more people who choose, for reasons of taste, to go without those necessities about which there is less consensus than others, but it is equally possible that people will rationalise their lack in this way among those necessities that are more 'marginal'.

To proceed any further, people's lack of items needs to be related to their income. This is also important to check that the people who say they cannot afford an item actually have a shortage of money.

The income measure

The income concept used is *net equivalent household income*. This means that the income measure is exclusive of housing costs, that it refers to the household and not the individual and that each household's income has been 'adjusted' to take account of the household's size and composition. The procedure and its problems are described in Appendix C (pp. 308–14). The discussion is placed in an appendix not because it is unimportant but because it is rather technical. Indeed, the conclusions of this technical discussion are extremely important.

For a wide variety of reasons, three key problems arose with this income measure. First, income is understated. Second, the extent of inequality, particularly in the lower half of the income range, is understated. Third, some households will have been misplaced in the income range; in other words, some people will have been grouped together as having the same or very similar incomes when in fact they have considerably different incomes. This means that the relationship between income and living standards described in the rest of this chapter will not be as tight as it is in reality.

Controlling for taste

The first question that needs to be examined is which measure of lack of necessities most accurately reflects the numbers going without because of lack of money. Should all those who lack necessities be taken? Or just those who say the lack is because of shortage of money? To answer this question, it is necessary to examine specifically those people who say they do not have an item or do not participate in an activity because they do not want to. If this group was primarily *forced* into this situation, they would be concentrated in the lower income groups.

Table 4.2 shows the relationship between those who do not have an item because they do not want it and their net equivalent household income. To find out whether the 'don't want' answers were independent of income we have calculated correlation coefficients. The correlation coefficient gives a measure of the way in which income affects people's answer: a negative correlation coefficient shows that those on lower incomes are more likely to be giving this answer than those on higher incomes, and a positive correlation coefficient shows the reverse. The statistical 'significance' of the relationship can also be calculated; that is, the probability that the relationship is real rather than occurring just by chance. Table 4.2 shows whether the correlations are significant at the 95 per cent confidence level. This means that the relationship would occur by chance only 5 times out of a 100; that is, 95 times out of a 100 it reflects real differences in behaviour.

The results show that to a large extent those who do not have an item because they do not want it are spread fairly evenly across the income range. For a majority of items, the relationship between income and lack of possession from

Table 4.2 *The lack of necessities from 'choice'*

The 26 standard-of-living 'necessities' in rank order	Net equivalent household income			Correlation coefficient
	Poorest 10%	Middle 10%	Top 10%	
	% not having item from choice[a]			
Heating[b]	—	—	—	—
Indoor toilet	1	2	0	− 0.044 NS
Damp-free home	1	3	2	− 0.001 NS
Bath[b]	—	—	—	—
Beds for everyone	0	1	0	− 0.048 NS
Public transport	3	8	5	+ 0.003 NS
Warm water-proof coat	5	2	2	− 0.056 NS
3 meals a day for children[c]	0	2	0	− 0.035 NS
Self-contained accommodation	2	0	0	− 0.044 NS
2 pairs of all-weather shoes	4	4	2	− 0.061 *
Sufficient bedrooms for children[c]	3	7	2	− 0.029 NS
Refrigerator	0	3	1	− 0.039 NS
Toys for children[c]	12	0	0	− 0.161 *
Carpets[b]	—	—	—	—
Celebrations on special occasions	3	8	1	− 0.052 NS
Roast joint once a week	4	10	6	− 0.031 NS
Washing machine	6	7	9	+ 0.015 NS
New, not secondhand, clothes	6	2	0	− 0.057 *
Hobby or leisure activity	15	11	4	− 0.131 *
2 hot meals a day (adults)	10	24	22	+ 0.083 *
Meat/fish every other day	10	10	7	− 0.068 *
Presents once a year	5	1	0	− 0.079 *
Holiday	9	11	2	− 0.089 *
Leisure equipment for children[c]	5	0	0	− 0.050 NS
Garden	10	8	4	− 0.046 NS
Television	3	0	2	− 0.001 NS

NS = not significant at 95% level.
 * = significant at 95% level.

[a]The percentages refer to respondents.
[b]Under 1% of sample.
[c]Families with children under 16 only.

choice is not statistically significant. However, there are seven items that those on lower incomes are significantly more likely to claim that they do not want than those on higher incomes: two pairs of all-weather shoes, toys for children, new clothes, hobby or leisure activity, meat or fish every other day, presents once a year, and holidays. For some of the items, the fact that the poor are the most likely not to want them may be explained by differences in lifestyles. In particular, the poor are generally less inclined than others to regard a hobby or a holiday as necessities (see Table 3.2, p. 61). For other items the differences are more difficult to explain but could stem from lower expectations. For two of the items, toys and presents, the proportions not wanting the item are very small, so not too much weight should be given to these particular findings. By contrast, there is one item that the better-off are significantly more likely not to want than others: two hot meals a day. This probably stems from differences in lifestyles – reflected in the fact that the better-off are less likely than others to regard two hot meals a day as a necessity (see Table 3.2, p. 61).

Overall, the relationship between income and lack of necessities because of lack of desire suggests that these people are, indeed, largely *choosing* to go without rather than being forced into this situation. To exclude this group from the measure of those who have an enforced lack of a necessity is therefore, to a large extent, to 'control for taste'. However, it is necessary to add some qualifications.

The first and most important qualification relates to the degree of 'choice' that the poor exercise. In Chapter 5 we shall see that, among those whose living standards fall below that of society generally, the exercise of choice is minimal. Those who lack three or four necessities will be seen to exercise a choice between whether to go without meat every other day or whether to go without a roast joint once a week, or between going without variety and adequacy of food and buying a coat. The choice seldom extends to whether to cut back on clothes or go on holiday – because holidays have already been cut back on. Those who are most intensely deprived have fewer choices left open to them – they cut back on all areas of life and within each area on many aspects. This means that, among those with the lowest living standards, lack of a necessity because they do not want it is likely to stem from very different causes from those whose choice is based on an ability to afford alternatives.

Consider, for example, two hot meals a day. Many of those who are better-off choose not to have this, but this does not mean that their diet will be in any way deprived, simply that they are choosing to concentrate their eating into one meal a day. Among those whose living standards are low who 'choose' not to have two hot meals a day it is likely that this lack will not be made up for in other ways. The feeling that choice is being exercised may be real enough, in that a decision is being made between two limited options, but it is not necessarily a choice that would be made if they had enough money. Tricia, for example, started cutting back on food for herself to buy toys for her children, and in one sense she chose to go without two hot meals a day. Moreover, she is now in the habit of eating just one meal a day – a tea of something like beans on toast with the children – and no longer misses regular food; in that sense, she no longer wants it:

> It's just something I've got used to, you know, so I don't think I could eat every day if people put it in front of me. It's just what I've got used to, the way I've got used to living because you are limited to what you can buy and what you can spend and you get into that way of life, and it's hard to get out of it. And it would take a lot to change it.

Recently, Tricia has been suffering from dizziness, which may well have been either caused or exacerbated by her inadequate diet. Thus, although the lack of necessities may be based on a choice, among the poor this lack may nevertheless be a deprivation.

The second major qualification relates to the number of necessities people choose to go without. The number of necessities a person lacks is, generally, of more importance than the particular necessities they lack. Those who lack one or even two necessities will generally find that the difference this makes to their lives is relatively small. Those who lack many necessities, by contrast, will find their whole way of life is affected. The number of necessities lacked through choice is shown in Table 4.3.

The significance of 'taste' as an influence on people's purchasing of, or participation in, necessities is best measured in the context of the rich, in other words of those who face no financial constraints with regard to their standard of living at this minimal level. While a significant number of the rich choose to go without one or even two necessities, only 4 per cent choose to go without three or more necessities. In the light of the limitations on the income data, this proportion is insignificant. The rich do not choose the lifestyles associated with the lack of necessities. Thus, the role of 'taste' is seen not to affect most people's purchases of necessities at all and never to affect people's purchases of necessities in more than the most marginal of ways.

Table 4.3 *The multiple lack of necessities from 'choice'*

Number of adult necessities[a] lacked	Adults[b]	Households in income deciles[c]									
		1st	2nd	3rd	4th	5th	6th	7th	8th	9th	10th
		% not having items from choice[d]									
0	57	55	42	53	50	48	44	53	50	58	59
1 or more	43	45	58	47	50	52	56	47	50	42	41
2 or more	21	18	27	27	29	28	36	23	25	10	12
3 or more	8	14	10	10	18	11	13	5	10	5	4
4 or more	3	4	6	4	6	6	4	3	1	1	2
5 or more	1	1	2	3	1	3	1	0	0	0	0

[a] See page 106 for the list of the 18 items included.

[b] Households have been weighted by the number of adults to give the percentage of the adult population.

[c] Income deciles are formed by grouping all households into tenths according to their income: the 1st decile represents the bottom 10% of households, the 2nd decile the next 10%, etc.

[d] Only those who do not have an item because they say they do not want it are included.

In this context, it is interesting that there are some among the poor who appear to 'choose' to cut back on a number of necessities. 'Controlling for taste' could thus be seen to minimise, not just the enforced lack of each necessity, but more generally the measurement of levels of deprivation. This is discussed further on pp. 113–17 and in Chapter 6.

In view of the importance of this question, it is worth looking further at which groups of low-income households are the most likely to go without from 'choice'. One group stands out: the elderly. Table 4.4 shows the proportions of pensioners and non-pensioners on low incomes 'choosing' to go without different levels of necessities. Among pensioners on low incomes, 73 per cent 'choose' to go without at least one necessity compared to 57 per cent of non-pensioners, and 24 per cent of pensioners 'choose' to go without three or more necessities compared to 9 per cent of non-pensioners. While this will to some extent reflect a lower degree of 'need' among pensioners, it will also reflect lower expectations and aspirations.

Ernie is a 79-year-old pensioner living on his own. He can no longer cook for himself and instead relies on meals-on-

Table 4.4 *The lack of necessities from 'choice' among the elderly*

Number of adult necessities[a] lacked	Households in bottom 40% of income range	
	Pensioners	Non-pensioners
	% not having items from choice[b]	
0	27	43
1 or more	73	57
2 or more	44	19
3 or more	24	9
4 or more	12	3
5 or more	4	1
6 or more	4	0
7 or more	0	0

[a]See page 106 for the list of the 18 items included.
[b]Only those who do not have an item because they do not want it are included.

wheels. But he does not get a lunch every day, only every other day. He eats half the main course at lunch-time, and half the sweet in the evening. The rest he saves for the next day. His motives are mixed:

> I can't eat them. To be fair to myself, I know I haven't got the appetite I used to have. Therefore I just have enough to eat and then I have the rest the next day. It's an economic idea to have as much as you can afford. You can't go beyond your means. I mean, the point is I get the meals Mondays, Wednesdays and Fridays and that costs over a pound, £1.40 for that. I would have to pay twice that if I had it Tuesdays and Thursdays. See what I mean.

Ernie would say that he was going without two hot meals a day from 'choice'. Like many elderly people his appetite is small and in that sense the 'choice' reflects a lower level of 'need'. However, the 'choice' also reflects low expectations stemming from lack of money. The result is that he does not in fact eat as much as he needs, and is gradually losing weight. Even when he is hungry, he does not eat any more because he has to save the rest for another meal. By the standards of today, his eating habits are inadequate: he does not eat enough, his diet lacks variety, and the conditions in which he saves the food and reheats it are unhygienic. In these respects, his lack of food, though perceived in part to stem from choice, would be seen by others to be nevertheless a deprivation.

This is just one example of the low expectations that are typical of many of the elderly. Although the elderly themselves may not feel deprived, they may still be judged on these criteria to be deprived by the standards of society as a whole. To the extent that the elderly's lack of necessities from 'choice' reflects these low expectations, the exclusion of those who do not have necessities because they do not want them is not so much 'controlling for taste' as limiting the measure of poverty only to those who recognise their impoverished situation – which is not the same thing as a more objective measure of poverty.

In summary, the findings suggest that it is worth 'controlling for taste'. There are a few people who lack a range of necessities who are in a position to exercise real choice, so that if 'taste' was not controlled for they would be unjustifiably counted among the deprived. However, the findings also suggest that the importance of 'taste' can be easily overestimated; in particular, the criticisms of the Townsend study that emphasise the role of 'choice' (see Chapter 2) run this risk. Moreover, 'controlling for taste' by simply excluding those who do not have a necessity because they do not want it does have serious limitations. The effects on the overall measures of the extent of deprivation are examined on pp. 113–17 and a slightly more sophisticated approach to the question of controlling for taste is developed in Chapter 6 in relation to the measurement of poverty. For simplicity, however, the study proceeds in the main to 'control for taste' simply by excluding those who do not have a necessity because they do not want it from the measure of the enforced lack of necessities. As such, these measures present only a *minimal* picture of the extent of deprivation.

An enforced lack of necessities

Central to this study of poverty is the concept of 'an enforced lack of necessities'. Those who do not have necessities because they do not want them have been excluded, in the main, from this measure to ensure that it is interpreted strictly; but there still remains a questionmark over whether those who lack necessities because they say they cannot afford them are really being 'forced' into this situation.

There are a number of reasons why those who are relatively well-off may say that there are one or two necessities they cannot afford. Most importantly, they may interpret the necessities in such a way that what they are referring to no longer reflects a basic standard of living but their own expectations. They may, for example, say they cannot afford a holiday – but a week in a caravan in Skegness is hardly what they have in mind. Clearly, a measure of poverty is not interested in whether a family is able to fly to the Bahamas, even if this is their interpretation of not being able to afford a holiday. As survey questions are always open to an interpretation not intended in their design, it is important to check whether those who say they cannot afford a necessity are doing so for reasons that reflect genuine financial pressures.

If such 'misinterpretations' were dominant, then people's answers to the question of whether they could not afford necessities would be randomly related to income. This is unlikely because the room for interpretation in most of the questions is relatively limited – but it is important to check. Table 4.5 shows the relationship between those who do not have an item because they cannot afford it and their net equivalent household income. The results show that not being able to afford the necessities is indeed sharply related to income: those on lower incomes are very much more likely to go without necessities because they cannot afford them than are those on higher incomes. The relationships between income and lack of necessities shown in Table 4.5 are under-estimates owing to the limitations of the income data. Even so, the relationships are highly significant: for the large majority of items the statistical significance is at the 99.5% level; that is, the likelihood that this relationship is a product of chance is less than 0.5 in every 100.

The figures paint a bleak picture of the day-to-day lives of poor families. The great majority of the population hardly thinks twice about spending money on the activities and items in the list of necessities. Buying the Sunday joint, turning on the central heating, buying new clothes, for example, are activities that are largely taken for granted. For the poor, this is not so. Every penny has to be accounted for in a constant struggle to make ends meet.

Table 4.5 also shows, however, that there are some rich people who say they cannot afford necessities. Overall, this is marginal: the rich can all afford nineteen of the necessities and the proportions unable to afford the remaining seven are all small. That there are a few rich people who say that they cannot afford one or other necessity is in itself unimportant.

Table 4.5 *The lack of necessities from 'shortage' of money*

The 26 standard-of-living 'necessities' in rank order	Net equivalent household income Poorest 10%	Middle 10%	Top 10%	Correlation coefficient
	% not having item because they can't afford it[a]			
Heating	17	6	0	− 0.146 *
Indoor toilet	9	1	0	− 0.104 *
Damp-free home	18	4	0	− 0.174 *
Bath	11	1	0	− 0.107 *
Beds for everyone	5	0	0	− 0.085 *
Public transport	3	3	0	− 0.036 NS
Warm water-proof coat	17	6	1	− 0.185 *
3 meals a day for children[c]	12	1	0	− 0.121 *
Self-contained accommodation	2	2	2	− 0.053 NS
2 pairs of all-weather shoes	29	7	0	− 0.184 *
Sufficient bedrooms for children[c]	18	2	0	− 0.155 *
Refrigerator	3	3	1	− 0.067 *
Toys for children[c]	13	0	0	− 0.156 *
Carpets	8	3	0	− 0.090 *
Celebrations on special occasions	14	4	0	− 0.146 *
Roast joint once a week	20	7	4	− 0.119 *
Washing machine	17	3	2	− 0.102 *
New, not second-hand clothes	20	4	0	− 0.180 *
Hobby or leisure activity	16	5	0	− 0.134 *
2 hot meals a day (adults)	7	4	0	− 0.073 *
Meat/fish every other day	23	8	0	− 0.172 *
Presents once a year	13	2	0	− 0.146 *
Holiday	49	17	7	− 0.230 *
Leisure equipment for children[c]	40	9	0	− 0.231 *
Garden	9	3	6	− 0.037 NS
Television[b]	—	—	—	—

NS = not significant at 95% level.
 * = significant at 95% level.

[a]The percentages refer to respondents.
[b]Under 1% of sample.
[c]Families with children under 16 only.

There is always, at the margins, some room for misinterpretation and error – and Table 4.5 shows that this is very much just at the margins.

There are, however, a significant number of people in middle-income groups who cannot afford one or other of the necessities. There may, of course, be some misinterpretation among this group about what is being asked for – although the insignificant levels of lack among the rich suggests that this is unlikely to be of any importance. What is far more likely is that this inability to afford necessities among a small minority of those on middle incomes reflects real financial difficulties. Once income rises above the median, the inability to afford necessities drops very sharply.

The reasons why any particular individual cannot afford any particular necessity are complex. Though the immediate cause is shortage of money, there are many other factors that lead to this situation (this is discussed further on pp. 127–32). As a consequence, some people with incomes that are not among the lowest cannot afford one or other of the necessities; while others, on lower incomes, possess these necessities. Similarly, among households on low incomes, some will go without one particular necessity and others without another, for a wide variety of reasons (this is discussed in detail in Chapter 5). Income can be expected to provide a measure only of the *likelihood* that a person will be forced to go without; it is not a complete guide to spending patterns and choices. In these terms, the results are clear-cut: for any one of the necessities, the poor are more likely to go without for lack of money than are others, and for the vast majority of the necessities the differences are sharp.

What is of far more importance than who lacks each of the necessities is the way in which the lack of necessities clusters among certain households. This provides a measure of the extent of different degrees of deprivation. To do this, the necessities must be examined together and not separately. But should all the necessities be included? It has been argued that only those people who have an enforced lack of necessities should be counted as deprived, which means that only those necessities that turn out in practice not to be open to any misinterpretation should be included. Table 4.5 shows that this holds for the overwhelming majority of necessities, but there remains some doubt over a small minority.

There are three items for which the correlation with income is not significant: lack of money for public transport, lack of self-contained accommodation and lack of a garden. The reasons for this are not entirely obvious. The small proportions of people unable to afford public transport and self-contained accommodation call for caution: these results could be a statistical aberration. However, it is possible that the results have been influenced by the fact that the cost and accessibility of all these items is very dependent on where a person lives; certainly the wide differences between councils in the degree to which they subsidise transport provision in their area could affect this result. Further, as far as public transport is concerned, people in middle-income brackets may have in mind not being able to afford the first-class fare by train from, say, London to Edinburgh whereas the poor are thinking of the bus fare down the road.

Because these reasons may mean that respondents have interpreted their lack of these three specific items in a way that does not reflect the basic standard of living intended, or that their interpretation of not being able to afford these three items does not reflect financial constraint in the way intended, these three items have been excluded from the measurement of deprivation and, in turn, poverty. Being able to afford a television has also been excluded because the numbers who cannot afford it are so small as to make it impossible to test the significance of the relationship with income. (In fact, it makes very little difference whether or not these four items are included, partly because the numbers involved are anyway very small and partly because of the way in which the lack of necessities tends to cluster.)

The remaining twenty-two items enable a tight measure of deprivation and poverty to be examined. For any of these items, the inability to afford it is highly related to income. This is confirmed by looking at households on supplementary benefit (see Table 4.6). There is even greater deprivation among these households than among those on low incomes

Table 4.6   *The lack of necessities from 'shortage' of money among supplementary benefit claimants*

22 standard-of-living 'necessities' in rank order	Households on supplementary benefit		
	Pensioners	Families	Others[a]
	% not having item because can't afford it		
Heating	11	25	24
Indoor toilet	12	5	8
Damp-free home	15	23	34
Bath	10	5	10
Beds for everyone	3	3	3
Warm water-proof coat	33	28	20
3 meals a day for children[b]	—	15	—
2 pairs of all-weather shoes	19	41	30
Sufficient bedrooms for children[b]	—	12	—
Refrigerator	11	5	5
Toys for children[b]	—	13	—
Carpets	1	19	7
Celebrations on special occasions	8	21	15
Roast joint once a week	11	23	30
Washing machine	18	21	15
New, not secondhand clothes	24	24	29
Hobby or leisure activity	3	29	25
2 hot meals a day (adults)	8	17	11
Meat/fish every other day	9	41	20
Presents once a year	13	24	16
Holiday	27	67	54
Leisure equipment for children[b]	—	46	—

[a]These include some families with children over 16 and households with more than one claimant.
[b]Families with children under 16 only.

generally. The problems are greatest for families with children under 16, suggesting that the supplementary benefit rate for children is too low. Problems are also great among households on supplementary benefit with children over 16 and households with more than one claimant (the last column in Table 4.6). Only pensioners appear to fare relatively well – and even then one-third cannot afford a warm, water-proof coat, and one-quarter have to rely on secondhand clothes. Further, much of this difference between pensioners and others is accounted for by the fact that pensioners are more likely to say that they do not want these goods and activities (see Table 4.4; this question is discussed further on pp. 115–16).

In summary, taking those who go without necessities because they say they cannot afford them provides a useful approximation for those who have an enforced lack of necessities. It is only an approximation, not so much because there are a few at the margins who could objectively be said to be able to afford the necessity, but because there are three key reasons for thinking that the measure is an under-estimate.

First, there may be a few people who say they have a necessity when in fact they do not. They may simply be too embarrassed to admit it. Some items, such as three meals a day for children, are particularly likely to have a great deal of stigma attached to their lack.

Second, there will be some among the poor who say they 'have' a necessity when by the standards of society at large their possession could be seen to fall below the most minimal level. Consider heating: there may be some, especially among the elderly, who say they have heating in their living areas, when in fact they can afford to have it on only for an hour or so in the evening, and usually wrap up in rugs or go to bed to keep warm. Because of low expectations, they do not feel that they are forced to go without heating, but this does not necessarily mean that they are not deprived.

Lastly, these low expectations may also mean, as has been seen, that there are some among those who go without necessities from 'choice' who have been 'forced' into this situation. By and large, we would not expect the influence of the first two factors to be great, since the poor's standards are very similar to those of others when measured in other less personal ways (see Chapter 3). The influence of the third, however, is significant and will be dealt with on pp. 113–17 and in Chapter 6. All in all, the measures taken of an enforced lack of necessities should be seen as *minimal*.

Levels of deprivation

To examine how many people are forced to go without necessities and the degree to which some people fall below the minimum standards of society requires an analysis of the necessities collectively, rather than separately. There are three types of necessities in the list of twenty-two selected for further examination: those that affect all members of a household; those that affect primarily just the respondent, that is the adult members of the household; and items specifically for children. To examine deprivation among adults, the household items and adult items have been grouped together forming a group of eighteen necessities:

- heating
- indoor toilet
- damp-free home
- bath
- enough beds
- refrigerator
- carpets
- celebrations on special occasions
- a roast joint once a week
- a washing machine
- new clothes
- meat or fish every other day
- presents for family or friends once a year
- a holiday away from home for one week a year
- a warm water-proof coat
- two pairs of all-weather shoes
- a hobby or leisure acitivity
- two hot meals a day.

To examine deprivation among children, the household items have been grouped with the children's items, forming a second group of eighteen necessities:

- heating
- indoor toilet
- damp-free home
- bath
- enough beds
- refrigerator

- carpets
- celebrations on special occasions
- a roast joint once a week
- a washing machine
- new clothes
- meat or fish every other day
- presents for family or friends once a year
- a holiday away from home for one week a year
- three meals a day
- enough bedrooms for every child over 10 of different sex to have his or her own
- toys
- leisure equipment.

Table 4.7 shows the distribution of deprivation among adults and Table 4.8 shows the distribution of deprivation among families with children. Two important findings emerge. First,

Table 4.7 *Levels of deprivation among adults*

Number of adult necessities[a] lacked	Adults[b]	Households in income deciles[c]					6th 7th	8th 9th 10th
		1st	2nd	3rd	4th	5th		
		% not having items because can't afford it[d]						
0	66	29	42	55	54	56	65	82
1 or more	34	71	58	45	46	44	35	18
2 or more	19	52	35	32	35	28	16	7
3 or more	12	39	25	22	25	17	8	4
4 or more	10	34	18	20	17	11	6	3
5 or more	8	29	16	14	16	10	4	2
6 or more	5	21	9	10	11	4	2	1
7 or more	4	19	4	9	7	1	1	0

[a]See page 106 for the list of the 18 items included.

[b]Households have been weighted by the number of adults to give the percentage of the adult population.

[c]Income deciles are formed by grouping all the households into tenths according to their income; the bottom five deciles, the next 20% and the top 30% are given.

[d]Only those who do not have an item because they say they cannot afford it are included.

Table 4.8 *Levels of deprivation among children*

Number of children's necessities[a] lacked	Children[b]	Families in income deciles[c]					6th 7th	8th 9th 10th
		1st	2nd	3rd	4th	5th		
		% not having items because can't afford it[d]						
0	54	17	26	35	47	50	61	81
1 or more	46	83	74	65	53	50	39	19
2 or more	29	64	42	49	29	27	11	6
3 or more	20	55	33	32	24	24	2	2
4 or more	14	47	27	23	13	13	0	1
5 or more	11	39	21	22	13	8	0	0
6 or more	9	28	18	18	8	0	0	0
7 or more	7	23	8	18	8	0	0	0

[a]See page 106–7 for the list of the 18 items included.

[b]Families have been weighted by the number of children to give the percentage of all children lacking necessities.

[c]Income deciles are formed by grouping all the households into tenths according to their income; families in the bottom five deciles, the next 20% and the top 30% are given.

[d]Only those who do not have an item because they say they cannot afford it are included.

the poor in Britain today fare very badly, not just compared to others, but more particularly by the standards set by the majority of people as minimal. Of the bottom 10 per cent in the income range, over one-half cannot afford at least two necessities, over one-third cannot afford four or more necessities, and over one-fifth cannot afford six or more necessities. Over one-quarter of these low-income households, however, say that there are no necessities they cannot afford – but this does not mean that they actually have all the necessities; this discrepancy is discussed on pp. 114–15. Secondly, families with children fare particularly badly. Comparing Tables 4.7 and 4.8 shows that, in each income decile, families fare worst: looking again at those in the bottom decile shows that two-thirds lack two or more necessities, nearly one-half lack four or more necessities and over one-quarter lack six or more necessities. In addition, families with children are more concentrated in the lower income ranges than households generally, with relatively few families at the top of the income range. Together, these two factors mean that overall deprivation among children is much higher than deprivation among adults: nearly one-half of all children lack at least one necessity because their families cannot afford it compared to one-third of adults; and one-fifth of all children lack three or more necessities compared to just over one-tenth of adults.

The findings also show that deprivation is not confined just to those on the very lowest incomes. This is shown graphically in Figures 4.1 and 4.2, which plot the proportion of each income group lacking various levels of necessities for all households and families, respectively. To some extent this spread of deprivation stems from an element of 'misinterpretation': just as with each of the necessities separately there was a small minority of the better-off who said they could not afford that necessity, so too with the necessities collectively. Looking at those who lack one or more necessities, there is a significant proportion in the upper half of the income range. This also holds, though to a lesser extent, for those who lack two or more necessities. To some extent, people who are better-off put themselves in a position where they have to cut back on necessities – but *only* at the margins. A family who is better off may, for example, sacrifice the annual holiday the year they are buying a larger house, they may even hold back on buying a new deluxe washing machine when their old one breaks down – but they do not make sacrifices that entail cutting back to any greater extent at this basic level.

Looking at the families who lack three or more necessities in Figure 4.2 shows that vulnerability to multiple deprivation does not extend to families in the top half of the income range. Whatever variations there are in the expenditure patterns of better-off families, they do not entail cutting back on necessities to this degree. This division is sharper for families than for households generally. The examination of families on their own avoids many of the problems of classification that lead to households being misplaced in the income range (see Appendix C). This suggests that the small number

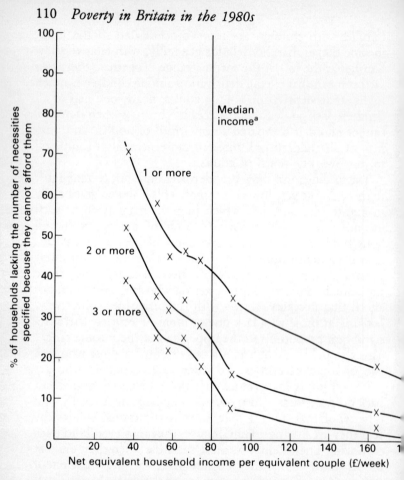

a The median is the income level below which 50% of household incomes fal

Figure 4.1 Levels of deprivation among adults

of better-off households showing multiple deprivation among adults (see Figure 4.1 and Table 4.7) are misclassified.

Vulnerability to deprivation does, however, extend throughout the households comprising the bottom half of the income range. While the levels of deprivation are considerably higher among the bottom decile than the others, significant proportions of families in the second and third, and to a lesser extent also the fourth and fifth, deciles face deprivation. This also holds for households generally.

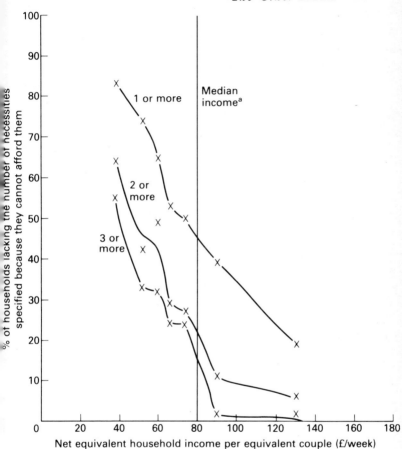

a The median is the income level below which 50% of household incomes fall.
Figure 4.2 Levels of deprivation among families

The reasons why households with different incomes nevertheless face similar levels of deprivation are examined on pp. 127–32. At this stage, it is worth noting that in the bottom half of the income range the income differences between large numbers of households are not all that great. Further, there is likely to be a greater degree of week-by-week interchange among those in the bottom income groups because their earnings fluctuate regularly. Those on lower incomes are much more likely to face periods of being out of work and when in work their earnings will vary according to the extent of overtime. This means that levels of deprivation among the second and third deciles, and to some extent also the fourth decile, do not vary greatly.

Overall, the patterns are clear. Those in the bottom decile of the income range are by far the most likely to be deprived; those in the next three deciles, and to some extent the fifth decile as well, are vulnerable to deprivation; those in the top half of the income range may occasionally lack one or even two necessities but they virtually never suffer multiple deprivation.

The problems of the poorest are highlighted by looking at those households on supplementary benefit. This is shown in Table 4.9. Most families on supplementary benefit face high levels of deprivation and a significant minority are intensely deprived (over one-third lack six or more necessities). A similar picture emerges for other non-pensioner households on supplementary benefit. The picture for pensioners is very different, however. This sharp distinction between pensioners

Table 4.9 *Levels of deprivation among households on supplementary benefit*

Number of adult necessities[a] lacked	Households on supplementary benefit		
	Pensioners	Families	Others[c]
	% not having items because can't afford it[b]		
0	41	13	24
1 or more	59	87	76
2 or more	45	74	63
3 or more	37	60	50
4 or more	36	45	45
5 or more	32	41	40
6 or more	16	34	28
7 or more	7	28	17

[a]See page 106 for the list of the 18 items included.
[b]Only those who do not have an item because they say they cannot afford it are included.
[c]This group includes some families with children over 16 and households with more than one claimant.

Table 4.10 *The enforced lack of necessities among the elderly*

Number of adult necessities[a] lacked	Bottom 40% of households	
	Pensioners	Non-pensioners
	% not having items because can't afford it[b]	
0	58	41
1 or more	42	59
2 or more	29	43
3 or more	13	37
4 or more	9	26
5 or more	8	22
6 or more	3	16
7 or more	3	12

[a]See page 106 for the list of the 18 items included.
[b]Only those who do not have an item because they say they cannot afford it are included.

and others is confirmed by looking at all households in the bottom 40 per cent (the households that are most vulnerable to deprivation). This is shown in Table 4.10. For example, 13 per cent of pensioners go without three or more necessities because they cannot afford them compared to 37 per cent of non-pensioners. It has already been seen (in Table 4.4) that the elderly are much more likely to go without necessities from 'choice' than others and the implications of this in relation to these apparent differences in levels of deprivation between pensioners and others will be discussed in the next section. What is clear from Table 4.10 is that there are widespread problems among non-pensioners on low incomes.

A wider view of the extent of deprivation

Deprivation has so far been measured in terms of those who lack necessities because they explicitly say they cannot afford them. So what has been the effect of excluding those who go without necessities because they say they do not want them?

Tables 4.11 and 4.12 show the extent to which adults and children, respectively, go without necessities for whatever reason.

The increase in the number who go without necessities is most marked for higher-income households at the level of one or two necessities. Large numbers of households choose to go without one or even two necessities for reasons of taste (see Table 4.3). When this group is combined with the smaller numbers of high-income households who lack necessities because they cannot afford them, there is a high proportion of better-off households going without one or two necessities for one reason or another: around half of those in the top 30 per cent go without one or more necessities. But, again, the proportion of better-off households going without three or more necessities is small.

More pertinent to the question of the extent of deprivation is the effect on low-income groups. Among these households,

Table 4.11   *Levels of going without necessities among adults*

Number of adult necessities[a] lacked	Adults[b]	Households in income deciles[c]						
		1st	2nd	3rd	4th	5th	6th 7th	8th 9th 10th
				% going without items[d]				
0	40	12	15	29	28	29	28	49
1 or more	60	88	85	71	72	71	72	51
2 or more	39	66	65	54	56	51	42	26
3 or more	25	57	41	37	39	33	22	12
4 or more	16	45	32	30	31	21	12	8
5 or more	11	35	23	24	21	15	7	2
6 or more	7	25	15	15	20	8	4	1
7 or more	5	22	6	10	12	6	3	0

[a]See page 106 for the list of the 18 items included.

[b]Households have been weighted by the number of adults to give the percentage of the adult population.

[c]Income deciles are formed by grouping all the households into tenths according to their income; the bottom five deciles, the next 20% and the top 30% are given.

[d]Going without refers to both those who do not have an item because they cannot afford it and those who do not have it because they do not want it.

Table 4.12 *Levels of going without necessities among children*

Number of children's necessities[a] lacked	Children[b]	Families in income deciles[c]					6th 7th	8th 9th 10th
		1st	2nd	3rd	4th	5th		
		% going without items[d]						
0	39	14	24	26	32	35	44	74
1 or more	61	86	76	74	68	65	56	26
2 or more	40	71	56	61	49	40	23	12
3 or more	25	62	43	37	28	26	7	7
4 or more	20	52	35	30	21	26	3	5
5 or more	15	42	29	28	19	9	1	0
6 or more	10	36	19	19	8	4	0	0
7 or more	8	24	16	19	8	1	0	0

[a]See page 106–7 for the list of the 18 items included.

[b]Families have been weighted by the number of children to give the percentage of all children going without necessities.

[c]Income deciles are formed by grouping all the households into tenths according to their income; families in the bottom five deciles, the next 20% and the top 30% are given.

[d]Going without refers to both those who do not have an item because they cannot afford it and those who do not have it because they do not want it.

going without necessities from 'choice' can, at least for some, be seen to be a deprivation. Looking at those on the lowest incomes, the proportion who show no signs of deprivation drops considerably: 12 per cent of households and 14 per cent of families in the bottom decile are left possessing all the necessities. A proportion of these households are not in fact on low incomes and have been misplaced in the income classifications. This can be seen by looking at households on supplementary benefit, a category where there is much less room for confusion. Table 4.13 shows that virtually *all* of the families on supplementary benefit are deprived in one way or another: a mere 3 per cent have all the necessities.

The difference between these two measures of deprivation is particularly sharp for pensioners: for example, while 37 per cent of pensioners on supplementary benefit lack three or more necessities because they say they cannot afford them,

Table 4.13 *Levels of going without among households on supplementary benefit*

| Number of adult necessities[a] | Households on supplementary benefit | | |
| | Pensioners | Families | Others[c] |
	% going without items[b]		
0	12	3	6
1 or more	88	97	94
2 or more	79	81	88
3 or more	73	76	73
4 or more	50	61	64
5 or more	40	44	54
6 or more	37	41	36
7 or more	29	31	29

[a]See page 106 for the list of the 18 items included.

[b]Both those who do not have an item because they say they cannot afford it and those who do not have an item because they say they do not want it are included.

[c]This group includes some families with children over 16 and households with more than one claimant.

73 per cent actually go without three or more necessities. Measured in terms of their total lack of necessities, deprivation among pensioners on supplementary benefit is high. When pensioners were compared to others on supplementary benefit in terms of the numbers of necessities they could not afford, pensioners appeared to be significantly less deprived (see Table 4.9). But when pensioners are compared in terms of those who simply do not have the necessities, the differences are much smaller. Pensioners do, nevertheless, remain slightly better off (they are, after all, generally on a higher rate of supplementary benefit), although the differences are slight and most are within the range of statistical error.

Other pensioners on low incomes appear, however, to be somewhat better off than non-pensioner households even when measured in terms of their total lack of necessities. This can be seen in Table 4.14. To a large extent, these differences will reflect the past financial positions of the two groups. Among those pensioners whose current income is low, there will be a significant proportion who can call on savings

Table 4.14 *The total lack of necessities among the elderly*

Number of adult necessities[a]	Bottom 40% of households	
	Pensioners	Non-Pensioners
	% going without items[b]	
0	17	22
1 or more	83	78
2 or more	62	63
3 or more	33	47
4 or more	26	37
5 or more	19	28
6 or more	14	20
7 or more	8	14

[a]See page 106 for the list of the 18 items included.

[b]Both those who do not have an item because they say they cannot afford it and those who do not have an item because they do not want it are included.

for emergencies and for special occasions and holidays, and many will have made sure that their household goods and furnishings were in good condition before they retired. When children are off their hands, many couples go through a period of less financial pressure when they can build up resources for their retirement. Many low-income families, by contrast, will have never experienced times when money was anything but in extremely short supply.

Overall, Table 4.14 indicates that deprivation among those on low incomes may be more extensive than that suggested by people's own judgements of what they can afford and what they want. Among non-pensioner households on low incomes, nearly 50 per cent go without three or more necessities for one reason or another compared to 37 per cent who go without this level of necessities because they explicitly say they cannot afford it. The extent of deprivation in relation to, for example, an enforced lack of three or more necessities clearly lies somewhere between these two positions.

The question of 'fecklessness'

It is sometimes claimed that those on low incomes are not really deprived, simply 'feckless'. The poor's lack of basic goods is said to reflect extravagant or wasteful expenditure in other aspects of life. For example, David Walker, writing in *The Times*, argues:

> The 'problem' of poverty in Britain is a tissue of inadequacy and even fecklessness as well as material want . . . Affecting vignettes of life among the Hackney poor do not of themselves make a case for increased social security payments. They might, instead, suggest that the women of poor families need help and guidance on household management. (Walker, 1983)

This 'thesis' can, to some extent, be tested by examining the possession of items that were not classed as necessities. Although the number of goods classed by the majority of people as only 'desirable' rather than 'necessary' is relatively small, they do reflect a range of goods and activities

Table 4.15   *The lack of other goods from shortage of money*

The 8 'desirable' standard-of-living items in rank order	Net equivalent household income			Correlation coefficient
	Poorest 10%	Middle 10%	Top 10%	
	% not having item because can't afford it			
Best outfit	26	12	0	− 0.190 *
Telephone	27	13	0	− 0.214 *
Outing for children once a week[a]	32	20	7	− 0.192 *
Dressing gown	4	2	0	− 0.112 *
Children's friends round once a fortnight[a]	38	14	12	− 0.180 *
Night out once a fortnight	34	20	3	− 0.186 *
Friends/family round once a month	31	12	5	− 0.184 *
Car	37	14	4	− 0.249 *

NS = not significant at 95% level.

* = significant at 95% level.

[a]Families with children under 16 only.

(cigarettes are discussed separately on pp. 124–6). Table 4.15 shows that the relationship between lack of these 'non-necessities' because of shortage of money and low income is highly significant for all the items. Indeed, the relationship between income and the inability to afford goods is stronger for the non-necessities than it is for the necessities. Moreover, for half these 'non-necessities', the poor are also more likely to go without them because they do not want them (see Table 4.16). Overall, this in turn means that the poor are actually far less likely than others to possess these 'desirable' goods. Indeed, lack of these goods among the poor is widespread and in general far greater than their lack of necessities: for example, well over half of the poor do not have a car, over half do not go out socially and nearly half cannot even have their family or friends round.

The enforced lack of these items would generally be accepted as diminishing people's lives, even though the lack

Table 4.16 *The lack of other goods from 'choice'*

The 8 'desirable' standard-of-living items in rank order	Net equivalent household income			Correlation coefficient
	Poorest 10%	Middle 10%	Top 10%	
	% not having item because don't want it			
Best outfit	5	8	3	– 0.037 NS
Telephone	7	15	2	– 0.112 *
Outing for children once a week[a]	8	12	16	+ 0.018 NS
Dressing gown	13	9	3	– 0.095 *
Children's friends round once a fortnight[a]	11	20	0	– 0.089 *
Night out once a fortnight	22	26	28	– 0.046 NS
Friends/family round once a month	15	28	14	– 0.023 NS
Car	21	24	2	– 0.151 *

NS = not significant at 95% level.
 * = significant at 95% level.

[a]Families with children under 16 only.

is not of such importance that the items are classed as necessities. In that sense, the poor not only miss out on necessities but also miss out, to an even greater extent, on the many other activities and goods that make life simply pleasanter or more enjoyable.

However, while the poor are, in general, much less likely to possess these non-necessities, it is still possible that those of the poor who lack necessities are those who spend their money on non-necessities. This too can be tested by looking at the extent to which those who cannot afford necessities also cannot afford the non-necessities. These non-necessities can, as with the necessities, be separated into those that affect all members of the household (a telephone; a car), those that affect primarily just the respondent (a 'best outfit'; a dressing gown; a night out once a fortnight; friends or family round once a month), and children's items (an outing once a week; their friends round for tea once a fortnight). A group of six goods affecting adults can be formed by combining the household goods and those items for adults, and a group of four goods affecting children by combining the household goods with the children's items. Table 4.17 shows the

Table 4.17 *The extent to which the deprived miss out in other ways: adults*

No. of other adult goods[c] lacked[a]	Households lacking[a] the adult standard-of-living necessities[b]						
	0	1 or more	2 or more	3 or more	4 or more	5 or more	6 or more	7 or more
	% lacking[a] other adult items[c]							
0	81	25	13	9	7	1	0	1
1 or more	19	75	87	91	93	99	100	99
2 or more	5	48	63	76	80	86	94	92
3 or more	0	24	36	53	58	61	70	73
4 or more	0	13	21	32	35	39	43	47
5 or more	0	3	6	8	11	11	16	16
6	0	1	2	3	4	5	7	5

[a]Throughout, 'lack' is taken as those who do not have an item because they cannot afford it and excludes those who do not have it because they do not want it.
[b]See page 106 for the list of the 18 items included.
[c]See above for the list of the 6 items included.

relationship for adult items between those households who cannot afford necessities and those who cannot afford the non-necessities and Table 4.18 shows this relationship for children's items.

The reality is completely the reverse of accusations of 'fecklessness'. The more a household goes without the necessities, the more it goes without other goods as well. For example, for both adult items and children's items, all those who lack six or more necessities lack at least one non-necessity and over half lack more than half of the non-necessities; by contrast, only about one-fifth of those who lack none of the necessities lack any of the non-necessities and none lack over half of the non-necessities.

There are, however, some who lack necessities who do not lack any of the 'non-necessities'. This is particularly notice-able for the group lacking one or more necessities: 25 per cent of this group do not lack any 'non-necessity'. The lack of more necessities, however, does involve much more serious financial problems: a large majority of those who lack two or more necessities will have cut back on other goods.

Moreover, Tables 4.17 and 4.18 give a minimal measure of the differences between those who are unable to afford

Table 4.18   *The extent to which the deprived miss out in other ways: children*

No of other children's goods[c] lacked[a]	Families lacking[a] the children's standard-of-living necessities[b]							
	0	1 or more	2 or more	3 or more	4 or more	5 or more	6 or more	7 or more
	% lacking[a] other children's items[c]							
0	78	30	21	18	17	9	0	0
1 or more	22	70	79	82	83	91	100	100
2 or more	5	43	56	64	67	78	93	95
3 or more	0	17	27	33	36	45	58	56
4	0	4	7	9	11	14	16	20

[a]Throughout, 'lack' is taken as those who do not have an item because they cannot afford it and excludes those who do not have it because they do not want it.
[b]See page 106–7 for the list of the 18 items included.
[c]See page 120 for the list of the 4 items included.

necessities and others. Those lacking necessities are not only much more likely to go without other goods because they cannot afford them, they are also more likely to go without these goods because they do not want them. The extent to which those who are unable to afford necessities do not *have* other goods is notably higher.

Nevertheless, at all levels of deprivation, households who cannot afford necessities do to a greater or lesser extent possess 'non-necessities'. The extent of possession of 'non-necessities' will depend on past circumstances, the particular current situation of the individual and the relative costs of these 'non-necessities'.

For example, nearly all those who cannot afford necessities do have a dressing gown – an item considered by most people as a 'non-necessity'. Such items may be relatively unimportant compared to heating but are not current day-to-day expenses and are anyway relatively cheap. Some may have 'non-necessities' that cost somewhat more, but that have a limited re-sale value.

A few of those who lack necessities will possess a car, a 'non-necessity' that entails some day-to-day expense and that many people who are not deprived will have cut out in order to be able to afford necessities. This does not necessarily mean that the small minority of households that lack necessities but possess a car are not deprived. The disabled, for example, are quite likely to possess a car through the state's mobility scheme but be forced to cut back substantially in other ways. Others will also face special circumstances that make it worth facing additional burdens in other areas in order to have the mobility a car provides. Mavis Long, aged 58 and unemployed, lives with her infirm, octogenarian mother. Although unable to afford new clothes, unable to heat the house adequately, and unable to eat properly, she does have a car. She bought it some nine years back, long before her current financial problems arose. Writing in *The Guardian*, she explains why she keeps it:

This year has been particularly hard. Mother has had weeks in hospital . . . Without the car I could not have gone to see her, so far are we from the hospitals in which she has been cared for. There is no help forthcoming either with public transport fares or with petrol which is less expensive ... It's hard to keep the car going but well worth the effort. We have no other vice, than that of breathing. We do not smoke, or drink, or gamble. But we can go out into the country, taking our food with us, and get a change, ('Nine years out of work: 3,000 job applications rejected', *The Guardian*, 23 June 1984)

Any study of poverty and deprivation depends on generalisations about people's needs and circumstances that will not fit every single individual. While the list of necessities is indicative of a minimum standard of living, certain people will, in preference, choose goods or activities that are not on that list. Often these goods and activities will have a marginal effect on their ability to afford necessities (for example, the dressing gown), and some may entail no additional expense (like the family coming round, which may even result in help). Sometimes, however, these activities will entail cutting back on necessities; this usually reflects differences in circumstances that lead to particular needs.

It should also be remembered that to some extent people from different social classes have different priorities (see Chapter 3). In particular, social security recipients place far greater emphasis on a television than the middle classes. The centrality of the television to the lives of some of the poor will mean that a *few* possess not just a television but also a video-recorder, an item that, though not tested in the survey, is unlikely to be regarded as a necessity by society as a whole. Such examples clearly raise the hackles of some people, in particular those of middle-class backgrounds who anyway disapprove of the television (see, for example, the letters pages of *The Sunday Times*, 28 August 1983). But these cases should be seen in the context of the way that the lives of the poor often become denuded of opportunities and outside interests (see Chapter 5). A culture arises that places an emphasis on aspects of life that meet the disapproval of others whose lives are remote from such deprivations.

In general, however, such differences in priorities are infrequent.

There is, nevertheless, one area of spending among the poor that is not just controversial but also common. A substantial proportion of those who lack necessities smoke (see Table 4.19). Indeed, the poor are more likely to smoke than others. Although, clearly, people who spend money on smoking do not have this money for other things, smoking does not explain why people have inadequate living standards. Those who lack necessities are more likely to smoke regularly than others – but the difference is not that great. Moreover, a majority of the deprived (56 per cent of those who lack one or more necessities) do *not* smoke regularly. Even among the deprived, regular smoking does not explain the differences in their living standards: those who lack more necessities are not notably more likely to smoke. So, while smoking is greater among the deprived, it cannot be put forward as the cause of low living standards.

Nevertheless, some people argue that people who smoke cannot be classed as being in poverty. This view is largely based on a misunderstanding of the situation of the poor and their financial problems. Although at the margins there are some people among those who cannot afford necessities who could afford them if they did not smoke, this is not generally the case. A rough indication of this can be gained by looking at how much more money households who lack three or more necessities need to enable them to afford all the necessities

Table 4.19   *The extent of smoking among the deprived*

	Lack[a] of adult standard-of-living necessities[b]						
	0	1	2	3	4 & 5	6 & 7	8 or more
% having a packet of cigarettes every other day[c]	34	43	39	60	37	56	50

[a]'Lack' is taken as those who do not have an item because they cannot afford it and excludes those who do not have it because they do not want it.

[b]See page 106 for the list of the 18 items included.

[c]Percentages refer to respondents and have not been weighted to give the percentage of adults.

(this is discussed in Chapter 6). Most (around 70 per cent) need at least £10 a week more and very many need as much as £30 a week. The £4 to £6 a week spent on a packet of cigarettes every other day (or even £10 a week) does not make a substantive impact on this 'short-fall': stopping smoking would *not* solve the financial problems of most of the poor.

The fact that the people who are the most deprived are, in general, the most likely to smoke – despite their financial problems – raises the question of why they smoke. Clearly, in some respects they have 'chosen' to do so, but there is also a sense in which their very deprivations *lead* to smoking or at least reinforce the habit and make it more difficult to give up. While, to our knowledge, the question of smoking and deprivation has not been studied specifically, it is our strong impression (based on very many extensive and in-depth contacts with poor households across the country) that smoking often provides the *one* release of tension people have from the constant worries that stem from circumstances that are often desperate and depressing. Elaine struggles to bring up her three young children on the wages her husband brings home from the night-shift at the local factory:

> We don't go out, we don't drink; the only thing we do is smoke. Fair enough, it's an expensive habit but it's the only thing we do. All the money we have, it either goes on bills or food or clothes and, apart from smoking, we don't have anything. We're sort of non-existent outside, we *never* go anywhere. I'm in here seven nights a week. Four of those nights Roy's at work and we have had a lot of trouble round here. I've had threatened rape. I mean Roy works nights and I'm in this house on my own. It's terrible.

That people spend a small proportion of their income on goods that are not essential, whether cigarettes or the other 'non-necessities' identified, does not make their lack of necessities any less of a deprivation. This point is critical. The purpose of identifying the basic needs to which everyone is entitled is to expand people's choices in life and not to limit personal freedom (see Chapter 2). This is also implicit in the survey's finding of what a minimum standard of living should entail. People did not view necessities in terms just of survival but in terms also of quality and of a life with a degree of pleasantness and enjoyment (see Chapter 3). For example, people considered a hobby or leisure activity as a necessity. If Mavis Long's trips of up to ten miles to take her elderly mother to the countryside are viewed as, say, a leisure activity, then the possession of an old car is in her circumstances in keeping with the view of minimum standards indicated by society as a whole.

This debate on the extent to which the poor should be 'allowed' to spend money on anything other than necessities goes back as far as the discussion of poverty itself. It is this question that led Rowntree to separate 'primary' from 'secondary' poverty. In general, 'primary' poverty excludes the possibility of spending any money on anything but basic needs, while 'secondary' poverty makes some allowance for people's *actual* spending patterns. Rowntree himself, recognising that 'primary' poverty represented an idealised view of the world that bore little relationship to reality, moved in his second study in 1936 to a measure of 'secondary' poverty that made allowance for spending on non-necessities such as beer and tobacco. For such reasons, studies of poverty from then on have taken this view. Similarly, in our view, it is necessary to take account in measures of deprivation and poverty of people's *actual* behaviour patterns rather than take a moral view of what they *should* be in an idealised sense.

In summary, it is not, in the main, the case that those who go without necessities do so because they are more likely than others to be spending their money on other goods. The priorities of the poor are similar to those of society at large. Nearly all those who are forced to cut back on necessities have already cut back in other less essential areas. Of course, some of the poor are 'bad managers', as indeed are some of the rich. In general, however, people face deprivation not because they are 'bad managers', spending rashly on unimportant goods, or because they are 'feckless', but because they lack money.

Indeed, the poor often 'manage' their money very carefully – and still fail to get by. Tricia is a single parent bringing up two school-aged children on supplementary benefit. She finds herself forced to cut back on heating and food even though she accounts for every penny she spends:

What I do is draw my money on a Monday, and I come home and I sort all my bills out, what I've got to pay there and then paid. Whatever I've got left, then I work from day-to-day. I do my shopping day-to-day. I've tried doing it in bulk but by the time you picked up what you think you need, the time you've paid for it you've got nothing left. So you can't shop like that, you've got to shop from day-to-day. You've got to be careful with what you buy. You can't just buy anything, you go for the cheapest. No matter what it is, you've got to go for the cheapest.

I mean, when I go into Stockport I always walk because it's 30p down and it's 30p back, and if you walk there and back you are saving yourself 60 pence and that's just for one person. You can get a lot with 60p, you can get a loaf and you can get margarine.

Usually by the time you get to Saturday, when most people are doing the shopping, you are down to your last pound. It's very hard for other people to realise what it's like to manage off that type of money.

Other influences on living standards

Although low living standards stem primarily from lack of income, other influences are important. There are considerable differences in the intensity and degree of deprivation between households on very similar incomes. For example, one-quarter of families on supplementary benefit lack only one or two necessities, while over one-quarter lack seven or more necessities. In addition, there are some who are not on the lowest incomes who nevertheless have low living standards: for example, one-quarter of families in the fourth and fifth income decile lack three or more necessities.

To some extent these variations reflect the inadequacies of the income data and the problems of household classification and equivalence (see Appendix C), as a result of which some households are placed in the wrong income group. This helps to explain the small minority of apparently 'better-off' households who cannot afford a range of necessities and the small minority of apparently 'poor' households who show no signs of deprivation. Nevertheless, to a large extent the differences are a reflection of reality.

So why is it that people with similar current incomes have different living standards? Let us compare the situation of Tricia, the single parent with two school-aged children, with that of Pamela, also a single parent. Tricia has two children aged 8 and 11 and Pamela a baby of 9 months. Both families live on the short-term rate of supplementary benefit and both are deprived. Their living standards are very different, however. The reasons are numerous and varied.

Tricia was divorced last year and, though her current income is low, she has known far better times. There were periods in the past when both Tricia and her husband worked, and they could afford new furniture, toys and clothes. Though Tricia's ex-husband is now unemployed and makes no financial contribution to the children, and though Tricia herself can no longer work because her mother, who looked after the children, is now ill, the past stock of resources is still around. Pamela, by sharp contrast, has never had anything. She had worked in a few temporary waitressing jobs before she was pregnant, but never earned enough to buy anything but day-to-day goods. Unmarried, with no help from the baby's father, she has nothing to fall back on.

Tricia's parents live on the same estate in Stockport. They are both now ill, but they can still help out with the more special things like presents for the children. Her husband, though unemployed, takes the children out regularly. Through the local council, a holiday for the children has been arranged and paid for.

Pamela came to London from Scotland where she had been brought up in a children's home. She has no contact with her mother or her stepfather. Her father is now dead, and anyway beat her when she was a child. A lone parent with a young baby living in an unknown city has few opportunities to make close friends. Her contacts with the social welfare agencies are limited. There is no one to turn to.

The housing conditions of the two families also bring sharp contrasts. Tricia lives in a pleasant, semi-detached council house, in good structural condition. Pamela is in a privately rented attic flat, decaying and decrepit. A newcomer into an area of great housing stress, her chances of getting any council place are limited and her chances of getting a decent council house non-existent. Living in appalling housing conditions causes other problems and other expenses. She has nowhere to wash and dry the nappies and so buys disposable ones. She cannot keep food in the house because mice infest the whole place. So when she eats, she goes to the local cafe. The area is run-down, the crime rate is high, the street itself is known for prostitution and pimps. Pamela keeps a guard dog. Overwhelmed by problems, often depressed, always worried, Pamela smokes. It relieves tension and a cigarette at lunch-time depresses the appetite – to buy a proper meal would be more expensive. But, of course, smoking adds to the financial difficulties. Tricia, on the other hand, gave up smoking when her financial problems intensified. From a much more stable background, with help from family and friends around, she copes with her problems. Tricia, as we have seen, is nevertheless forced to cut back on basic necessities. Even in her relatively favourable circumstances, supplementary benefit is not enough to manage on. For people like Pamela, with additional problems and no resources, the same inadequate income leads to a life of intense deprivation.

These two families illustrate a few of the very many reasons why people on the same income have different living standards. In general, the causes fall into five main areas. First, the demands people face may be different. Families with, for example, an elderly relative nearby may well be worse off than those with no one dependent on them. Parents who have to pay for child care in order to go out to work will be worse off than those who can leave the children with friends or relations. While the list of necessities gives a general guide of what most people need, some people will have additional needs. The disabled, for example, often require additional equipment or special diets and, although the state makes some provision for this, it is often inadequate (indeed, the situation is worsening: the government has recently announced a reduction in the amount disabled people on supplementary benefit are allowed to keep as part of their special diet allowance).

The second major area is the household's background. People's incomes are not static from year to year or even month to month. In each income group there will be some people who were in the recent past better off and some who were worse off; and this will have a significant impact on their living standards. Some will have built up resources, from financial savings to a well-furnished house. Others will be struggling to save up just these kinds of resources. Yet others who are not at present on the lowest of incomes will have problems hanging over from when their income was less. Past debts are particularly important in lowering people's current living standards (see pp. 158–60). In general, the greater the length of time a household is on a low income, the lower their living standards will slip. Among pensioners, for example, those who have recently retired fare adequately – but, as they become older, resources dwindle, clothes wear out and the financial problems mount up. Among the unemployed, those who have been on the short-term rate of supplementary benefit for a week or two may be just about coping, but, as the months go by, clothes need to be bought, household items replaced, fuel bills come in, the children change school and need a uniform and the local authority has cut out school uniform grants. For the long-term unemployed, who are still on the short-term rate of supplementary benefit even after a year, the situation is often desperate.

The third main area contributing to the variations in living standards among those on apparently similar incomes is the fact that their *actual* incomes may be different. The survey's measure of current income was by no means comprehensive.

Some people will have a second job in the 'black economy' and their income will be undeclared. Some people on benefit will also be making a bit of pocket money on the side, although other studies suggest that the extent of this is relatively limited (see, for example, The Economist Intelligence Unit, 1982). More significantly, fringe benefits will be unevenly spread, again making some households better off than they appear. These benefits will accrue in the main to those who are anyway better off, and by definition to those in work, making the differences between those in work and out of work on similar current incomes sharper than they appear. Even among those dependent on state benefits, there will be some differences in terms of one-off grants that are claimed or unclaimed.

The fourth set of reasons relates to the degree of outside support households receive from, on the one hand, family and friends and, on the other hand, the various welfare agencies – voluntary and state. Even between people with very similar needs and incomes, the extent of this outside help will vary considerably. Some of the elderly, for example, will have children who regularly do the weekly shopping for them; some will have an old people's club nearby where they can go for cut-price lunches and warmth as well as companionship; some will live in areas where the local council services are comprehensive and wide-ranging; while others will have none of these benefits.

The final area is that of housing. This affects people's level of deprivation both directly, in that housing indicators are used in the measure of deprivation, and indirectly, in that bad housing can lead to other deprivations. Access to decent housing is less dependent on income than in the past. The state provision of public housing has improved housing conditions among the poor and weakened the link between poverty and bad housing. Nevertheless, the link is not totally broken. Some poor households fare much worse than others.

For such reasons, the living standards of those on the lowest incomes vary. All are deprived in one way or another, but some end up far worse off. These influences also mean that there are some who are not on the lowest incomes who nevertheless have low living standards, though seldom the very lowest.

The extent of deprivation

Deprivation in Britain in the 1980s is widespread. Our findings show that vulnerability to deprivation extends throughout the bottom half, and particularly the bottom 30 to 40 per cent, of society. Families with children are especially vulnerable. This suggests that the tax–benefit system generally is not redistributing money where it is needed; this question is pursued further in Chapter 6. Those in the top half of society, by contrast, are comfortably off, able to ride the additional problems that crop up from time to time and that force those who are worse off into deprivation. While a minority of those in the top half cut back on one or even two necessities, they do not cut back to any greater extent on these basic aspects of living.

We have argued that one criterion for the classification of those in poverty is that their lack of necessities is enforced. In this chapter we have seen that nearly all those who lack three or more necessities are forced into this situation. The measurement of poverty will be pursued in Chapter 6. But first the impact of these deprivations on people's lives will be discussed; this is the subject of the next chapter.

It is already clear, however, that the state's minimum income is too low to maintain the minimum standards of society today: all those on supplementary benefit faced deprivation to some degree or other. At the start of the last chapter, Mavis – who is blind, partially deaf and diabetic and who lives on her own on supplementary benefit – was quoted as asking:

A standard of living surely should give you the benefit of making a choice of whether you have a piece of beef or a small chop. A piece of beef would last you two or three days where a chop would last you one. Surely living standards should be able to give you the choice of being able to buy a small joint?

In the last chapter it was seen that the large majority of people in Britain today agree with this sort of description of minimum living standards. This chapter has shown that for those living on the minimum income provided by the state today, there is only one answer – the one that Mavis gives:

You can't do it.

5

Just Existing
The impact of deprivation

> You query the price of things so much when you go out. Can I afford this? Can I afford that? I like meat, I like vegetables, and things like that. But I've got to query it, I might have vegetables twice a week, I might have meat twice a week, otherwise I've got to live on eggs and things like that and this isn't a standard of living. It's existence.
> [A disabled woman on supplementary benefit]

The impact of deprivation is more intense for some than others. Among the poor, the types and range of the deprivations suffered vary.

A picture of these variations can be drawn by looking at which of the necessities the poor are most likely to be unable to afford. This will depend on the overall level of deprivation the household faces, that is the overall number of necessities lacked. For both the eighteen necessities identified for adults and the eighteen necessities identified for children (see pp. 106–7), the households lacking necessities have been divided into four groups. First there are those who lack one or two necessities – about 20 per cent of the population. Second, there are those who lack three or four necessities – about 5 per cent of the population. Third, there are those who lack five or six necessities – accounting for a further 4 per cent of the population. Finally, there are those who lack seven or more necessities – a level of intense deprivation that affects about 5 per cent of the population.

Of course, the divisions between people are not that rigid: many households will find that their level of deprivation varies, sometimes even from week to week. But grouping households in this way enables an examination of the form and extent of deprivation among those with low living standards. Table 5.1 shows, for each of the individual necessities relating to adults, the proportion of households in each of these overall groups who lack that necessity. In Table 5.2, the proportions going without some aspect or other of heating, housing, food, clothing, household goods, social activities and leisure activities are given. Finally, a picture of the deprivations faced by children is given in Table 5.3.

The implications of these tables are discussed in this chapter. This provides a picture of the impact of deprivation; a picture that in turn throws light on the question of the extent of poverty, which is pursued in Chapter 6.

Table 5.1 *The living standards of the deprived*

Deprivations	Lack[a] of necessities			
	1 or 2	3 or 4	5 or 6	7 or more
	% of households facing each deprivation			
Inadequate heating	6	20	35	46
No unshared indoor toilet	1	4	17	13
Damp home	9	16	51	42
No unshared bath	1	4	15	15
Not enough beds	1	5	9	4
No warm water-proof coat	5	20	45	65
Less than two pairs of all-weather shoes	9	26	37	88
No refrigerator	2	5	9	13
Not enough carpets	2	7	2	31
No celebrations on special occasions	4	9	13	53
No roast joint each week	8	29	44	48
No washing machine	10	22	25	31
Second-hand clothes	4	13	46	66
No hobby or leisure activity	6	36	35	61
Less than two hot meals a day	3	11	28	28
Meat/fish less than every other day	10	27	33	88
Not enough money to give presents once a year	4	24	18	55
No holiday	47	65	76	96

[a]Throughout, 'lack' is taken as those who do not have an item because they cannot afford it and excludes those who do not have it because they do not want it.

Two factors should be remembered throughout. First, people's lack of each of the necessities is seen only in terms of those who do not have the necessity because they say they cannot afford it and excludes those who go without from 'choice'. This provides a *minimal* measure of the *numbers* of people facing deprivation (see Chapter 4) and it also provides a *minimal* measure of the *extent* of their problems. Second, the study underestimates the differences between those who are deprived and those who are comfortably off because the measures of *quality* are limited. The indicators of deprivation were restricted to simple matters of possession in terms of quantity and regularity. This means that, in describing the living standards of the poor, they will at times be classed as possessing an item when in fact the quality of that item is inadequate.

Even on these minimal measures of the deprivations faced by those with the lowest living standards, the picture that emerges is of a life worn down by not being able to make ends meet. It is a picture that comes disturbingly to life when the poor speak for themselves.

Table 5.2 *The impact of deprivation*

	Lack[a] of necessities			
	1 or 2	3 or 4	5 or 6	7 or more
Main areas of deprivation[b]	% of households facing each area of deprivation			
Inadequate heating	6	20	35	46
Bad housing	16	34	62	62
Lacking household furnishings and equipment	16	26	38	56
Poor and inadequate clothing	17	48	89	98
Unbalanced and unattractive diet	18	52	64	93
Missing out on important social functions and obligations	7	28	22	72
Cutting out leisure activities	53	85	90	96

[a]Throughout, 'lack' is taken as those who do not have an item because they cannot afford it and excludes those who do not have it because they do not want it.

[b]This classification is described in the text under the sections dealing with each of these areas.

Table 5.3   *Deprivation among children*

	Lack[a] of necessities			
	1 or 2	3 or 4	5 or 6	7 or more
Areas of deprivation (children)	% of families facing each area of deprivation			
Overcrowding	23	17	16	47
Insufficient food	1	4	17	40
No money for toys and/or leisure equipment	15	46	72	79

[a]Throughout 'lack' is taken as those who do not have an item because they cannot afford it and excludes those who do not have it because they do not want it.

Living in a rubbish dump

It's very bad with the damp, the rain coming in through the window, the mice, the rats, the bugs, beasts, the lot. And it's tiny in here. I can't get room to move about, I can't put my child on the floor to play. And if I put her on the floor she goes straight for the door and down the stairs. And when it rains in here, the floor gets soaking wet. And as for repairs, the landlord won't do anything to do with repairs. Nothing at all. It's just ridiculous to have ended up in a rubbish dump, that's what I call it, a rubbish dump.

Pamela lives with her 9-month old baby in an attic flat in a decaying row of terraced houses in inner London. Her flat is privately rented, but her feelings are reflected by many in the public sector of housing. Marie lives with her two children in a council flat in Vauxhall, Liverpool:

It's full of damp. And there are rats and there's all kinds of, well, crawlies all over the place and you can't get nothing done. The corporation, they'll not come out and do a thing for you. The windows don't shut and bins don't get emptied. They just won't do nothing at all. The housing condition itself is just terrible. It's just rubbish because that's all it is, we're just living in rubbish really.

These neglected council estates of the inner city are a conspicuous form of housing deprivation. For others – the homeless, the overcrowded, those forced to share with friends and relatives – the housing problems may be less visible but they are no less serious. Kathy and her husband are homeless. The council has placed them 'temporarily' in a hotel room. For the last seven months, they have been trying to cope with bringing up their baby son in this one tiny room:

> It's dirty. It's noisy. Outside our window there's rubbish and a ten foot brick wall. You can't open the window because all the insects come in. It's so small there's nowhere to cook. I'd rather give him food I'd normally eat but I can only manage packet foods. You know, just boil the kettle and pour it and mix it up. I can't give him normal food because there's nowhere to do it. I mean, you name it – everything's wrong with this place. It's just a dump. (Quoted in *The London Programme*, 20 January 1984, LWT)

Bad housing is the single most serious form of deprivation identified by the *Breadline Britain* survey. Of all the items identified as necessities, five out of the top eleven related to housing conditions: an indoor toilet not shared with another household, a bath for each household, a damp-free home, self-contained accommodation and enough bedrooms for older children to have their own. Each of these housing items was classed as a necessity by over three in four people.

Pamela, like many in privately rented accommodation, lives in a multi-occupied block sharing basic facilities. She finds it particularly difficult to ensure that baby Emma's conditions are hygienic:

> There's twelve altogether living in the house and we have to share one bathroom between the whole house. Three toilets. Sometimes the toilets don't even work.

They get blocked up so it starts overflowing and gets all over the place. But there's only one bath in the whole house. I can't put her in the big bath because it's too disgusting because people wash their clothes there. They do everything in there and they never think to clean it afterwards. So I have to bath her in this small bath but I haven't got water up here so I take a bucket from the kitchen, go down to the bathroom, fill it up with hot water and then take it back up here.

Lack of such basic facilities is concentrated among those with the lowest living standards (see Table 5.1). Of those who lack three or four necessities, only 4 per cent are forced to share an indoor toilet and 4 per cent a bath, whereas, of those lacking five or six necessities, 17 per cent share an indoor toilet and 15 per cent a bath, and, of those lacking seven or more necessities, 13 per cent share a toilet and 15 per cent a bath. Lack of these basic facilities is concentrated in the privately rented sector. This means that, while in general it is the poor who are likely to be in the worst privately rented blocks, these tenants are not necessarily among the very poorest.

Although a minority of the poor still lack these basic facilities, the situation has improved considerably since the war. Access for all to these basic housing conditions has been a key aim of postwar housing policy and in these limited terms it has had some success. Improvements in this area continued throughout the 1970s: according to official figures, the proportion of dwellings lacking one or more of these basic facilities fell from 11 per cent in 1975 to just over 2 per cent in 1981. The *Breadline Britain* survey found that the lack of these basic facilities remained about the same in 1983 but, as Table 5.1 shows, this lack is heavily concentrated among those who are multiply deprived.

Ending overcrowding has also been an important aim of housing policy and again has met with some success (Lansley, 1979, p. 76). However, among the poor it still remains a problem. In the *Breadline Britain* survey, overcrowding was measured only for families with children, who were asked whether they had sufficient bedrooms for each child of a different sex over the age of 10 to have their own. Table 5.3 shows that this is most concentrated among those with the very lowest living standards: nearly half of the families who lack seven or more necessities are living in overcrowded conditions. Outside this intensely deprived group, there does not seem to be an overlap between overcrowding and the extent of lack of other necessities.

In other areas of housing, problems have remained more widespread. In particular, there has been a continuing problem of damp. Elaine and her husband Roy live on a pre-war, inner city council estate with their three young children, Michael and Darren who attend the local infant school and Melanie, aged 3:

> There's damp in the living room and bedroom. They did that two years ago but it just came back. They just, I don't know, they just don't seem to care. It's as though they think oh, she's got repairs, we'll do them eventually. I mean, it's so cold and damp and we can't get the house warm. It's been affecting Melanie's health. She's had bronchial pneumonia. She went to the hospital and a fortnight later she got it again. So she went back to the hospital and they said the dampness in the house wasn't helping her health. But even then, they refused to do it, to come and sort out the damp.

Faced each year with thousands of requests for repairs and thousands of older properties needing substantial improvements, councils have been unable to keep up with the investment needed to sustain the fabric of the council stock. This means that many properties are in need of major structural repairs and as a consequence tenants face problems, in particular that of damp. Such problems are not confined to older estates, however. The council block that Marie and her two children live in was built in the late 1960s:

> The rooms are soaking with damp. I dread the winter coming. The poor child will end up with pneumonia

when the winter comes because they're so full of damp.
You get that back kitchen, even in the hall, damp just
falls off the walls.

Among the estates built in the 1960s and 1970s, a small but
nevertheless significant proportion turned out to have
structural problems that led to persistent dampness and
condensation. For these reasons, the problem of damp is
concentrated in the council sector: 14 per cent of council
tenants in the survey faced the problem of damp compared
to 5 per cent of those buying their home on a mortgage.

This, in turn, means that the problems of damp housing
have remained closely associated with low income. Since the
First World War, successive governments have implemented
a number of measures with at least the partial aim of
improving the access of the poor to decent housing at
reasonable cost. The most important of these measures has
been the building of local authority housing. So failures to
maintain this stock have a very direct effect on the living
conditions of the poor. Table 5.1 shows that the problem of
damp is faced by over half of those who lack five or six
necessities and 42 per cent of those who lack seven or more
necessities. This compares with 9 per cent of those who lack
one or two necessities.

The last of the housing necessities – self-contained
accommodation – was not found to be correlated with
income (see Chapter 4). It is not surprising therefore that lack
of self-contained accommodation is not so concentrated
among those with the lowest living standards as are the other
aspects of housing deprivation. Of those who lack seven or
more necessities, only 8 per cent share accommodation,
although 21 per cent of those lacking five or six necessities
face this problem. Accommodation is shared by 9 per cent of
those who lack three or four necessities and 2 per cent of
those lacking one or two necessities.

Overall, however, housing deprivation is concentrated
among those whose living standards are low in other respects.
Table 5.2 shows these five housing items grouped together.
One-third of those who lack three or four necessities, over 60

per cent of households lacking five or six necessities, and 60 per cent of households lacking seven or more necessities, live in bad housing.

It is interesting, none the less, that housing problems are not as sharply concentrated among those with multiple deprivations as are other aspects of living standards. This is because council housing has to some extent reduced the link between lack of money for basic necessities and bad housing (Lansley, 1979, ch. 3; Murie, 1983). Table 5.2 shows that those who are intensely deprived (lacking seven or more necessities) are in the main less likely to face housing problems than other problems. As a result of the postwar public housing programmes, there are some who are multiply deprived in all other aspects of life who nevertheless live in decent housing. That said, the findings suggest that the poor tend to live in the worst housing.

These five items do not, of course, give anything like a complete picture of what it is like to suffer from inadequate housing. The list excludes other standard amenities such as a sink, washbasin or an adequate hot and cold water supply. It does not include poor structural conditions other than dampness. In a separate section of the survey, some of these aspects were covered. Respondents were asked if their present home had broken windows, a poor heating system, or poor decoration inside and outside. On the basis that the findings on necessities can be seen as a guide to the kind of standard of living regarded as minimal for living in Britain today, these items too could be seen as deprivations. Again, those who in other respects have low living standards are also the most likely to face these problems, as Table 5.4 shows. Again, however, bad housing is seen to be less closely tied in to generally low living standards than the other aspects of living standards are tied in to each other. Again, too, these problems are heavily concentrated among council tenants. For the poor, their housing conditions are, in effect, out of their control. They cannot afford to buy their way out of the council sector and so the standards of their housing conditions will depend above all on public housing investment and improvement programmes. Often the poor

Table 5.4 *A broader view of housing deprivation*

| | Lack[a] of necessities | | | | |
| | 0 | 1 or 2 | 3 or 4 | 5 or 6 | 7 or more |
	% facing additional housing problems				
Broken windows	4	10	10	23	18
Poor heating system	12	28	37	48	54
Poor decoration inside	4	10	9	14	34
Poor decoration outside	8	13	15	2	13
1 or more of these four problems	22	42	52	72	66

[a]Throughout 'lack' is taken as those who do not have an item because they cannot afford it and excludes those who do not have it because they do not want it.

are concentrated in 'dump estates' where not just the housing conditions will be bad but also the whole environment. Marie's estate in Vauxhall, Liverpool, though it was built twenty years ago, has now decayed through neglect. It is almost literally sinking into filth:

> When the flat opposite came empty all the sewerage was coming out of the front door. It was seeping across into the next door flat and the two children there ended up with dysentry and the family had eventually to be moved out because it was so bad. The corporation wouldn't go in, the health wouldn't go in, nobody would go in the flats. Then we couldn't get the bins emptied at all then because nobody would come in. Nobody would come in the block because the smell was that bad. In the end the firemen stopped it, I don't know how.

Going to bed to keep warm

I put the gas fire on after supper because I only have one 50p to put in it each day. There's no more fifty pences, just that one for the simple reason that I can't afford any more in the gas. If I was to run it properly you're talking about £2 a day and this gas fire is the only heating we have got in the house. There's nothing upstairs. So when that goes we go to bed because we keep warm in bed. Last winter we were freezing. You find that fifty pence doesn't last very long in winter – it was cold all the time. I mean, it was so cold, there were three of us in one bed to keep warm.

Tricia is a single parent bringing up two children on supplementary benefit. Like many single parents in this situation, she cannot afford to heat her home properly. Inadequate heating is sharply concentrated among the very poorest: nearly half of those who lack seven or more necessities cannot afford heating, compared to only 6 per cent of those who lack one or two necessities (see Table 5.1).

Heating, which in the public's perception of necessities was top of the list, is an aspect of living standards that people struggle to afford, even at the expense of cutting out other important aspects. Among those with the very lowest living standards, the proportion lacking heating is lower than the proportion who cut back on other aspects of life (see Table 5.2).

A household's ability to afford heating by cutting back on other areas will, however, depend in part on the intrinsic costs of heating their home. Some methods of heating are more expensive to run than others, and some houses are more expensive to heat – for example, those that are drafty or have inadequate insulation. In general, these problems are concentrated on council estates (Bradshaw and Harris, 1983). Many prewar estates have inadequate heating systems, and many remain unmodernised. The problem has been further compounded by disastrous design blunders in public sector house building during the 1960s and 1970s. The legacy of cheap-to-install and expensive-to-run heating systems hangs over many tenants. The *Breadline Britain* survey found that more than one-third of council tenants thought their accommodation had poor heating. These problems are often further aggravated by inadequate ventilation: two in five council tenants in the survey complained of condensation.

Households with heating costs they cannot afford face

intolerable choices. Some, like Tricia, cut back on heating. But this leads to coldness and condensation, and sometimes to health problems. Anne, whose husband is unemployed, has a son with bronchial asthma:

> We can't afford to heat upstairs. It's very cold upstairs for him. He has to have two pillows to prop him up at night-time, because, if he's got bronchitis, he's coughing most of the night. Some nights he's crying all the night with the cough 'cause it's hurting that much to cough. Some nights he's slept with me when he's been that bad, and his dad's slept in his room. All last year when he was bad, he really got us worried.

If the heating is not turned off, the debts mount. Debt, in turn, leads either to borrowing or to turning the heating off to pay the bill, either voluntarily or through disconnections. Mavis – blind, partially deaf and disabled – had mounted up a gas bill of £80 in one quarter from using the central heating in her north-facing council flat. Because she knew that she could not pay the bill, she turned the gas central heating off. Throughout the winter months, she relied, instead, on a small and ineffective electric heater:

> I very often go to bed during the day to keep warm. Pile on as much as I can find maybe a couple of old coats 'cos I've only got one blanket and a sleeping bag that I've had for years. And I just stay there. Sometimes I fall asleep and I wake up about 7 p.m. I get up and I see what I've got to drink and eat and then I come quickly back again. And that works out my day.

While the problem of 'fuel poverty' is hardly new, it is becoming increasingly serious. This is in part because of the design faults on council estates, but it also stems from the end of cheap fuel a decade ago (Cooper, 1981). Since 1979, the problem has been aggravated by moves towards the 'economic pricing' of energy, leading to sharp increases in the price of fuel. Those on low incomes have become increasingly vulnerable to having to live without adequate heating.

Overall, the consequence of these pricing policies and housing failures has been that heating has remained a serious problem for the poor. Fifteen years ago, Townsend found in his survey of poverty in Britain that 5.2 per cent of the population did not have adequate heating. The *Breadline Britain* survey found that, if anything, the problem had grown: 6 per cent of the population could not afford heating in the living areas of their homes.

Eggs, eggs, and more eggs

> Eggs this week. I had one on Sunday for lunch, and I had some tomatoes on toast for the evening meal. What did I have yesterday – just plain bread and butter and toast. At the moment, an egg on toast. I shall look like an egg by the end of the week.

For Mavis, living on her own on supplementary benefit, her diet has an endless monotony: eggs, eggs, and more eggs. It is a monotony shared by many of the poor. Elaine's husband works the night-shift in a local factory but she too finds that eggs provide the staple meal for them and their two children:

> It's very rare we have meat whereas at one time it was meat every night of the week but now you just can't afford it. We've had to give that up. We more or less live on chips and eggs and something cheap like that. There's just no way I can give the kids a varied sort of diet 'cos I just can't afford it. And Sunday is terrible. I mean at one point we had a joint every week but now we can't afford it.

The extent to which the deprived go without food is striking. Table 5.2 shows a summary measure of how people's eating patterns are affected in terms of the three food items in the list of necessities. Over half of those who lack three or four necessities and 93 per cent of those who lack seven or more necessities cut back on food in some way or another. It is interesting to compare this summary measure of eating standards with each of the food items separately (see Table 5.1). This shows that as people's living standards worsen they find that they are forced to cut back not just on one or other aspect of food but on many: nearly nine out of ten of the households that lack seven or more necessities cut back on meat or fish alone, and half cut back on a roast joint once a week. At this level of deprivation, the adequacy of food for children can also be affected. Table 5.3 shows that, among those families who lack seven or more necessities, 40 per cent cannot afford three meals a day for children.

These items are not, of course, a comprehensive list of all the problems that the poor face in simply feeding themselves. Those who are so short of money that they are having to cut back on meat are likely to cut back also in other areas. The variety of their diet will be affected in all sorts of ways. Mavis's diet, for example, is monotonous not only in that she can seldom afford meat but also in many other ways:

> Sometimes somebody will give me an apple which is always attractive. But I make do with what I've got: a piece of bread, I may have some cottage cheese which is rather nice on toast though that's a bit expensive.

Further, these measures give little indication of quality. Those who have difficulty in affording a roast joint each week but manage it by cutting back on meat at other times will be buying only the cheapest cuts. Anne, with her husband unemployed and three school-aged children, shops around very carefully:

> Most of the week we have chips and sausage, or eggs and chips. I have meat twice a week. I go down to the cheap butchers and we have liver and belly draft which are cheap. I mean we do have a joint at the weekend either a shank of lamb or a piece of pork or a chicken. It's much cheaper than beef. I think beef is over £2 a pound and

to feed the five of use it would be too expensive. We haven't had a joint of beef now for two years.

In buying food, as in all areas of regular expenditure, the poor find they are juggling around with not enough money to cope adequately. In general, the findings suggest that people put a high priority on food. Those who are only on the margins of poverty, lacking only one or two necessities, are much less likely to cut back on food than they are on leisure activities. It is only when money is very short and things like holidays have already been cut out that, in general, people start cutting back on food. In particular, families place a high priority on giving their children enough food: only 4 per cent of families who lack three or four necessities cut back on three meals a day for their children; in general, it is only when many other aspects of expenditure have already been cut back that families reduce the quantity of food given to children.

Without enough money to eat properly, the particular ways each household copes will vary from circumstance to circumstance – Anne has a cheap butchers round the corner; Mavis is blind and cannot shop around. Among those who lack a number of necessities the particular ones they lack will vary according to their situation, and may vary from week to week. At times a household may be managing to have meat two or three times a week and a roast joint at the weekend, then the electricity bill comes in or the children need a pair of shoes and so they will cut back on food.

Often, problems in one aspect of life lead to problems in other areas. Pamela, like many single parents, puts her priority on feeding her child. Her situation, however, is made worse by the fact that her flat is so unhygienic that she cannot cook at home. She goes to the local cafe to eat but it costs more. With just supplementary benefit to live on, she ends up cutting out meals:

I come in here every day of the week. At the beginning of the week when I get paid, I have like a ham salad or something. During the week I'll have a cheese roll and a cup of tea. That's all I'll have all day. Then at the end of the week, sometimes I just don't have anything at all. Sometimes I have to go hungry, in order to feed the child, to buy her nappies and her milk. For two or three days, I go without food. I just drink a cup of tea. That's all I'll do.

Living in other people's cast-offs

The raincoat, somebody found it for me but they didn't realise it was split in the first place and it's not water-proof anymore and the sleeve linings are going and it's split in both sleeves. Whether somebody wore a lot of woollies and split it I don't know, but it lets in water and if I've been caught out in heavy rain I've got very wet shoulders. That's the only one I've got, I can't afford another one.

Many of the poor will live in other people's cast-offs. For Mavis, this means her coat is neither warm nor water-proof. For others it will mean a loss of dignity in knowing that all their clothes come from jumble sales.

The poor find that clothing is a constant problem. Table 5.2 gives the proportion who lack at least one of the three clothing items in the list of necessities (a warm, water-proof coat; new, not second-hand, clothes; and two pairs of all-weather shoes). Around half of those who lack three or four necessities have problems with some aspect of clothing, and of those who are multiply deprived virtually all find they cannot afford to clothe themselves adequately.

Comparing this summary measure of clothing standards with each of the clothing items separately (Table 5.1) presents a similar picture to that found for food. For those lacking three or four necessities, the proportion cutting back on clothing in general is far greater than that cutting back on any specific aspect. They cannot afford to clothe themselves adequately but there remains some discretion. As living standards worsen, however, any remaining degree of choice goes. Households find that it is not enough just to cut back, everything begins to go. Of those who lack seven or more necessities, 88 per cent cannot afford two pairs of all-weather shoes, 66 per cent cannot afford new clothes and 66 per cent cannot afford a warm, water-proof coat. There is also a sharp distinction in the clothing standards of those who lack only one or two necessities and those who lack three or four: under one-fifth of the former group cut back on clothing compared to around one-half of the latter group.

The problem of clothing is often particularly acute for those with children. Mary is a single parent with a school-aged son living in a small village in a rural area of the West Country:

> I cannot go for a job interview even if I could get one, as after three years of unemployment my clothes are virtual rags, and I cannot buy any more, as it costs so much to keep my son decent – scruffy children have their lives made a misery at school and whatever else I do without, he will *not* have to go through that.

Shoes, in particular, are a problem for children. They wear them out quickly, they cannot be bought second-hand and they are expensive new. Sandra has three children to bring up on the low wages her husband brings home:

> I used to walk the youngest 100 yards to school but that one closed and now I've got to go right the way down Moss Lane. It's alright in summer but you bring them in the cold weather then you get to school and they say you mustn't keep those damp shoes on. You've got to take two pairs of shoes. Sometimes you can't afford two pairs of bloody shoes. And you can't put the children into them plimsols. They say don't bring those things in they're bad for their feet. You can't afford it all the time.

Furnishing the home from the rubbish tip

I found the front room carpet in the rubbish bin. There's a big bin there. I felt it and it felt fairly good to me so I thought, oh, we're having some of that. So I decided to take it in. I've got to negotiate it, three steps with the carpet dragging, dragging the carpet round the corner and along and in. Then I've got to lay it. I did this all by my own, though somebody very kindly did that bit in the bathroom for me and they cut it to fit. That was found in the bin as well, though I didn't bring that in at the same time.

Mavis, despite her blindness, laid the carpet in her sitting-room – a carpet that someone else placed in the communal rubbish bin.

In general, those with low living standards are more likely to have household goods than other items. Table 5.2 gives a summary measure of the lack of household furnishings and goods, in terms of those who cannot afford at least one of the four household items in the list of necessities (beds, carpets, a refrigerator and a washing machine). Only among those who lack seven or more necessities does the proportion lacking household furnishings reach one-half. There are a number of reasons for this. These household goods are often easier to pick up second-hand than more personal items and are more likely to be handed on from family or friends than day-to-day purchases. Often, such goods will have been bought when times were better and there was some spare cash around.

When times are worse, these goods are still there – although their quality diminishes. Carpets become threadbare. Washing machines break down. For those whose living standards are in other respects low this causes particular problems. Tricia, a single parent, has an 8-year old son:

Tony's only got one pair of school trousers and when he gets them dirty they've got to be washed and dried for the next morning. I did have a washing machine but it's now broke and the only way of doing my washing is in the sink. It does cause problems with the drying because though I can squeeze them out it's not as good as putting them in a spinner. If you put them in a spinner they come out almost dry; where you're ringing them by hand they're dripping wet, you just can't get them any drier than that. It's very difficult to get things dry especially if it's raining. The only way I can get things dry when it's raining is putting them in front of the fire.

As she has only 50 pence a day to spare for the gas meter, that, in turn, causes problems.

The poor are vulnerable. When a problem comes along they have no resources to fall back on and it is difficult to cope. Mary, a single parent with a 5-year old son, lives on supplementary benefit:

He wets the bed and has to wear nappies. His sheets and bedding must still be washed every day. When my washer broke, I asked if the DHSS could help, and was told that the washer was not regarded as a necessity, and I should use the laundrette. As this is 9 miles away and there is no bus service, this is ludicrous. I borrowed £100 for the repair, and pay £15 a month for that.

Santa is dead

He has not had either birthday or Christmas presents since he was 2. He asks for Lego and cars from Santa, but Santa is dead in this house; how does one explain that to a child of 5?

Mary and her son have been living on supplementary benefit for the last three years. She now finds that it is impossible to manage anything other than day-to-day essentials. Table 5.3 shows that, among families with the lowest living standards, an overwhelming majority cannot afford either toys or leisure equipment for their children: 79 per cent of those lacking seven or more necessities, and nearly a half of those lacking three or four necessities – a sharp contrast once again with those who lack one or two necessities. Overall, about 1½ million children go without toys or, for older children, leisure equipment.

Alongside the problem of not having enough money for toys is the problem of Christmas and of birthdays. Roy, father of three, has been unemployed for three years:

> It was my son's birthday three months back, he's still waiting for his present. It was my wife's last month and she's still waiting for hers. You know, they're going to mount up and mount up and if and when I do get a job, I'm going to spend the first few months just getting presents – just the backdated ones.

Table 5.2 shows the problems that those with low living standards have in meeting these social obligations of Christmas and giving presents, although it is a problem in the main for the poorest of the poor: 72 per cent of those lacking seven or more necessities could not afford at least one of these social obligations, but only around one-quarter of those lacking three to six necessities.

None the less, most of the poor find that in some way or another their life outside the immediate day-to-day personal and household needs is diminished. In particular, the poor cut back on leisure activities (a holiday and a hobby). Indeed these are the first areas to go: over half of those who lack only one or two necessities, as many as 85 per cent of those who lack three or four necessities, and virtually all of those who are multiply deprived cannot afford leisure activities. Among those with some financial difficulties, most will cut back in these areas to ensure minimum standards in other areas, although a few will trim back elsewhere to ensure a holiday. For those facing intense deprivation, however, such choices are a long gone luxury: they have already cut back on holidays and leisure activities to pay for food and clothing; now they also cut back on food and clothing. There is no way they can cut back further on these day-to-day items to go on holiday or pursue a hobby.

These problems of not having enough money to do anything interesting are again most concentrated among families. Elaine's children are aged 7, 5 and 3:

> The children have never had a holiday. They don't know

what it's like to have a holiday. They go out with the
school. When the school holidays come, we go down to
the playscheme, we go out for days. But they don't
know what it's like for a proper holiday.

And during the school holidays, Roy's three children just
have the local park in their district of inner Birmingham:

They get a bit frustrated and bored because we can't
take them anywhere during the holidays. They have to
stay around this area 52 weeks of the year. They don't
get out of it on nice days. You'd like to take them out
somewhere but you just can't afford to. They get a bit
frustrated when I say you can't go, we haven't got the
money. They go off sulking somewhere, or crying. And
it makes you feel rotten.

Part of the problem is the cost of public transport. Roy's wife
Anne explains:

When we all go out we walk. We walk a lot. It's very rare
we use buses. Cost of coaches, the trains, they're all
expensive. I think it's important for kids to get out of
the city so they can see the things they probably
wouldn't see otherwise, like wild flowers. I mean when
I was a kid, we used to go bluebell picking in the woods
and that. But it's just impossible.

A lonely living

What do I do most of the time? Try and clean the flat.
Put the radio on and get fed up with it, turn it off. Put
the talking book on, get fed up with it, turn it off. Put
my coat on, go out for a walk. Can't do that if it's cold.
What else do I do? Sit here and think – think about the
past quite a lot and I shouldn't be doing that at my age
I know. Sit here and wish that somebody would ring me
up or knock on my door to come and visit me. Get very

lonely. And that's about all I do. You wish you had more money so that you could get out an' perhaps take yourself for a meal or something like that. Ah, just I don't know, get very, very lonely.

Mavis, being blind and partially deaf, is more at risk of social isolation than others, but it is her acute lack of money that in the end completely cuts her off from society. For the poor struggling to afford the basic necessities, there is no spare money for just socialising. While this in itself is not, on the methodology adopted in this study, a mark of deprivation – in general, the survey found that those aspects of our standard of living that relate specifically to social relationships were classed as only 'desirable' and not as 'necessities' – it does mean that those who are deprived are also socially isolated. Mary and her 5-year old son live in a rural area of Cornwall:

> I have no chance of getting out to meet people; a baby sitter here costs £1.50 an hour, and even then there is nowhere I can go as I don't have transport and there is no bus service. A night out alone at the cinema would cost me over £20, and yet my doctor tells me I must get out at least once a week. I have no relatives to help out, and since I can no longer entertain or go out I have literally no friends. So I spend every day alone and every night.

The poor become cut off from the rest of society in that they cannot afford to meet people socially, either at home or out. They are also to some extent excluded from the mainstream of society by their unacceptably low standard of living in itself. The diversity of lifestyles in society does not apply to these basic aspects of living. Once people have a way of life that excludes them from a number of these basic necessities, then they do stand out as different. The poorest tend, as a consequence, to be ashamed about their living conditions. This can lead to a reluctance about inviting people in. The house may be cold, the carpets may be threadbare, there may be embarrassment about offering only a cup of tea. The poor are thus often isolated and lonely.

Yet more problems

> I sat down and worked out, roughly, what you spend per week. And now you've got washing up liquid, you got toilet paper, you got soap to wash with, you've got to keep yourself clean, you want disinfectant, or anything like that. Well what is it, you go out and you think to yourself, now if I buy washing up liquid I can't have a loaf of bread. Which do you do? Buy the loaf of bread or the washing up liquid? You've got to keep yourself clean and you've got to eat. So which way do you sway?

Mavis has to juggle her money between not just the necessities specifically examined but also a host of other important goods. While the picture presented has given an insight into the main consequences of deprivation, the necessities identified are not a comprehensive list of a person's needs. Those who are unable to eat properly or to clothe themselves decently are likely to suffer problems in the other areas of life that depend on day-to-day expenditure. If a more comprehensive list of indicators had been used, a fuller picture of the problems faced by those who have anyway been seen to be surrounded by problems could have been presented.

In addition, those suffering deprivations that stem from lack of income are also the most likely to be deprived in other ways. The poor are likely to live in the worst environments; and the very poorest are concentrated in the decaying areas of the inner city. The schools and the general practitioner service in these areas are likely to be worse than elsewhere. The leisure facilities are often inadequate. Marie, in Vauxhall, Liverpool, finds that the decay of the area and the lack of opportunities have their effects on the local children:

> The kids just more or less end up running wild some-
> times because there's nothing for them to do and

nowhere for them to go. The kids get bored so the next thing you know the windows in the empty houses – there's that many empty houses around – get smashed. Teenagers do it but the little ones see the teenagers doing it, so the little ones then tend to do it themselves. So like, it's only babies more or less of about 5 kicking stones up and lashing them at the empty windows.

A vicious circle is thus set up whereby a bad environment becomes worse.

Although such factors are an important aspect of a person's quality of life, their investigation was outside the scope of the survey. Instead, we concentrated on those deprivations that stem more directly from lack of money rather than from inadequate services. This chapter has so far examined the direct consequences of these deprivations. The problems that people face have been seen to be great, but the cumulative effect of all these problems has many other consequences for people's lives.

Failing to make ends meet

You are just living from day-to-day. We can't live from week-to-week, it's day-to-day. Because the money's just so tight. We just can't manage on the wages Roy is bringing home.

Even though Roy works the night-shift to try and push up his wage, his wife Elaine finds that with a family of three young children she cannot manage. Though they cut back on their living standards, they still have difficulty in making ends meet.

Each week, the poor find that they are down to their last pound. There is no leeway if for one reason or another their money one week is late. When Mavis's supplementary benefit Giro does not arrive, she is down to literally a penny ha'penny in her purse and a few slices of stale bread and some eggs in the house:

It's alright when your book comes through and you can go to the post office and get your money. But when it's like this, the end of a book or they're adjusting your money and you're waiting for your money and they say they're going to send you a Giro and it's in the post and that's it. You try and scrounge but there aren't any neighbours round here that I can scrounge off. In any case, I don't like knocking on doors and saying 'please can you let me have some of this' and 'please can you let me have some of that'.

When money runs so low each week, any delay in benefits arriving, any unexpected drop in earnings or, on the other hand, any unexpected expenditure can cause immense problems.

To investigate the extent to which people run out of money, the survey asked respondents whether there had been any time in the last year when they did not have enough money to buy food that they, and their family, needed. Table 5.5 shows that those who have to cut back on a range of necessities are also vulnerable to running out of money altogether and so simply missing out on meals: while virtually none (3 per cent) of those who had all the necessities had experienced running out of money for food, one-third of

Table 5.5 *The consequences of failing to make ends meet*

	Lack[a] of necessities					Income: Bottom decile
	0	1 or 2	3 or 4	5 or 6	7 or more	
	% who had faced problem during past year owing to shortage of money					
Missing out on meals; not buying food	3	19	33	44	68	37
Borrowing from family/ friends for day-to-day needs	7	22	40	47	69	28

[a]Throughout, 'lack' is taken as those who do not have an item because they cannot afford it and excludes thosed who do not have it because they do not want it.

those who lack three or four necessities had faced this problem. This vulnerability rises sharply for those who are multiply deprived: over two-thirds of those who lack seven or more necessities had experienced running out of money for food.

Faced with such problems, many find that they are forced to borrow from family and friends in order to pay for their day-to-day needs. This is also shown in Table 5.5. However, borrowing provides only a temporary solution, as Pamela, the single parent with a 9-month old baby living on supplementary benefit, explains:

Sometimes in the middle of the week I've got no money and I've got to go and find some money in order to buy nappies for her. So I have to go and ask people. If I haven't got the money I have to borrow the money from friends and that. And I have to give that back when my next pay comes so that leaves me short again.

On top of the problems of simply getting through the week, there is the constant problem of how bills will be paid. Ernie, a 79-year-old pensioner, often pores over the stack of bills he's faced with:

That's the telephone bill – £19.59, I haven't had that no time. £168 – that's the gas bill, it's fantastic. What's this one – £23, I can't account for that. Talk about being bamboozled . . . This has to be paid £20. Oh golly, they're a headache to me.

Confronted with bills they cannot pay, the poor are faced with either cutting back further on their living standards or running into debt. Mavis, the blind, partially deaf and diabetic claimant, finds this an impossible choice:

To make ends meet is terrible. It really is, You have it in one hand and it's out with the other. Your electricity's got to be paid for to start with, so you either eat or you pay the electricity? What do you do? You just can't make things balance. You can't do it. You're below the breadline.

Mavis, like many others in this situation, has fallen into debt. Table 5.6 shows that over half of those who lack seven or more necessities and one-third of those lacking three or four necessities are in debt, a sharp contrast to those households lacking none of the necessities, of whom only 7 per cent are in debt. The incidence of debt is thus sharply related to lack of necessities. In general, people do not run into debt out of extravagance; indeed, those most likely to fall into debt are those who have already cut back to the extent that their living standards fall below minimum levels.

Interestingly, debt is more closely related to low living standards than it is to low incomes. The last three columns in Table 5.6 show the incidence of debt for those on the lowest incomes. Those with low incomes do, of course, overlap considerably with those with low living standards (see Chapter 4) and, not surprisingly, many of those in the bottom decile are in debt: about 40 per cent. However, over 30 per cent of households in the second and third deciles are also in debt. The combination of the concentration of debt among those with low living standards and the spread of debt

Table 5.6 *The distribution of debts*

	Lack[a] of necessities					Income:		
	0	1 or 2	3 or 4	5 or 6	7 or more	Bottom 10%	Next 10%	Next 10%
			% seriously in debt during past year					
Rent	2	7	25	28	39	22	15	11
Gas	2	3	22	10	36	14	15	12
Electricity	2	9	20	22	42	22	11	11
Goods on HP	1	4	6	6	19	11	3	5
Mortgage	1	3	3	3	—	3	2	1
Rates	3	3	5	14	5	7	3	5
At least one debt	7	19	32	43	56	40	36	31

[a]Throughout, 'lack' is taken as those who do not have an item because they cannot afford it and excludes those who do not have it because they do not want it.

among the lower income groups suggest that debt is an important reason why some who are not on the lowest incomes are nevertheless among those with the lowest living standards. These debts may stem from past periods when the household income was lower; the effects carry over so that living standards continue to be low, even when the household income is somewhat higher.

For Elaine and Roy and their three children their problems really started when Roy was put on short-time:

> About three years ago Roy went on short-time working and the wages were cut by half. No warning, he just went into work one night after his holidays, and came home the following day and said they was on short-time. At that time I had a gas bill of over £100, and other bills as well. And we went all over the place trying to get help with paying the bill, the gas bill; they had cut me gas off, and I was three months without gas. We went down to the social security, and they said, when we first went down, they said yes, you're entitled to help, and then they said no, we were not entitled to help. And we got into arrears with the rent.

Elaine would have been entitled to rent rebate but did not know that. The debts mounted and, although Roy is back on full-time work and takes home about £80 a week, the problems continue, as Elaine explains:

> We are trapped by our debts, if we could get rid of the debt and start off with a clean slate, we'll probably be a lot happier and the children would probably be a lot happier as well. But there's no way I can do it. We are just doing it slowly which isn't very easy. Once you get into debt it's very hard to get out of it.

For those who accumulate debts but find that their income remains at the level that led to the debts, the problems are even worse. Living standards drop even further and the problems of debt, in turn, become worse. Table 5.7 shows

Table 5.7   *Sinking deeper into debt*

	\multicolumn{5}{c}{Lack[a] of necessities}				
	0	1 or 2	3 or 4	5 or 6	7 or more
	% owing multiple debts during past year				
At least one debt	7	19	32	43	56
Two or more debts	2	6	24	22	44
Three or more debts	—	3	19	11	29

[a]Throughout, 'lack' is taken as those who do not have an item because they cannot afford it and excludes those who do not have it because they do not want it.

that, among those who lack seven or more necessities, 44 per cent have more than one outstanding debt. Mavis got into debt with the gas and, in trying to pay off that, she built up other arrears. Money for these debts is now being deducted from her supplementary benefit:

> I get a total of £29.05. What am I supposed to do with it? They're deducting £1.65 for this and £1.90 for that and so it works out. And I'm supposed to live on it. Oh well.

Feelings of despair

> I'm just fed up with the whole thing and the money is ridiculous. I can't cope on the money and I can't cope in living here. I can't sleep at night, and she's up all night. I nearly went through a nervous breakdown because of the conditions. You know, I can't cope anymore.

Pamela finds that bringing up a 9-month old baby on the money she gets from supplementary benefit in an unhygienic, decrepit attic flat is just getting too much for her. In the long run, poverty affects a person's well-being both psychologically and physically. Because of the constraints of time and money, the *Breadline Britain* survey did not explore whether those with low living standards suffered worse health as a consequence. The one question on health that was asked related to long-term illness, and this is as much a cause of poverty as it is a consequence; this is discussed in Chapter 6.

However, the survey did explore whether people *felt* that their lack of money was affecting their emotional well-being and personal relationships. Table 5.8 shows that those with low living standards experience a whole range of worries. The contrast between those well below minimum living standards and those firmly above is sharp: 90 per cent of those lacking seven or more necessities are faced with worries compared to 28 per cent of those who lack none of the necessities. Comparing the experiences of those with different levels of deprivation shows that the financial concerns of those lacking three or four necessities are as great as those lacking five or six necessities and significantly greater than those lacking one or two necessities: about 80 per cent of those who lack three to six necessities experience regular worries stemming from lack of money compared to just over 50 per cent of those who lack one or two necessities.

Table 5.8 *The personal consequences of deprivation*

	Lack[a] of necessities					Income: Bottom decile
	0	1 or 2	3 or 4	5 or 6	7 or more	
	% facing worries during past month owing to lack of money					
Been depressed	10	21	55	50	54	29
Worsened relations with friends	2	2	7	3	12	9
Worsened relations with family	2	9	11	8	28	14
Been bored	9	20	31	35	40	17
Worried about not having enough money for day-to-day living	7	19	47	47	75	41
Felt looked down upon by others	1	5	16	14	18	13
Felt a failure	3	8	17	12	36	16
Lacked hope for the future	12	25	39	40	62	36
Felt your family was let down	4	14	29	14	34	25
At least one worry	28	57	81	79	90	69

[a]Throughout, 'lack' is taken as those who do not have an item because they cannot afford it and excludes those who do not have it because they do not want it.

Throughout this chapter it has been seen that those who lack three or four necessities are distinguished from those whose lack is less by the extent to which their lives are affected by their lack of money. The greater concentration of worries among those lacking three or four necessities reinforces the findings that their deprivations are of a far more wide-ranging nature and, moreover, suggests that the problems they face are, in general, more similar to those who are more deprived.

For some, the lack of money for day-to-day living puts a strain on relationships. When there is not enough money to go round, it adds a sharp intensity to general bickering about money. Parents can even find that never being able to escape from the constant problems that surround them damages their relationship with their children. A single parent explains:

> I get so angry I take it out on my daughter, because I can't go out. I end up taking it out on her. Instead of me taking it out on myself, I end up taking it out on her. I get so angry with her sometimes when she starts crying. I just can't be bothered, I just leave her.

Others feel that they are letting their families down because their living standards are so low. Some, as a consequence, feel a failure, others that they are looked down upon. Roy, during his three years of unemployment, has experienced a mixture of these emotions:

> I get so frustrated, knowing I'm stuck at home, feeling useless, that's how you feel, useless. You can't feel like a man. They won't let you, the system won't let you feel like a man. So until I get a job I have just got to sit down and suffer, what's the word, the indignities of being out of work 'cause you're looked down upon. Yes that's it, you are looked down upon as idle – you don't want a job, you're happy the way you are. Well, I'm not. I want to get back out there and feel useful again. You feel like an outcast.

Three concerns come through above all: a constant worrying about lack of money, depression and lack of hope for the future. Table 5.8 shows that nearly half of those who lack three to six necessities and three-quarters of those who lack seven or more necessities are worried about not having enough money for day-to-day needs. Roy, the night-shift worker, has tried doing a second job during the day to pay off their debts. But that just made him ill. So he is left with just worry:

> I do worry about money but I just don't like to show that I do worry. I more or less keep it to myself and try and work it out and try and make ends meet.

For Ernie, coming up to the age of 80 and with no hope of earning any extra money to help out, the bills he is faced with have become oppressive:

> I worry at night. I can't sleep. I go to sleep when it's daylight thinking how it's going to be done. I know I shouldn't worry because I'm too old to start worrying now about them. But I've still got to get by . . . in fact I don't know how I get by.

Worries about money and inadequate living standards lead in turn to depression. Table 5.8 shows that over half of those who lack three or more necessities have felt depressed in the last month. Roy, the unemployed father of three:

> Some days I'm alright and some days I just go into a black mood and I will not let anybody come near me. I just sit up the corner and just bang my head against a wall. And say why me?

Lack of hope is also widely shared, although this feeling is somewhat more concentrated among the very poorest: 62 per cent of those lacking seven or more necessities have felt this way compared to about 40 per cent of those lacking three to six necessities. For many of the poor their income is effectively out of their control and so there is very little they can do to improve their living standards. For those on supplementary benefit the levels are set by the state and any income the claimant earns above £4 is deducted from their benefit. For the low-paid, there is the trap of the tax–benefit system. Roy works in a local factory on the Trafford Park estate, Manchester, on the night shift to try and push up the money he takes home for his wife and three children. But he's beginning to wonder if there is much point:

> It's disheartening, any way you turn, you lose most of it with tax and insurance but you also lose your benefits as well for rebates and other small things. It makes me feel trapped 'cos it's not worth doing the overtime at all. Bar another job and more pay and that, to raise my standard of living, I don't think I'll ever get out of the trap. I might be lucky but I don't think I will. For the simple reason that there's the unemployment nowadays. I don't feel very optimistic about it all, or very hopeful about anything really nowadays.

It is interesting, in the light of all these worries, to look at people's feelings of satisfaction as regards their living standards. Table 5.9 shows that the lower a person's living standard the more likely they are to be dissatisfied with it. Among those with very low living standards (lacking seven or more of the necessities), dissatisfaction is high: 80 per cent

Table 5.9   *Satisfaction with living standards (percentages)*

Feelings about standard of living	Lack[a] of necessities					Income: Bottom decile
	0	1 or 2	3 or 4	5 or 6	7 or more	
Satisfied	84	66	61	47	19	45
Neither satisfied nor dissatisfied	7	12	6	4	2	7
Dissatisfied	9	20	34	48	79	46

[a]Throughout, 'lack' is taken as those who do not have an item because they cannot afford it and excludes those who do not have it because they do not want it.

are fairly or very dissatisfied, with a half being very dis-satisfied. In other respects, however, the results are very surprising. They show a widespread satisfaction among those who objectively have some of the worst living standards in society: some 60 per cent of those who lack three or four necessities and nearly half of those who lack five or six necessities are satisfied, and even among the most deprived nearly 20 per cent are satisfied. This picture of satisfaction also holds for those with the lowest incomes: nearly half of those in the bottom decile are satisfied.

On the other hand, a large majority of the very same people who express satisfaction with their living standards are worried in one way or another about problems stemming from lack of money. Their standard of living is in key respects being cut back because they cannot afford more. To view one's standard of living with satisfaction in these circum-stances suggests a high degree of resignation to one's situation and low personal aspirations. Maybe the answer is that the 'contented poor' exist not just in social science text-books but also in reality.

Feeling poor

I do feel poor. I'm not ashamed to admit it.

Roy's three years of unemployment have resulted in the family going without many necessities. The family is poor by the standard's of today – and they themselves feel poor. It is sometimes suggested, however, that the poor do not recognise their plight – a suggestion that is given some backing by the finding that some of the poor are satisfied with their standard of living, despite all their problems. On the other hand, it is possible that the poor may be relatively satisfied and yet realise that compared to others they are doing relatively badly. The judgement of satisfaction is essentially inward-looking, whereas feelings of being poor involve explicit comparison with others.

So, do those who are deprived by the standards of today

feel poor? The *Breadline Britain* survey asked people whether they could 'genuinely' say they were 'poor' always, sometimes or never. The results show a remarkably high degree of consistency between the socially defined measures of deprivation and the self-perception of being poor (see Table 5.10). The greater the number of necessities a person lacks, the more likely they are to see themselves as poor all the time, while the fewer necessities a person lacks the more likely they are never to regard themselves as poor. At the extremes, only 3 per cent of those who have all the necessities they want always feel poor, while only 9 per cent of those who lack seven or more necessities never feel poor.

Although a person's self-perception of their situation does not provide an adequate answer to the question of whether they are too poor, a high degree of overlap between the objective and subjective measures is not insignificant. It suggests that the objective measures are reflecting people's feelings about their situation and tapping something that is recognised by people as being of importance to them.

While those who lack necessities are more likely to feel poor than others, these feelings become notably more common once deprivation reaches the level of lack of three or more necessities: only 18 per cent of those lacking three or four necessities never feel poor. As living standards slip further, the regularity with which people feel poor increases:

Table 5.10　*The self-perception of being poor (percentages)*

'Do you think you could genuinely say you are poor now all the time, sometimes or never?'	Lack[a] of necessities					Income: Bottom decile
	0	1 or 2	3 or 4	5 or 6	7 or more	
All the time	3	13	38	49	73	39
Sometimes	23	38	41	40	18	34
Never	72	47	18	11	9	27
Don't know	2	2	3	—	—	—

[a]Throughout, 'lack' is taken as those who do not have an item because they cannot afford it and excludes those who do not have it because they do not want it.

around three-quarters of those lacking seven or more necessities feel poor all the time. Mavis is among those whose living standards are of the very lowest:

I feel destitute, not poor.

It is interesting to compare the feelings of those with low living standards with those on low incomes (see Table 5.10). Those who lack three or four necessities are slightly more likely to feel poor than those in the bottom decile and those who lack five or more are distinctly more inclined to feel poor. This suggests that people judge their situation by their standard of living as much as by income *per se*. This point may seem rather obvious, but it is of interest because most measures of poverty have been based on income; this study is unusual in placing its primary emphasis on the consequences and results of an inadequate income instead.

Just existing

The lives of all those who lack the necessities for living in Britain in the 1980s are diminished, even demeaned. An 'enforced lack of socially perceived necessities' is not just an academic description of deprivation but represents real problems for the poor.

Although there are no sharp divisions between those lacking necessities, those who lack at least three necessities have been seen to be likely to experience deprivation in many of the key areas of life. Most cut back on food, some cut back on clothing, some on heating and some on their social obligations; others live in bad housing; nearly all cut out leisure activities. All cut back in more than one of these ways; some in all of these ways. By contrast, of those who lack one or two necessities, the only areas that a majority cut back on is leisure activities: primarily a holiday – a deprivation by the standards of today, albeit on its own relatively minimal. Their lives are affected, but not in such a pervasive way. This is of importance when considering the measurement of poverty and is discussed in the next chapter.

For the poor, there is a constant balancing act between different sets of needs. It is a balancing act that never works. Impossible decisions have to be made about what needs will be left unmet. These decisions depend on a variety of factors, from personal ones such as health to the numerous differences in social circumstances. And, of course, people's personal priorities differ: for example, some may cut back on basic aspects of clothing to ensure that they eat properly, while others may put up with an unvarying diet so that their standards in the more visible aspects of life are acceptable. For such reasons, some of the poor will cut back in one area and others elsewhere. As living standards slip further and further below the minimum, even this limited degree of choice slips away.

Among the most intensely deprived the situation is desperate. There is little but worry about making ends meet. There is rarely any spare cash to enable a break, even for a few hours, from the monotonous and depressing routine.

Mary, the single parent living an isolated and lonely life with her 5-year-old son, has reached the depths of despair:

> There is no way out of this for me now. Work goes to kids on 'schemes' as they can be paid slave-labour rate – no-one wants a 43-year-old experienced office worker to whom they would need to pay £100 a week, so here I stay. My life is virtually at an end and I know that if I did not have my son, I would have taken my own life long before now rather than live like this; it is mere penurious existence.

6

Measuring Poverty

The implications of the findings on deprivation

It's a well-known fact that people on supplementary benefit get about £1 per day per child. That's to clothe and feed them on. And it's ridiculous because nobody can clothe and feed a kid on £1 a day. [A single parent with two school-aged children]

Deprivation in Britain in the 1980s is both extensive and, for some, intense. However, deprivation is not poverty. Although the two concepts overlap considerably, poverty has a narrower focus and somewhat greater implications for the individual.

The most important aspect of the *Breadline Britain* survey has been to throw light on the nature of relative deprivation, but it is useful to try to draw these findings together to form a measure of poverty. Although this runs the risk of over-simplifying the complex pattern of deprivation, a summary measure does help focus the debate on how many people face unacceptably low living standards.

The classification of people as being in poverty will aim, as far as possible, to be a descriptive exercise rather than one of personal value judgements. It will aim to measure the numbers of people whose *enforced* lack of necessities affects their *way of living*. The fact that there are no sharp distinctions between different levels of deprivation inevitably means, however, that such an exercise can only be rough and will include a degree of arbitrariness. This, in our view, is inevitable in any measure of poverty. To indicate the effects of this, a possible 'range' in the numbers in poverty will also be calculated.

In general, this chapter tries to draw together the findings of earlier chapters and use them to answer three broad questions. First, how many people live in poverty and how far do they fall below the minimum way of life to which everyone is entitled? Second, who are the people in poverty and who are the people most at risk? And last, is it possible to identify a level of income above which the risk of poverty is substantially diminished?

The principles underlying the measurement of poverty

Having identified minimum needs, there are at least two ways in which to identify the numbers in poverty. The first is to look *directly* at those whose needs are unsatisfied; in this study this means counting the numbers who lack necessities. The second is to look for a level of *income* below which people are unable to meet these minimum needs. This method entails drawing a *poverty line*: people with incomes below this line are counted as being in poverty. Both methods have advantages, although, as Sen points out, they embrace different conceptions of poverty:

> The direct method identifies those whose actual consumption fails to meet the accepted conventions of minimum needs, while the income method is after spotting those who do not have the ability to meet these needs within the behavioural constraints typical in that community. Both concepts are of some interest on their own in diagnosing poverty in a community, and while the latter is a bit more remote in being dependent on the existence of some typical behaviour pattern in the community, it is also a bit more refined in going beyond the observed choices into the notion of ability. A poor person, on this approach, is one whose income is not adequate to meet the minimum needs in conformity with the conventional behaviour pattern. (Sen, 1982, p. 28)

For such reasons, income has generally been used to measure poverty. However, there are immense problems in drawing a 'poverty line' based on income because of the relationship between income and deprivation (see Chapter 4). Simply, there are some people on the lowest current incomes who have a higher standard of living than others with a higher current income. Townsend tried to overcome this problem in his study by exploring whether there was an income level below which people were disproportionately deprived. While this 'income threshold' may have uses, it is not an adequate indication of poverty because there could still be people in poverty even if there was no threshold.

Although income remains central to any attack on poverty, this study turns to the *direct* method of identifying the numbers in poverty. This approach has its advantages:

> In an obvious sense the direct method is superior to the income method, since the former is not based on particular assumptions of consumption behaviour which may or may not be accurate. Indeed, it could be argued that *only* in the absence of direct information regarding the satisfaction of the specific needs can there be a case for bringing in the intermediary of income, so that the income method is at most a second best. (Sen, 1982, p. 26)

In the past, it has been argued that the main disadvantage of this direct method is that observing the people whose needs are unsatisfied without observing their ability to afford these needs ignores 'choice': the ascetic, for example, who fasts. By controlling for 'taste' this criticism has been taken into account. The measure of poverty used is, then, based on counting those who have an enforced lack of necessities.

In doing this, we have aimed to limit the role of personal value judgements. In particular, we have removed from our own judgement the key question of what aspects of life are so important that to go without is to be deprived. Instead, we have taken the consensual judgement of society at large. This has involved developing the concept of socially perceived necessities, which enables a much more descriptive, as opposed to prescriptive, view of deprivation to be taken.

However, it is not possible to remove subjective judgement altogether. Indeed, we do not claim to have come up with a 'scientifically' objective measure of poverty. Our definition of poverty is based on the concept of an enforced lack of necessities, which does not of itself provide an unambiguous measure of poverty. To move from the concept to a measure, it is still necessary to make judgements about the interpretation of the two main criteria at the heart of this definition. The first of these is the question of when a lack of necessities is *enforced*. This tells us when people are deprived and gives a measure of deprivation. Second, there is the question of how a measure of relative deprivation is translated into one of poverty – that is, what *level* of deprivation constitutes poverty.

Deciding when a lack of necessities is enforced, and when it is not, requires judgements about the extent to which choice and taste should be taken into account – how far, in particular, people's *self-perception* of their situation should be accepted. For example, take an elderly person who says they do not want a holiday. If they are poor and could not afford it anyway, should it be assumed that they are still deprived on the basis that their expectations are distorted – or that they genuinely do not want a holiday, even if they could afford it?

Another question in deciding whether the deprivations are enforced concerns people's *priorities* or the types and pattern of goods lacked. To what extent, for example, can people on higher incomes who say they cannot afford one or some necessities be said to have an enforced lack of necessities? Again, and more importantly, to what extent can people who say they cannot afford necessities be said to have an enforced lack of these necessities if at the same time they spend their money on goods that society as a whole considers to be less important? In what circumstances should these priorities be accepted as 'reasonable' and the deprivations stemming from them as enforced?

These questions need to be answered in order to determine

the patterns of enforced deprivation. All those who have an enforced lack of necessities are deprived in some way or another. Before we can estimate the extent of poverty, however, a further question remains. At what point does deprivation become poverty? Does a lack of one necessity constitute poverty? Or should it be several necessities? This again is a matter of judgement. In this study, we assume that poverty is a situation where such deprivation has a multiple impact on a household's *way of life*, affecting several aspects of living. Thus, a family which just about manages but to do so does without an annual holiday is deprived by today's standards; in our judgement, however, it is not in poverty. Deprivation has to have a more pervasive impact to become poverty.

With these criteria in mind, we shall estimate the extent of poverty and the sensitivity of such estimates to different assumptions on these questions. This helps to provide a range of estimates about the extent of poverty, based on judgements that are likely to be broadly acceptable. At this stage, it is as well to recall the implications of some of our data problems for these estimates. In particular, the problems of the income data (see Appendix C, pp.308–14) mean that some households are misplaced in the income distribution, giving a slightly weaker relationship between deprivation and income than would be expected to be the case. Some of the questions raised above would be easier to answer and the estimates of poverty more precise if the income data were better.

An enforced lack of necessities

In Chapter 4 the measurement of deprivation was examined. In light of the questions above, it is worth summarising briefly the main findings.

First, consider those who lack necessities because they say they cannot afford them. For each level of lack of necessities, can the lack be generally described as enforced? Two criteria have been applied: first, those who lack this level of necessities should have low incomes, falling in the bottom half of the income range; second, their overall spending patterns should reflect financial difficulty rather than high spending on other goods. This second criterion has been interpreted as meaning that at this level of lack of necessities households should be cutting back in other ways and that they should be more likely to do so than those who are not cutting back on necessities.

Using these criteria, a level of lack of one or two necessities is largely enforced, though not overwhelmingly. Around one-quarter could be considered to have 'chosen' not to afford the necessities even if they say they cannot afford them in the sense that they are in the top half of the income range (it is also the same percentage as those who lack none of the 'non-necessities', groups that overlap considerably).

A level of lack of three or more necessities is, by contrast, overwhelmingly enforced. Very few of the better-off lack this level of necessities. And nearly all those who lack this level of necessities cut back on non-necessities, a majority cutting back substantially. To a large extent, differences in *priorities* do not arise – people's priorities are similar.

Of course, there will be exceptions: there will be some whose standards of living are intensely low because they gamble or they go down to the pub every night, all night. While such exceptions may be of interest, they in no way invalidate the general conclusions. It is inevitable in any study of social circumstances that there will be exceptions because of the wide variety of highly individual factors that affect behaviour. What is important is that the circumstances described are, in the main, an accurate reflection of people's predicament – and there is no evidence to throw any substantive doubt on that.

To the extent that we feel there is room for doubt we shall investigate the effect of this. Using the dual criterion that those on high incomes and those with otherwise high spending patterns should be excluded, some 10 per cent of those who cannot afford three or more necessities are arguably not in real financial difficulties. Allowance will be made for this by calculating a downward limit to the numbers in poverty. We shall call this a *deduction for high spending*.

There is one other factor worth considering in this context of the extent to which the lack of necessities is enforced – namely, smoking. Some people have argued that no one who smokes can be described as being in poverty. While we have argued that, in the main, it is deprivation that leads to smoking rather than the reverse (see Chapter 4), there remains a small minority whose smoking could be said to cause their deprivations in that they would appear to have enough money to afford the necessities they lack if they did not smoke. We calculate this to affect around 15 per cent of those lacking three or more necessities. We will, therefore, make an allowance for this and call it a *deduction for the effect of smoking*.

Where there is, in our view, more room for interpretation is on the question of the extent to which people who lack necessities because they do not want them should be excluded from the measure of deprivation. The findings suggest that it is worth controlling for 'taste' in that there are many on higher incomes who choose to go without one or other necessity and a few who choose to go without a range of necessities. Among the poor, however, the exercise of 'choice' is limited: when someone who anyway cannot afford a necessity 'chooses' to go without it, the likelihood is that the lack is not being replaced by an adequate substitute. *Low expectations* do indeed appear to be an important influence, particularly among the elderly. For these reasons, while in the main the measure of deprivation taken has excluded those who lack goods because they do not want them, we shall also calculate what effect this factor of low expectations has on the numbers of those in poverty. That is, we shall calculate a measure of poverty based on all those who do not have necessities excluding only those of the people who 'choose' not to have a necessity who could afford that necessity if they so chose. This, of course, entails another judgement about those who could not afford necessities they say they do not 'want'. We have taken all those in the first, second, third and fourth deciles, where the concentration of deprivation based on those who cannot afford the necessity is notably higher.

To some extent, there are arguments for limiting this

'differential taste exclusion' to those in the bottom decile, where income constraints are clearly both sharpest and very intense. The point, however, is simply to give an indication of the degree to which excluding people on the grounds of 'taste' has had an effect on the upward limits of the numbers of people whose living standards fall below the minimum laid down by society as a whole. We shall call this *adjusting for low expectations*.

The effects of deprivation

In Chapter 5, the effects of deprivation on a person's way of life were examined. It was argued that the effect of a lack of one or two necessities is in the main relatively marginal, simply because people's lives are inevitably touched in at most one or two areas. By contrast, those who lack three or more necessities are generally cutting back in a range of ways: in particular, the distribution of the specific necessities lacked by this group showed that they were cutting back in ways that affected a range of *areas* of their life and not just one. Taking the criterion that those facing deprivation will be classed as being in poverty only if those deprivations have widespread effects, then all those with an enforced lack of three or more necessities are in poverty. In our view, this criterion is on its own sufficient. All fall below the minimum way of life laid down by society as a whole.

We will, therefore, take all those who cannot afford three or more necessities as an indication of the numbers in poverty.

However, some people would argue that a criterion of 'seriousness' should also be considered. It would be argued on this basis that a person is only in poverty when the deprivations faced are in some sense intense. It would be perfectly possible to make an estimate of the 'seriousness' of the deprivations faced. Although the survey did not directly test the comparative importance people placed on each of the necessities, some indication of this is given by the rank order of the necessities; that is, by the proportion of the population classing each item as a necessity (see Table 3.1, p. 54). This shows that some items are more likely to be considered as necessary than others (for example, heating as compared to holidays), but it is probably also true that the items for which there is a high degree of consensus are also the items about which each individual will feel most strongly are necessary. The deprivation suffered from a lack of these more 'important' necessities is likely to be more intense.

On this basis, the 'seriousness' of the deprivations faced could be taken into account in constructing a measure of poverty. One way of doing this would be to weight necessities so that those that are more 'serious' count for more than those that are less 'serious'. This approach is, however, based on a misconception of the nature of poverty. It assumes that those in poverty should, by definition, all face an equally 'serious' situation, whereas living standards at the bottom of society, as elsewhere, are likely to vary. There will be some in poverty whose problems are more serious than others – and this is a legitimate question for study. However, to try to produce a measure that 'equates' problems is to make an assumption about the nature of poverty that is, in our view, fundamentally incorrect.

The 'seriousness' of the deprivations faced could, none the less, be taken into account without coming up against these problems. It could be done by simply adopting the criterion that the deprivations faced must extend into areas that are 'serious' for the circumstances to be classed as poverty. This approach is, in our view, still misplaced. That the deprivations suffered by some do not extend into the more 'serious' areas does not diminish the fact that their way of life falls below the standards of society as a whole. Their deprivations may be less serious than others but they remain deprivations none the less.

We do not wish, therefore, to add a criterion of 'seriousness'. We will, however, estimate the effect of this assumption in the next section. This is, anyway, of some interest. Even if it is accepted, as we do, that the judgement of a straightforward majority of the population is sufficient to define the deprivations that count in the measurement of

Table 6.1   *The degree of concern about the deprived: adults*

The 18 adult standard-of-living items	Lack[a] of necessities			
	1 or 2	3 or 4	5 or 6	7 or more
	% of households lacking at least 1 item from each group			
Items classed as necessities by over 75% of people	33	68	91	100
Items classed as necessities by over 66% of people	51	95	100	100
Items classed as necessities by over 50% of people	100	100	100	100

[a]'Lack' is taken as those who do not have an item because they cannot afford it and excludes those who do not have it because they do not want it.

poverty, it is still useful to know the extent of public concern about the problems of those at different levels of deprivation. This is shown for adults in Table 6.1 and for children in Table 6.2.

Looking at those who lack three or four necessities shows that lack of 'important' items is widespread: *virtually all* (95 per cent) lack at least one item classed as a necessity by 66 per cent of the population and over two-thirds lack at least one item classed as a necessity by over three-quarters of the population. This is in sharp contrast to those who lack one or two necessities, where the items lacked are much more likely to be concentrated among the necessities about which there is less agreement: only about one-half of this group lack an item classed by over two-thirds of the population as necessary, even though the majority of necessities fall into this category.

Those who lack three or four necessities do, then, lack at least once necessity about which there is widespread agreement that to go without that item is an unacceptable deprivation. Even if a criterion of 'seriousness' was introduced, it would not make a great deal of difference. If 'seriousness' was judged in terms of two-thirds of the population thinking the deprivation is important then the numbers in poverty are only marginally affected. If 'seriousness' is judged in terms of three-quarters of the population

Table 6.2 *The degree of concern about the deprived: children*

The 18 children's standard-of-living items	Lack[a] of necessities			
	1 or 2	3 or 4	5 or 6	7 or more
	% of families lacking at least 1 item from each group			
Items classed as necessities by over 75% of people	56	72	95	100
Items classed as necessities by over 66% of people	86	96	100	100
Items classed as necessities by over 50% of people	100	100	100	100

[a]'Lack' is taken as those who do not have an item because they cannot afford it and excludes those who do not have it because they do not want it.

thinking the deprivation is important, then the numbers of those lacking three or more necessities who could be classed as being in poverty will be reduced. We shall call this an adjustment for *the marginality of deprivation*. However, using this criterion, it is arguable that those who lack one or two necessities should be included in the estimates of poverty if these necessities are 'serious'. One-third of those who lack one or two necessities lack an item classed by over three-quarters of the population as a necessity. We shall call this an adjustment for *the intensity of deprivation*.

The extent of poverty

With these criteria identified it is possible to calculate the extent of poverty in Britain in the 1980s. This is done by simply multiplying the percentage of adults and children in the survey sample in poverty by the numbers of adults and children in the population as a whole. (The statistical error will be around 2–3 per cent, which is minimal compared to the range that results from the assumptions outlined above.)

Taking first the simple measure of poverty as those who cannot afford three or more necessities, Table 6.3 shows that

Table 6.3   *The numbers in poverty (in millions)*

	In poverty	High spending	Effects of smoking	Adjustments[a] for: Low expectations	Marginality of deprivation	Intensity of deprivation
Adults	5.0	4.5	4.25	6.9	4.3	7.9
Children	2.5	2.25	2.15	2.8	2.4	3.8
Total	7.5	6.75	6.4	9.7	6.7	11.7
Percentage of the population	13.8	12.4	11.7	17.1	12.3	21.5

[a]The adjustments are taken separately and are not cumulative.

there are:

**5 million adults and
2.5 million children living in poverty; that is,
7.5 million people – around 1 in every 7 people.**

The effects of the adjustments discussed above are shown in Table 6.3.

- *Deduction for high spending:* that is, making an allowance for those whose income and spending patterns are such that their lack of necessities appears not necessarily to be enforced. On this basis, the bottom range of the numbers in poverty would be around 6.75 million people.
- *Deduction for the effects of smoking:* that is, making an allowance for those who would appear to have enough money to afford the necessities if they did not smoke. On this basis, the numbers in poverty would be around 6.4 million.
- *Adjustment for low expectations:* that is, making an allowance for those who have an enforced lack of necessities that is not recognised because of low expectations. Then the numbers in poverty increase to around 9.7 million
- Adjustment for *the marginality of deprivation*: that is, making allowance for the proposition that some who lack

three or more necessities find that their lives are less 'seriously' affected bcause of the type of necessities they lack. This brings the numbers in poverty down to around 6.7 million.

• Adjustment for *the intensity of deprivation*: that is, making allowance for the proposition that some who lack one or two necessities find their lives 'seriously' affected because of the types of necessities they lack. This brings the estimate up to around 11.7 million.

Taking the downward 'adjustments' together and the upward 'adjustments' together gives a range (accounting for overlap in both sets of adjustments) of between about 6 million and 12 million people in poverty. Taking all the adjustments together, the numbers in poverty are estimated to be about 8.5 million.

While it is worth trying to achieve a measure of the extent of poverty for which there is wide agreement, there is a danger that at the margins the argument becomes rather semantic. Whether one chooses to describe 12 million people as 'in poverty' or 12 million people as 'in or on the margins of poverty' and 6 to 8.5 million people as 'in poverty' is less important than the implications that both wordings imply – namely, that there are about 12 million people who are struggling by the standards of today; that, among this group, living standards gradually deteriorate so that somewhat over half of this group face wide-ranging and serious problems.

We shall refer to those who are unable to afford three or more necessities as *in poverty*, and we shall refer to those on low incomes who are unable to afford one or two necessities as *on the margins of poverty*.

What is clear, and it is worth emphasising, is that there are no sharp distinctions. At the margins of poverty, there are many people whose living standards are relatively similar. There are around 4.5 million people in the bottom four deciles who lack one or two necessities. The adjustments for low expectations and for the intensity of deprivation both have the effect of drawing this group into the estimates of poverty. Indeed, their living standards are not all that different from those on low incomes who say they cannot afford three necessities. People will move in and out of these two groups from month to month (or even week to week) as different problems or bonuses crop up: someone cutting back on two necessities one week may cut back on more the next week to pay, say, the electricity bill.

Similarly, among the 7.5 million people who have been classed as being in poverty, there is a wide variation in living standards. The adjustments suggest that there may be about 1.5 million people whose problems are not as serious as the rest, but even among the remaining 6 million living standards will vary considerably. All fall below the minimum standards of society today – but some will fall further below than others.

This can be demonstrated by looking at the extent of their deprivation. Those who cannot afford five or six necessities are generally finding life more difficult than those lacking three or four, while those lacking seven or more necessities are intensely deprived, cutting back in many ways in all areas of life (these differences are described in detail in Chapter 5). If the criterion of 'seriousness' is taken, nearly all those lacking five or more necessities and all those lacking seven or more necessities are also facing the more 'serious' deprivations (see Tables 6.1 and 6.2).

Broadly speaking, those who cannot afford five or more necessities are *sinking deeper* into poverty; and those who cannot afford seven or more necessities are in *intense poverty*. The numbers of people affected are shown in Table 6.4.

Table 6.4 *The depths of poverty (in millions)*

	In or on the margins	In poverty	Sinking deeper	In intense poverty
Adults	7.9	5.0	3.3	1.7
Children	4.2	2.5	1.4	0.9
Total	12.1	7.5	4.7	2.6
Percentage of the population	22.2	13.8	8.6	4.8

It is striking that there are 2.6 million people, including nearly 1 million children, who live in intense poverty: that is, about 1 in every 20 people. Their lives are diminished and demeaned in every way, so far do they fall below the minimum standards of society today.

The people in poverty

Who, then, are the people whose living standards are too low? There are five groups: the unemployed, single parents, the sick and disabled, pensioners and the low-paid. Of course, these groups overlap to some degree – some people, for example, will be both disabled and unemployed, some both single parents and unemployed – but each of these groups is significant in their own right.

In terms of *numbers*, the households split fairly evenly between those where the head of the household is in work, those where s/he is unemployed and available for work, and those where the head is not working and is unavailable for work. This is shown in Tables 6.5 and 6.6. (For the groups in poverty, the percentages should be treated as a guide to the scale of different factors rather than as a precise measure, as the overall numbers in these groups are relatively small; for statistical detail see Appendix A, pp. 287–8).

The tables show that *low pay* is an important cause of inadequate living standards: one-third of households where the adults are in poverty and 40 per cent of families in poverty have a head of household in full-time work. This affects about 1.75 million adults and 1 million children. Of those in work with inadequate living standards the overwhelming majority are in manual occupations. Low pay is, however, less significant as a cause of intense poverty, accounting for only about one-fifth to one-quarter of this group. Nevertheless, 400,000 adults and 160,000 children are in households where the head works full-time yet the household is in intense poverty.

Generally, as people slip deeper into poverty, the spectre of *unemployment* looms. In nearly one-half of households

Table 6.5   *The work status of the head of household for adults in poverty*

	Not in poverty[a]	All those in poverty	In Poverty Those who are sinking deeper	In intense poverty
		(column percentages)		
Full-time employment	66	35	31	25
Part-time employment	2	3	4	5
Not working	27	29	27	25
Unemployed	5	33	38	45
All	100	100	100	100

[a]Those who are not in poverty are taken as those who do not lack any of the necessities because they cannot afford them.

where the adults are in intense poverty and in two-thirds of families in intense poverty, the head of household is unemployed. The effect of the recession of the 1980s has been sharply to increase the numbers of adults and children suffering intense deprivation. Overall, there are about 1.65

Table 6.6   *The work status of the head of household for children in poverty*

	Not in poverty[a]	All those in poverty	In Poverty Those who are sinking deeper	In intense poverty
		(column percentages)		
Full-time employment	91	42	18	18
Part-time employment	(—)[b]	2	3	1
Not working	6	16	17	15
Unemployed	3	39	62	66
All	100	100	100	100

[a]Those who are not in poverty are taken as those who do not lack any of the necessities because they cannot afford them.
[b]Under 0.5 per cent.

million adults and nearly 1 million children in poverty as a result of unemployment; of this group, nearly half the adults and over half the children are in intense povety: that is, about 0.75 million adults and 0.5 million children.

Those in poverty where the head of household is not working and is unavailable for work fall into three main groups: the elderly, the disabled, and single-parent families.

The proportion of those in poverty who are *elderly* are on these measures relatively small: only about 13 per cent, representing about 0.65 million. The main reason why the elderly do not figure prominently is because of the methodology adopted. The elderly tend to have low expectations and, though many lack necessities, they tend to be excluded on a count based on those who explicitly say they cannot afford necessities. If an adjustment for low expectations is made, the numbers of elderly in poverty rise significantly to about 1.5 million, and would account for more like one-fifth of those in poverty.

Nevertheless, even after this adjustment, the elderly now represent a smaller proportion of those in poverty than throughout the postwar years. The Townsend study fifteen years ago found that the elderly accounted for about one-third of those in poverty. The measure adopted in the Townsend study is, of course, somewhat different from the measure adopted here, but this would not account for the bulk of the decline in the proportion of those in poverty who are elderly. Moreover, the numbers of elderly in the population have been rising, making the drop more significant than it appears. It therefore requires some explanation. The main reason is clear: it results from the impact of the recession. The numbers of unemployed have risen dramatically and have formed an ever-increasing proportion of those in poverty. In addition, other changes have improved the circumstances of some of the elderly: in particular, the state pension has fared relatively well compared to other benefits and an increasing proportion of the elderly have an occupational pension to add to their state pension.

Moreover, it is not only the case that the elderly form a smaller proportion of those in poverty generally, they also form a smaller proportion of those in intense poverty. While nearly half of the unemployed in poverty are in intense poverty, only about one-fifth of the elderly in poverty are in intense poverty (adjustments for low expectations have been taken into account). Nevertheless, this still represents about 300,000 elderly people whose circumstances are absolutely desperate. It is also worth noting that, although the elderly on supplementary benefit do receive a higher rate than the unemployed, they fare just as badly (see Table 4.13, p. 116). The significance of old age as a cause of poverty may have declined, in terms of both the overall numbers and the intensity of the deprivations, but the state's provision for the elderly remains inadequate.

The importance of *sickness and disability* is shown in Table 6.7. The survey asked people whether they had any long-standing illness, disability or infirmity. Overall, 23 per cent of the sample had some kind of illness or disability that had troubled them over a period of time. This proportion is slightly lower than that found in the General Household Survey, where, in an identical question, around 30 per cent of the population are estimated as having a long-standing illness or disability. The significance of disability as a cause of

Table 6.7   *The extent to which those in poverty are sick and disabled*

	Not in poverty[a]	Poverty among adults All those in poverty	Those who are sinking deeper	In intense poverty
		(column percentages)		
Long-term illness or disability	20	33	37	29
Fit	80	67	63	71
All	100	100	100	100

[a]Those who are not in poverty are taken as those who do not lack any of the necessities because they cannot afford them.

poverty may, therefore, be slightly underestimated. Among those in poverty, one-third are sick or disabled: that is, about 1.5 million adults. Many of these will also be elderly, but over half are not. Sickness and disability are, thus, important causes of poverty among those below retirement age.

The final group of the poor are *single-parent families*. The number of single parents in the sample was small, so no precise estimates can be drawn, but the data tentatively suggest that about one-fifth of children in poverty are in single-parent families.

Certainly, the *risk* of a single-parent family being in poverty is high. (The 'risk' of poverty is defined as the proportion of a particular group that is in poverty.) The study indicates that at least half of children under the age of 16 in single-parent families are in poverty and many are in intense poverty. In addition, the fact that one-parent families are headed by mothers means that there are many women who face a high risk of poverty; though, in general, women are not significantly more at risk than men. The risk of poverty is also particularly high among the unemployed: around two-thirds are on the margins of poverty and about a half in poverty.

In general, those whose risk of poverty is very low are those in employment with no dependent children – either single people or couples. Families are more likely to fare badly. In particular, children of large families are more likely to be in poverty than are those in small families: families with three or more children are about twice as likely to be poverty as those with just one child. And one-parent families and the unemployed are likely to fare the very worst.

One final characteristic of those in poverty was explored: *the area of the country* in which they live. There is a sharp north/south divide: over two-thirds of those in poverty live in Scotland, the north of England and the Midlands, while under half of the comfortably off live in these areas. This is shown in Table 6.8 (the figures refer to adults in poverty but the percentages for children are very similar). The concentration in the northern cities of those in intense poverty is stark. This reflects the massive extent of inner-city

Table 6.8   *The areas of Britain in which those in poverty live*

	Not in poverty[a]	Poverty among adults		
		All those in poverty	Those who are sinking deeper	In intense poverty
		(column percentages)		
London	14	13	11	11
Rest of the south	37	20	16	10
Northern conurbations	31	40	45	65
Rest of the north	18	27	27	14
All	100	100	100	100

[a]Those who are not in poverty are taken as those who do not lack any of the necessities because they cannot afford them.

decay in conurbations like Merseyside and the sharp impact of the recession in these areas.

The problems in estimating an adequate income level

The two groups most at risk of poverty – the unemployed and single parents – have one major factor in common. They both, by and large, are dependent on the state's minimum income – supplementary benefit. It was seen in Chapter 4 that supplementary benefit is inadequate (see, in particular, Tables 4.10 and 4.14). The question remains: what level of income *would* be adequate?

This is a difficult question to answer because of the nature of the relationship between income and living standards. The vulnerability to poverty extends throughout the bottom 40 per cent of the income range; indeed, there are few people whose exceptional circumstances mean that they fall into poverty when their incomes are above that level. Many of the problems of those in poverty whose incomes are not currently among the very lowest will have stemmed from times when their incomes were lower. This means that it is very difficult to estimate the precise long-term effects of rises in the minimum income level; it is not possible simply to assume that the proportions now found in poverty at any given income level would be the same if the minimum income level was higher: the proportions would undoubtedly be lower but by exactly how much is not known.

This problem is compounded by problems with the income data (see Appendix C). For example, Figures 4.1 and 4.2, and the accompanying Tables 4.8 and 4.9, suggest that for virtually everyone to be lifted out of poverty everyone's income would have to be above that of those currently in the middle. It is difficult to estimate to what extent this is caused by misplacement of households in the income range and to what extent it reflects real problems among a small minority of middle-income households.

The problems with the income data cause another quite separate problem. People's incomes have been understated in the survey (see Table C.2, Appendix C). This means that, when estimating an adequate income level, the income figures in the survey have to be adjusted so that they represent more accurately each household's real income. To compare these adjusted income figures with the supplementary benefit level, it is necessary also to take into account housing costs.

Finally, the housing indicators used in the measurement of poverty also cause a problem in estimating the impact of increases in household income on the extent of poverty. Rises in a household's income would not necessarily have any impact on improving their housing conditions. For this to happen there would need to be a substantial programme of housing investment.

These difficulties mean that it is possible to make only very broad estimates of the kind of level of minimum income that would be adequate. While this exercise is imprecise – and must be treated as such – it is worth trying to gain an idea of the *scale* of the problem.

The measurement of an 'income threshold'

Is it possible, therefore, to identify a minimum income level below which people's *risk* of going without necessities is sharply increased? This is the same question as is asked when attempts are made to define poverty on the basis of an income line or 'threshold'. This was rejected as a way of measuring those in poverty on the basis that, even if there were no such threshold, there may still be people in poverty. Indeed, even if there is a threshold, there may be people on current incomes *below* that level who are *not* in poverty and people *above* that level whose circumstances are such that they *are* nevertheless in poverty. However, the concept of an income threshold remains of interest in the context of identifying an adequate income. If there is a 'threshold' below which people's chances of being unable to afford the necessities increase disproportionately to the drop in their incomes, then this would be a 'cost-effective' point to identify as a minimum income level. So, do the data suggest that there is a 'threshold'?

This concept was pioneered by Professor Peter Townsend in his study *Poverty in the United Kingdom* (1979) and it is worth reviewing his approach briefly (the more general and theoretical aspects of Townsend's approach are discussed in Chapter 2). Townsend's method was to select a list of twelve indicators of styles of living from the sixty items he examined in his survey (see Table 2.1). A 'deprivation index' for each household was then calculated on the basis of the number of these twelve indicators the household did not have. The index was plotted against income and was found to be closely correlated with income, showing an increase in deprivation as income fell. Using this relationship between deprivation and income, Townsend went on to argue that there was also tentative evidence of a kink in the relationship at around 150 per cent of the supplementary benefit level, indicating a 'threshold' separating the poor from the non-poor. On the basis of this income level, Townsend estimated that some 23 per cent of the population lived in poverty in 1969 (1979, p. 273). Townsend's approach has been criticised on both conceptual and technical grounds. The conceptual objections have been discussed in Chapter 2. The technical objections were that Townsend had not provided statistical support for his contention of an income threshold and that the evidence remained ambiguous (see, for example, Piachaud, 1981).

Subsequently, a set of more rigorous statistical tests were applied to the Townsend data by Professor Meghnad Desai (1981). The central issue is whether there is a discontinuity in the relationship between deprivation scores and income level. In other words, does a given fall in income mean a much sharper rise in deprivation at a lower income level than it does at a higher income level? This can be tested using a statistical technique known as regression analysis. Regression analysis involves fitting an equation to the data on deprivation and income, which shows both the nature and the strength of the deprivation/income relationship. Such an equation both provides a measure of the extent to which deprivation changes as income rises or falls, and shows whether the relationship is significant or not. To test for a threshold involves splitting the data into two groups of low-income and high-income households and fitting separate equations to each sub-sample. If the poor are distinct from the non-poor, then the relationship between income and deprivation would vary between sub-samples, giving two distinct lines instead of a single continuum. The question, statistically, is whether two equations fit the data (in the sense of minimising variations) better than one. In applying this method, Desai found that a break did occur as hypothesised by Townsend.

On our behalf, Professor Desai has applied an identical test to the *Breadline Britain* data to see if there is evidence of such a threshold. The 'deprivation scores' used are for the adult items identified as necessities. Only those items lacked because the household say they cannot afford them are counted in the deprivation score. The test reveals a clear break in the relationship between deprivation and income, at a net equivalent income of around £70 a week per equivalent couple. This point marks a discontinuity in the relationship between income and deprivation. Accounting for average housing costs and adjusting for biases in the income data, this level of income is roughly 150 per cent of the supplementary benefit scale rate. This result is similar to that found using the Townsend data. As the items in the Townsend index are different from those used in this study, this suggests that there is an income level below which people are forced to withdraw from a whole range of activities and are unable to afford a whole range of goods.

Households with incomes less than this level of about 150 per cent of supplementary benefit are *much* more likely to be deprived than those above. Indeed, the mean deprivation score of those below this level is more than five-and-half times that for those above this level. Moreover, a given percentage fall in income implies a much steeper rise in deprivation for those below than for those above this level. The results do, therefore, provide some additional support for the concept of the existence of a threshold below which there is a sharp increase in the likelihood of deprivation. In the context of the approach adopted in this study, this suggests that there is an income level below which people's *risk* of poverty is greatly increased.

The impact of raising the minimum income level

To demonstrate the impact of raising incomes to 150 per cent of supplementary benefit, we have estimated the effect on the numbers in poverty. It is also possible to make similar estimates for other rises in the minimum income level. Indeed, if there was no evidence of an income 'threshold', calculations of the impact of different minimum income levels on the numbers in poverty could be used as a basis for judging an 'adequate' income level. For illustrative purposes, we have also estimated the impact of a rise in minimum incomes to around 133 per cent of supplementary benefit and to around 115 per cent of supplementary benefit. (The calculation of minimum income in terms of supplementary benefit does not imply, of course, that these minimum income levels would be obtained by raising supplementary benefit itself – just that everyone's income, whether from earnings, national insurance benefits, supplementary benefit or, indeed, any other system, would be equivalent to that level.)

The estimates should be treated only as a guide to the scale of impact of various levels of minimum income and not as a precise measure for the reasons outlined earlier. The calculations are initially based on families with children as their income groupings were more reliable and the response rate on the income data was higher; the effect on the population as a whole is then calculated on the basis that the impact of the increases would be much the same for households generally as it is for families specifically. The estimates refer to the *immediate* impact of increasing minimum incomes. In the long term, the impact would be greater. As has been seen earlier, the problems of some of those in poverty, whose income is currently above these minimum income levels, stem from periods when their household income was lower; gradually the numbers in this situation would diminish.

If the minimum income level was equivalent to *150 per cent of supplementary benefit*, then the impact would be dramatic. The numbers in poverty would drop from the present level of about 7.5 million people to about 1.5–2 million people; in other words, only about 3 per cent of the population would still be in poverty compared to the current level of about 14 per cent. The impact on the numbers in intense poverty would be even more dramatic – poverty at that level would be virtually 'abolished'. (It should be added that this is conditional on a programme of housing investment to ensure that everyone's housing met the basic standards laid down.)

If it was assumed that the minimum income was equivalent to about *133 per cent of supplementary benefit*, then there would still be a considerable impact, with the numbers in poverty being at least halved. There would be about 3–3.75 million people left in poverty, about 6 per cent of the population. Again, the impact on those in intense poverty would be even greater: their numbers would be reduced from about 2.6 million people to about 0.5 million, about 1 per cent of the population.

If a somewhat more modest increase was implemented to raise everyone's income to around *115 per cent of supplementary benefit*, then the impact would also be more modest. Well over half of those in poverty would still be there: about 5.5 million people, or about 10 per cent of the population. The numbers in intense poverty would be reduced to about 1.5 million, that is, about 3 per cent of the population.

In summary, the evidence suggests not just that supplementary benefit is too low, but that it is *considerably* too low. Although the estimates are not precise, they do provide a firm indication of the scale of increase needed to be effective. To move towards 'solving' the problem of poverty would require raising the incomes of those on supplementary benefit (or equivalently low incomes) by some 50 per cent, though a rise of around one-third would have a significant impact, particularly on those in intense poverty. Rises of less than this would be much less effective and rises of, say, 5 per cent would have little impact on either the numbers in poverty or the numbers in intense poverty: it might make the lives of people on the lowest incomes marginally less difficult, but it would be a long way indeed from solving all their problems.

The implications of the findings for policy

In suggesting that those who lack at least three necessities can be taken as a rough measure of those in poverty, the *Breadline Britain* series was criticised by some for taking too broad a view of the problem. In essence, the alternative view favours a narrow conception of poverty in order to focus policy on those most in need. For example, Victoria Neumark, writing in the *Times Educational Supplement*, argues:

> Surely the half-million children who don't have three meals a day are a worse case than the the 10 million who can't afford a hobby or Christmas presents. LWT are wasting their firepower on a blunderbuss when this is a target urgently needing pinpointing. (Neumark, 1983)

Such comments miss the point. It is obviously the case that

among those who are below the minimum standards of society there are some who are more intensely deprived than others. Chapter 5 showed in detail how those who lack seven or more of the necessities find their lives diminished in every respect, lacking almost all elements of choice that would enable them to express their individuality. Day after day, and week after week, life turns into a deeply depressing experience. That there are some 2.6 million people, including nearly 1 million children, in this intense poverty is a matter that, in our view, requires urgent action.

However, although the situation of those at the very bottom is the most desperate, there are others who live below what they should be entitled to in Britain in the 1980s. It is this, in particular, that the *Breadline Britain* survey established by enabling minimum standards to be drawn up based on the view of society at large. The findings have shown that there are many people who, while they are not among the most deprived, *do* fall below what can be described as 'a minimal acceptable way of life'. In Chapter 2, it was argued that those who fall below this level can be said to be in poverty. It is in this sense that the 7.5 million people who have an enforced lack of three or more necessities can be described as living in poverty. While this group is not sharply defined and while it contains among its members some who are considerably worse off than others, all find their lives affected in more than a peripheral way. That there are among those in poverty some who are in more urgent need than others does not diminish the need they all face relative to others in society.

This debate between those who try to limit the concept of poverty (and the implicit call for concern) to only a very small minority of the very poorest and those who take a wider view of those in need is long-standing. J. C. Kincaid, writing a decade ago, notes exactly the same debate:

It is, of course, reasonable to say that among the many poor there are the smaller number of poorest, and that these should be the most immediate concern of politicians. But in most recent discussions the poorest have

somehow ended up as being presented as the only poor.
(Kincaid, 1973, p. 180)

In the past, this tendency to recognise only intense poverty
has resulted in action aimed only at helping this group.
Gradually since the national insurance acts of the postwar
Labour government, and more rapidly since the 1960s, there
has been a shift from universally based benefits to a piece-
meal arrangement of means-tested benefits. Yet, as this study
clearly shows, by the standards of today these measures have
failed. The very poorest remain excessively deprived.

This failure stems partly from a lack of commitment to
tackling even this intense poverty, but it stems also from the
misunderstanding of the nature of deprivation that results
when the recognition of poverty is sharply limited to just the
very poorest. Without the broader understanding of poverty,
the problems of those in intense poverty are completely
underestimated. Marginally raising their incomes would
improve their living standards but would not lift them out of
poverty. Moreover, like the risk of poverty, the risk of intense
poverty, though highest in the bottom decile, affects the
bottom 40 per cent of households (see Tables 4.7 and 4.8,
pp. 107–8).

Even if only those at the very bottom are considered to be
in urgent priority need, the action that is required to be
effective depends on this broader understanding of the
spread of poverty. Indeed, to successfully tackle the problems
of those in intense poverty requires substantial redistribution: the findings suggest an increase of at least one-
third in minimum income levels.

Moreover, attempts to tackle the problem of intense
poverty without a recognition of the problems of others in
poverty tend to push down the living standards of those
whose poverty is more marginal. This trend has also been
apparent over the last twenty years. Many of those who are
in poverty or on the margins of poverty are families where the
head of the household is in work, while those who are in
intense poverty are, in the main, excluded from the labour
market and dependent on benefit. Apart from the intro-

duction of Family Income Supplement in the early 1970s, the problems of low-paid families have worsened; in particular, the taxation burden has steadily shifted towards the low-paid and the state's support for children (now child benefit) has been eroded compared to its immediate postwar level. There has, moreover, never been any consistent attack on low pay.

The reasons for these trends are varied, and the blame cannot be entirely laid at the door of governments. None the less, the consequence is that low pay and the low levels of state support for children are still important causes of inadequate living standards. This holds despite the sharp rise in unemployment, which might otherwise have been expected to outweigh the significance of other factors.

Overall, the findings throw serious doubt on a basic assumption that is sometimes made: namely, that benefits to the poor can be improved to a level that makes a significant impact on their living standards without significantly affecting the overall distribution of income in society. For example, the SDP's proposals *Attacking Poverty* (1982) promise to 'eliminate' poverty on the basis of a plan that involves little redistribution. The survey's findings clearly show that any plan to reduce poverty will have to redistribute resources from the top half of society to the bottom half.

Poverty in the 1980s

The theme of Part I of this study has been that all those who are forced to fall below the minimum way of life of society today are in poverty. Some will be intensely deprived, others less so – but all are entitled to a better standard of living. This entitlement stems from a widespread consensus about what level of living is unacceptable for Britain in the 1980s. This ability to assess people's unmet needs, in our view, provides the basis for assessing anti-poverty policies and, in particular, the tax–benefit system. This is of immediate political significance.

In the spring of 1985, a series of government 'reviews' of the social security system are due to report. The 'reviews' themselves have a narrow outlook; their compositions are designed to favour the government's approach. They have, however, opened up the debate on the benefits system, with many bodies submitting evidence to the review panels. Much of this evidence has been about the technical workings of various approaches to the tax–benefit question: from, for example, the negative income tax proposed by the Institute of Fiscal Studies (1984) to the general view of a wide range of options compiled by the National Consumer Council (1984).

These technical questions about the mechanism for distributing income are important, but they are, in our view, subsidiary to the question of how much income should be redistributed and to whom. This primary question can be answered only on the basis of an assessment of people's needs.

It seems unlikely that the review panels will tackle this basic question. Set up in the spring of 1984, the evidence to them has been rushed and no work has been commissioned into what people need and the extent to which the benefit system fails to meet these needs. The motivation behind the reviews has been very different: namely, to find ways of cutting social security spending. Few would dispute that there *is* room for more efficiency. However, the most important objective of any changes in the social security system should be to reduce poverty.

Part I of our study has provided a basis for assessing any proposals that come out of these reviews in terms of this central question: 'what is the effect on the numbers in poverty?'. While it is outside our scope to assess the technical mechanisms for redistributing income, we have indicated the *level* of income support needed to tackle poverty.

The basis for all these assessments has been the consensual view of people's needs. Whether the *policy* implications that emerge would also gain the consensual support of society is another question altogether. It is to this question that we turn in Part II.

PART II

Attitudes to Anti-Poverty Measures

7

The Will to Act?
Public attitudes to the poor and to equality

> You get people saying people are scroungers on SB. Well they can't
> be because nobody wants to live like that. I mean, I surely don't, not
> for the rest of my life anyway. There's no way. It's very difficult to
> manage from day to day. [A single parent on supplementary benefit]

In Part I it was argued that around 1 in 7 people are living
in poverty in Britain. But how far is there the will to do
anything about it? The extent to which the public will back
the policies necessary to tackle poverty and inequality
depends on many factors: how they view poverty, why they
think people are in need, and how they balance social justice
against their own self-interest. Each of these is examined in
this chapter.

At the outset, it is important to note that public attitudes
on these questions are highly complex and not always easy to
interpret. Indeed this is highlighted by the often contradictory and inconsistent nature of research in this area. Such
views are also unstable, changing through time and with
different social and economic circumstances. Moreover, public opinion is only one of the factors determining the policy
decisions of successive governments. It is, none the less,
unquestionably an important influence, helping to set
political agendas and imposing constraints on action. With
these provisos, we begin by looking at how the context of the
debate has shifted.

The persistence of poverty

Throughout the 1950s and into the 1960s, it became widely
assumed that poverty had been largely eliminated. The post-

war social reforms and the emergence of near full employment led to a growing confidence of a newly affluent, secure and more equal Britain, rid of the insecurity, inequalities and harsh social conditions that disfigured the interwar years. This view was reinforced by Rowntree's third and last survey in York in 1951, which showed a sharp fall in poverty among the working class from nearly one-third in 1936 to less than 3 per cent in 1951 (Rowntree and Lavers, 1951).

Subsequent research has revealed that this confidence, or complacency, was little more than a comfortable myth. Yet the problem of poverty did not reappear as a political issue until the mid-1960s. During the 1950s, academics such as Richard Titmuss and Peter Townsend had been arguing for a new relativist approach to the measurement of poverty. (Rowntree, as seen in Chapter 2, had adopted an essentially subsistence approach, although he did update his poverty line over the course of his three surveys to make some allowance for social developments.) In the early 1960s Brian Abel-Smith and Peter Townsend, using a contemporary relative poverty line, found that there was widespread poverty – affecting up to 14 per cent of the population (Abel-Smith and Townsend, 1965).

Combined with the emergence of new pressure groups such as the Child Poverty Action Group and Shelter and the showing of social documentaries such as *Cathy Come Home*, public concern about poverty was rekindled. Such concern, however, seemed shortlived and did not generate changes in policy sufficient to make a noticeable impact. The Wilson government of 1966–70 was too preoccupied with economic crises to give priority to the social and wider reforms that would have been needed. Indeed, despite rising welfare expenditure, there has been little if any significant change in the extent of income inequality and relative poverty over most of the postwar period (Fiegehen *et al.*, 1977; Lansley, 1980). Looking at trends in the distribution of income over a longer period of time, Rudolf Klein has argued that 'the major shifts in income distribution took place *before* the major expansion of the welfare state in Britain and elsewhere' (Klein, 1980, p. 26).

In the last few years, interest in and anxiety about poverty have been revived. The emergence of mass unemployment on a greater scale than even in the depths of the 1930s' depression, the rising number of families dependent on state benefits and the re-questioning of the role of state intervention and high levels of public expenditure have led to a new concern about poverty and its roots. Against this background of persistent, if partially hidden, and then rising poverty, what stance has the public taken?

Attitudes to the causes of poverty

When asked about the broad objective of tackling poverty, the public have tended to show overwhelming support. In the British Election Survey of 1974, as many as 86.9 per cent thought it very or fairly important to increase government spending on getting rid of poverty (Table 7.1), roughly the

Table 7.1 *Attitudes to tackling poverty and the redistribution of wealth (percentages)*

Respondent's attitude to increased government spending on getting rid of poverty	1974	1979
Government spending on poverty:		
Very important it should	51.8	47.8
Fairly important it should	35.1	35.7
Doesn't matter	6.4	7.9
Fairly important it should not	4.5	6.6
Very important it should not	2.1	2.0
Respondent's attitude to government redistribution of wealth		
Government redistribution:		
Very important it should	23.9	26.1
Fairly important it should	32.4	29.2
Doesn't matter	15.7	16.5
Fairly important it should not	18.0	17.4
Very important it should not	10.1	10.8

Sources: Whiteley (1981), Table 1; British Election Survey, 1979.

same proportion that supported increased spending on the National Health Service (see Table 9.1). Even in 1979, despite the growth of antipathy towards some aspects of welfare spending and towards some claimants, this figure still stood at 83.5 per cent.

When it comes to particular groups of the poor and to detailed policies, however, public opinion has been more discriminating and changeable. Partly, this is explained by differences in why people are thought to be poor. Those who think poverty is mainly or wholly the fault of the individual are more likely to show hostility than those who blame it on wider social and structural factors. Over time, attitudes to the causes of poverty have tended to fluctuate.

In an EEC survey of poverty in 1976, respondents were asked why people live in need. This revealed that the UK public were the most unsympathetic in the European community in their attitudes to the poor (Table 7.2): 43 per cent of the UK sample attributed living in need to 'laziness and lack of willpower', whereas the EEC average was 25 per cent and the nation with the next highest figure was Luxembourg with 31 per cent.

A similar question was asked in the *Breadline Britain*

Table 7.2　*The public's view in the 1970s of why people live in need (percentages)*

'Why in your opinion are there people who live in need? Here are four opinions – which is closest to yours?'	EEC, 1976		Breadline Britain 1983
	EEC	UK	GB
Because they have been unlucky	16	10	13
Because of laziness and lack of willpower	25	43	22
Because there is much injustice in our society	26	16	32
It's an inevitable part of modern progress	14	17	25
None of these	6	4	5
Don't know	13	10	3
All	100	100	100

Source: EEC (1977), Table 29; LWT/MORI survey, 1983.

survey. This showed a remarkable shift in public opinion towards much greater sympathy for the poor (Table 7.2). By 1983, the public were much more inclined to blame wider social factors than the individual: the proportion identifying 'laziness and lack of willpower' halved from 43 per cent in 1976 to 22 per cent in 1983, while the proportion blaming injustice doubled from 16 per cent to 32 per cent.

Table 7.3 shows that people's own living standards are an important influence on their views. In 1983, the poor themselves, whether defined as those with the lowest incomes or those lacking necessities, were more likely to blame injustice and less likely to blame laziness than the average. Thus only 5 per cent of those lacking five or more necessities blamed laziness compared with 25 per cent of those lacking none of the necessities. In contrast, 40 per cent of those without five or more necessities blamed injustice compared with 32 per cent of those with all the necessities.

Attitudes to the roots of poverty also vary with people's self-perceptions of whether they are poor. Twice the proportion (26 per cent) of those who think they are 'never poor' blame poverty on 'laziness and lack of willpower', as those (13 per cent) who believe they are poor 'all the time'. Those who think they are poor 'all the time' are much more likely to blame injustice (40 per cent) than those who think they are never poor (26 per cent).

The poor themselves are therefore more likely to blame poverty on wider structural factors; but this is not exclusively so. Thus, 13 per cent of those feeling poor all the time still attributed living in need to laziness. This is a much lower figure, however, than in Townsend's survey, where in answer to a similar question nearly one-third of those feeling poor all the time blamed poverty on the people themselves. This led Townsend to conclude,

> Some of the poor have come to conclude that poverty does not exist. Many of those who recognise that it exists have come to conclude that it is individually caused, attributed to a mixture of ill-luck, indolence and mis-management, and is not a collective condition

Table 7.3 *The public's view in the 1980s of why people live in need (percentages)*

'Why, in your opinion, are there people who live in need? Here are four opinions – which is closest to yours?'	All households	Net equivalent household income		AB	C1	C2	D	E
		Poorest 10%	Richest 10%		Social class			
They have been unlucky	13	13	3	15	12	11	11	16
Laziness and lack of willpower	22	14	13	21	20	23	24	20
Too much injustice in our society	32	50	48	24	32	33	36	34
Inevitable part of modern progress	25	19	24	30	26	26	23	20
None of these	5	3	11	7	7	4	6	4
Don't know	3	1	1	4	3	3	0	6
All	100	100	100	100	100	100	100	100

'Why, in your opinion, are there people who live in need? Here are four opinions – which is closest to yours?'	Political affiliation			None/ Don't know	Sex	
	Conservative	Labour	Lib/SDP		Male	Female
They have been unlucky	13	12	14	12	10	15
Laziness and lack of willpower	32	11	21	22	22	21
Too much injustice in our society	14	44	41	35	36	29
Inevitable part of modern progress	29	26	22	20	24	26
None of these	7	4	2	7	6	5
Don't know	5	2	1	5	2	4
All	100	100	100	100	100	100

'Why, in your opinion, are there people who live in need? Here are four opinions – which is closest to yours?'	Are you poor?			Lacking necessities			
	All the time	Sometimes	Never	0	1 or 2	3 or 4	5 or more
They have been unlucky	14	10	13	11	13	10	24
Laziness and lack of willpower	13	16	26	25	20	16	5
Too much injustice in our society	40	41	26	32	32	33	40
Inevitable part of modern progress	23	26	25	25	28	32	18
None of these	1	4	7	6	5	3	3
Don't know	8	3	3	2	3	7	10
All	100	100	100	100	100	100	100

determined principally by institutionalised forces, particularly government and industry. In this they share the perceptions of the better-off. Divided, they blame individual behaviour and motivation and unwittingly lend support to the existing institutional order.
(Townsend, 1979, p. 429)

While this attitude was also evident among some of the poor in the *Breadline Britain* survey, it was much less pronounced.

Some of the sharpest differences, however, are found between people with different political affiliations. Conservative supporters are much more likely to blame the victim and much less likely to identify injustice. Thus, 14 per cent of Conservatives blamed injustice compared with 44 per cent of Labour and 41 per cent of Liberal/SDP supporters. Nearly three times as many Tories blamed laziness as Labour supporters. There were also some differences by age, with pensioners much more likely to blame the victim and much less likely to blame wider social and structural factors than were non-pensioners. Differences in attitude between men and women and across occupational groups, in contrast, were small.

The deserving and undeserving poor

The public's attitudes to the causes of poverty also affect their views on anti-poverty policy. Some groups and policies are likely to be viewed with greater sympathy than others. Partly this is a reflection of the public's image of who the poor are. Surveys have found that, even where it is accepted that poverty exists, some groups are more likely to be seen as poor and therefore more deserving of help than others. In Golding and Middleton's survey in the late 1970s, for example, while only 5 per cent completely denied the existence of poverty, most had in mind the elderly and the disabled. Few mentioned the unemployed or lone parents, although slightly more mentioned the low-paid (1982, p.189). With the emergence of mass unemployment and the growth in the number of single parents, the public might now be more likely to recognise poverty among these groups.

The main explanation underlying the public's discriminating outlook is that, even where they recognise that groups such as the unemployed and single parents face financial hardship, they have tended to view them with much less sympathy than pensioners and the disabled.

> The nineteenth century distinction between the deserving and undeserving poor seems to be alive and kicking – despite the efforts of social reformers to abolish it over the past 70 years – in the minds of a majority of the people. (Klein, 1974, p. 411)

This 'moralistic' stance on welfare issues reflects a view that some groups are poor or in need more because of their own personal failings than society's. If people are perceived to be poor because of individual inadequacies such as fecklessness, mismanagement or feebleness, they are much more likely to be viewed with disapproval. State support is more likely to be seen as an undeserved and indiscriminate handout and indeed as a discouragement to the individual effort required to escape from poverty. In the past, the unemployed, and to a lesser extent single parents and large families, have been especially likely to be viewed as undeserving. In an ORC survey conducted in 1968, for example, it was found that:

> 89 per cent agreed that 'too many people don't bother to work because they can live well enough on the dole', 78 per cent agreed that 'we have so many Social Services that people work less hard than they need to' and 87 per cent agreed that 'too many people take advantage of unemployment and sickness benefits by taking time off work'. (Klein, 1974, p. 412)

These views can be reinforced by the way welfare services and benefits are operated and delivered. Different groups of claimant, for example, are entitled to different levels of benefit, both national insurance and supplementary benefit.

The sick and unemployed, for example, receive a lower benefit than pensioners and the disabled. This gap, which has steadily widened since the mid-1970s, has been officially defended as reflecting the lower needs of short-term as against long-term claimants, yet the unemployed are not entitled to the long-term rate of supplementary benefit even after a year of unemployment.

Past surveys have also shown that distinctions between the deserving and undeserving poor tend to be held on a relatively uniform basis. 'One of the most striking features of the distinction between deserving and undeserving groups is the homogeneity of opinion across the population... the groups most likely to suffer the needs accounted undeserving express very little more support for welfare in these areas' (Taylor-Gooby, 1983a). In Golding and Middleton's study (1982, p. 170–2), hostility towards welfare claimants was found to be strongest among the low-paid and unskilled workers, who felt themselves to be no or little better off than those on the dole. Unemployment and sickness benefits were often seen as blunting motivation and independence and encouraging work-shyness and scrounging, a view fuelled by a feeling that claimants were often those least in need.

A similar hostility was also voiced by claimants themselves – and not only among pensioners, whose resentment was often born out of a view that the unemployed have it too easy compared with when they were young. This hostility is partly bred within the process of claiming itself. The experience of dependency on welfare – of the DHSS office, of the local authority housing department, of the social services – is often frustrating, debilitating and humiliating. In the *Breadline Britain* survey, supplementary benefit claimants were asked how they felt about claiming benefit. Although most (85 per cent) said it was a right they were entitled to, as many as 40 per cent said they were embarrassed about claiming it. And, although the majority (60 per cent) were satisfied with the service they got from their local DHSS office, more than 1 in 4 (27 per cent) were dissatisfied. In an identical question asked in a MORI survey of poverty in Greenwich in December 1983 (MORI, 1984), the level of dissatisfaction was much higher at 40 per cent. This seems to confirm a view that the problems faced by claimants are more serious in urban areas where the offices are under much greater pressure.

Sometimes the stigma associated with the way means-tested benefits are administered, or perceived to be administered, leads to outright rejection. Moreover, in responding to meeting need, welfare policies also operate a system of sanctions, such as encouraging unemployed claimants to find work. This, combined with the policing role that such sanctions require and the emphasis on preventing abuse in many offices can inflame the unpopularity of services. It is perhaps not surprising that the resentment that often arises from this process can turn not only against the institutions themselves but also against other claimants who may be perceived as less deserving but somehow getting a better deal.

> Shielded from any broader view of social injustice, those crushed by inadequate and censoriously administered welfare benefits on the one hand, or by poverty wages on the other, find their fears and resentments readily channelled into bitter and divisive contempt for those alongside them at the bottom of the economic ladder. (Golding and Middleton, 1982, p. 181).

While this distinction in the public's mind between the deserving and undeserving poor has prevailed throughout the postwar period, it has been held with varying intensity. It seems, for example, to have been especially widespread in the second half of the 1970s. Golding and Middleton have documented with particular force the mood of 'scroungerphobia' that prevailed in this period, producing 'a shrill and mounting antagonism to the welfare system and its clients' (1982, p. 59). As in other surveys, however, it was mainly the unemployed who were the targets of this antagonism. When asked who they thought most deserved to get money from the welfare, it was the old and sick who were nominated; only 5.9 per cent mentioned the unemployed and 2.4 per cent the low-paid, even though up to three answers were coded (p. 169). This rising tide of hostility towards claimants was also found to be especially strong among the working class. This was attributed to three main factors; first, to the 'drop in real incomes experienced by many on low or average wages' in the years after the mid-1970s; second, 'the tax net was dragging in more and more of the low paid so that large numbers of ill-rewarded people found their pay packets irritatingly rifled for dubious purposes' – that is, the protection of benefit levels; third, 'there had been, real, visible and irreversible rises in the costs of welfare' (pp. 231–3).

The waning of the welfare backlash

Since the late 1970s, however, there is evidence of some softening in public attitudes. This is reflected both in overall attitudes on the need to tackle poverty and in attitudes to particular groups of claimants and types of benefit. We have already seen how the tendency to blame the victim is much weaker now than in the past. In the *Breadline Britain* survey, respondents were also asked whether they thought that the government is doing too much, too little or enough to *help those lacking necessities*. A majority (57 per cent) thought that it was doing too little, one-third thought that it was about the right amount, and only 6 per cent thought it was too much (Table 7.4).

The poor themselves, both those on the lowest incomes and those lacking the most necessities, were nearly twice as likely as those who are best-off to argue that too little is being done. Similarly, working-class groups were much more likely than the middle class to think that too little is being done, while Labour supporters were nearly four times as likely to think so as Conservatives.

In the 1976 EEC survey, respondents were asked whether they thought the authorities were doing too little, too much or about what they should do *for people in poverty*: in the UK 36 per cent said too little, 20 per cent too much and 35 per cent the right amount. As in the answers to why people

Table 7.4 Public attitudes towards government help for the poor (percentages)

'Still thinking about people who lack the things you have said are necessities for living in Britain today, do you think that the Government is doing too much, too little, or about the right amount to help these people?'

	All households	Net equivalent household income		Social class				
		Poorest 10%	Richest 10%	AB	C1	C2	D	E
Too much	6	2	3	4	8	5	6	7
Too little	57	81	42	35	51	62	68	63
About the right amount	33	16	54	56	39	28	23	26
Don't know	4	1	1	5	2	6	2	4
All	100	100	100	100	100	100	100	100

'Still thinking about people who lack the things you have said are necessities for living in Britain today, do you think that the Government is doing too much, too little, or about the right amount to help these people?'

	Political affiliation				Lacking necessities			
	Conservative	Labour	Lib/SDP	None/Don't know	0	1 or 2	3 or 4	5 or more
Too much	11	4	3	4	7	4	12	1
Too little	23	80	58	68	49	69	67	86
About the right amount	62	13	33	23	40	23	20	9
Don't know	3	3	6	5	4	4	1	4
All	100	100	100	100	100	100	100	100

live in need (Table 7.2), this revealed a much less supportive attitude to the poor than in the European Community as a whole, where 54 per cent said too little and only 7 per cent too much. Although this question was differently worded than in the *Breadline Britain* survey, the sharp differences in the answers indicate some shift towards greater public support for actions to help the poor.

The *Breadline Britain* survey also suggests that attitudes towards those on benefit are much less hostile than they appeared to be in the late 1970s. In particular, the traditionally undeserving poor and traditionally unpopular benefits are now viewed with greater sympathy than in that period. A majority think not only that pensions are too low, but also that supplementary benefit is too low, while 40 per cent think that unemployment benefit is too low compared with 9 per cent too high. (This is discussed further in Chapter 9.) In August 1976, in contrast, a Gallup poll found that 37 per cent thought unemployment benefit was too high and only 9 per cent too low.

This change in attitude towards claimants, especially the unemployed, is mainly explained by the personal impact of the recession, soaring unemployment and the sharp rise in the number of claimants. Since 1979, the number of unemployed supplementary benefit claimants has more than tripled from 560,000 in 1979 to 1.9 million in August 1983. The unemployed now account for 43 per cent of all claimants compared with 20 per cent in 1979. For the first time since the war, there are now more unemployed than pensioner claimants. With this trend, the old antipathy towards the unemployed seems to have weakened markedly. By mid-1980, a Gallup poll showed that unemployment had displaced inflation as the most important problem facing the country, whereas, in April 1975, only 26 per cent mentioned unemployment compared with 65 per cent mentioning inflation. The public also seem much more aware of the underlying structural causes of unemployment, and of the lack of jobs available compared with the number looking for work. In an NOP poll in August 1982, 31 per cent blamed the government for unemployment, 20 per cent blamed the world recession and only 5 per cent mentioned laziness. In September 1977, in contrast, in a Gallup poll, one-third mentioned 'people not wanting to work'. Moreover, with the spread of unemployment, more and more people have had direct experience of life on the dole within their families. In the *Breadline Britain* survey, 26 per cent said that unemployment was a problem facing them or their family, while more than one-third of families (36 per cent) were worried about employment prospects for their children. As many as 34 per cent said that they or someone in their family were or had been unemployed, or had someone in their family unemployed in the past year. It is not surprising, therefore, that people are much less likely to blame the victim and that the unemployed are less likely to be labelled undeserving.

That the recession has had a moderating impact on social opinion and helped to weaken the old distinction between the deserving and undeserving poor is also confirmed in people's attitudes towards supplementary benefit claimants. In contrast to earlier attitudes, Table 7.5 shows a clear majority (69 per cent) strongly agreeing or tending to agree that most people claiming supplementary benefit are in real need. As many as 74 per cent also agreed that a lot of people who are entitled to claim supplementary benefit don't claim it.

How far do attitudes vary across social groups? As we have seen, earlier surveys have shown that hostility to claimants was not confined to the middle classes but also existed among the working class and to a lesser extent among the poor themselves. Table 7.5, however, shows that the poorest – both those with the lowest incomes and those lacking the most necessities – are much more likely to agree strongly that claimants are in real need than are the richest, although still 17 per cent of those with the lowest incomes disagreed, compared with 30 per cent of the richest. The working class are also much more likely to agree strongly with the prevalence of need among claimants than are the middle class.

The answers are particularly strongly correlated with political affiliation – though slightly less strongly than with other attitudinal questions. In general, Conservatives display a more reactionary view, being less likely to agree that claimants are in need, and less likely to acknowledge a failure to claim among those entitled.

These findings do not mean that the equivocation found in other studies no longer exists at all. As we shall see in Chapter 9, public spending on social security is afforded a relatively low priority compared with other spending, even if it is not as low as in the past. Tackling poverty is also relatively low in people's rankings of current problems. In a Harris poll conducted in May 1984, when asked which three of a list of nine were the most serious problems during the past five years, 22 per cent said 'getting rid of poverty'. While expectedly way behind unemployment (86 per cent) and inflation (44 per cent), it was also given a lower priority than industrial relations (32 per cent), the crime rate (30 per cent) and the competitiveness of British industry (28 per cent). It was also only slightly ahead of the need to encourage people to work harder (17 per cent). Against this there was over-whelming concern about the government's record on poverty: 38 per cent thought the government unsuccessful and only 1 per cent successful (*The Observer*, 6 May 1984).

There also appears to be some concern about the incentive effects of welfare spending. Table 7.6 shows that 57 per cent agreed with the proposition that 'Britain's welfare system removes the incentive for people to help themselves', whereas 35 per cent disagreed. Even so, this does not necessarily imply an opposition to the welfare system. It may simply mean that the public are aware of the problem of the 'poverty trap' facing low-income families whereby increased earnings simply lead to loss of benefits, so that they may be no better off. This question of incentives is discussed further in Chapter 9 (pp. 258–60).

Further, in the *Breadline Britain* survey, as many as 62 per cent strongly agreed or tended to agree that 'many people claiming supplementary benefit are on the fiddle', with only 23 per cent disagreeing (Table 7.5). Given the clear majority saying that supplementary benefit recipients are in real need, this could be said to reveal a basic contradiction in the public mind. This is not necessarily so. People may well

Table 7.5 Attitudes to supplementary benefit claimants (percentages)

'I'd now like to ask you some questions about supplementary benefits. I'm going to read out some statements and I'd like you to tell me how strongly you agree or disagree with each one.'	All households	Households on SB	Net equivalent household income		Social class				
			Poorest 10%	Richest 10%	AB	C1	C2	D	E
Most people claiming SB are in real need:									
Strongly agree	25	54	49	25	16	17	25	23	41
Tend to agree	44	36	28	38	51	46	38	47	41
Neither agree/disagree	8	3	1	4	9	8	9	9	4
Tend to disagree	16	7	16	23	17	16	22	16	8
Strongly disagree	3	0	1	7	4	7	3	2	0
Don't know	4	1	5	4	2	5	3	3	6
A lot of people who are entitled to claim SB don't claim it:									
Strongly agree	23	28	33	19	24	14	25	26	24
Tend to agree	51	47	46	63	48	57	55	48	47
Neither agree/disagree	8	5	6	9	10	11	5	6	7
Tend to disagree	10	8	4	8	13	12	9	8	10
Strongly disagree	2	3	1	1	0	3	0	4	2
Don't know	6	8	10	—	4	4	5	7	11
Many people claiming SB are on the fiddle:									
Strongly agree	25	22	23	29	20	19	28	32	22
Tend to agree	37	30	32	36	36	39	35	41	33
Neither agree/disagree	9	8	7	5	10	10	9	9	8
Tend to disagree	17	17	15	21	23	19	19	8	17
Strongly disagree	6	15	11	7	6	8	3	5	9
Don't know	7	8	12	2	6	5	6	7	10

'I'd now like to ask you some questions about supplementary benefits. I'm going to read out some statements and I'd like you to tell me how strongly you agree or disagree with each one.'

	Political affiliation				Lacking necessities			
	Conservative	Labour	Lib/SDP	None/ Don't know	0	1 or 2	3 or 4	5 or more
Most people claiming SB are in real need:								
Strongly agree	11	40	25	23	18	28	48	50
Tend to agree	51	38	47	39	46	43	35	25
Neither agree/disagree	9	3	7	13	10	6	3	5
Tend to disagree	22	13	15	15	17	16	9	16
Strongly disagree	3	3	2	5	3	4	1	1
Don't know	5	2	4	5	4	3	3	3
A lot of people who are entitled to claim SB don't claim it:								
Strongly agree	17	24	32	20	21	24	30	36
Tend to agree	55	56	45	47	52	53	50	41
Neither agree/disagree	10	6	6	7	7	10	5	1
Tend to disagree	11	5	12	14	11	7	7	12
Strongly disagree	1	2	1	2	1	4	1	4
Don't know	5	6	4	10	7	3	8	6
Many people claiming SB are on the fiddle:								
Strongly agree	26	20	27	27	25	27	19	17
Tend to agree	41	36	31	37	37	35	37	44
Neither agree/disagree	7	7	11	13	9	10	8	10
Tend to disagree	14	21	21	13	18	14	17	15
Strongly disagree	3	11	5	4	5	5	13	11
Don't know	9	6	4	7	7	9	6	4

Table 7.6 Public attitudes towards the impact of welfare on incentives (percentages)

'Please tell me whether you agree or disagree with the statement that Britain's welfare system removes the incentive for people to help themselves.'

	All households	Net equivalent household income			Social class				
		Poorest 10%	Richest 10%	AB	C1	C2	D	E	
Agree	57	44	54	62	53	59	59	51	
Disagree	35	44	41	34	44	32	31	37	
Don't know	8	12	5	3	3	9	11	12	

'Please tell me whether you agree or disagree with the statement that Britain's welfare system removes the incentive for people to help themselves.'

	Political affiliation			
	Conservative	Labour	Lib/SDP	None/Don't know
Agree	76	44	49	56
Disagree	21	46	43	34
Don't know	4	10	8	10

acknowledge the existence of fiddling but still accept that claimants are in need. Whether or not such fiddling is disapproved of or accepted as sometimes necessary because of the inadequacy of benefit levels is unclear from the findings. We have seen how concern about abuse and fraud, about work-shyness and about incentives has existed throughout the postwar period, and was especially strong in the late 1970s. Such concern has persisted but is now mixed with an apparently genuine concern about the position and needs of the poor, and seems to be a lot less dominant and powerfully held than in the recent past. People seem to accept that, even if fiddling or abuse occur, a generous system of benefits is still required to ensure that those perceived as in genuine need are adequately supported.

Thus, acknowledgement of fiddling is not associated with the widespread hostility or the welfare backlash apparent in the late 1970s. It could be argued that the lack of a public reaction to unprecedentedly sharp cuts in benefit levels represents a sort of backlash by default. This seems unlikely, however. The lack of a widespread reaction to these cuts is probably as much to do with ignorance, or concern with self-preservation, or at worse, apathy in the face of a lack of alternatives as with any quiet endorsement of government policy. In the late 1970s, apparently high public spending levels and their beneficiaries – the poor and the unemployed – were convenient and easy scapegoats on which to pin the blame for wider austerity. This view was, after all, at least implicitly acknowledged by the then Labour government, which had already begun the process of cutting welfare programmes. Since 1979, although the present government has accelerated the process of cuts initiated by Labour, rising unemployment has made people much more sceptical of the case for cutting welfare spending. It is much less easy now to single out such easy targets.

Attitudes to redistribution

Above it has been seen that there is public support for the broad principle of tackling poverty and some evidence of a growth in sympathy for the position of the poor. In Chapter 9 we shall look more closely at how far support in principle is matched by support for the policies required to tackle poverty. First, we look at the related but wider issue of redistribution.

Like poverty, the question of redistribution has been highly controversial. If poverty is defined in terms of subsistence only, its elimination involves a relatively limited degree of redistribution that is compatible with widespread inequality. If, on the other hand, poverty is defined in a generous relative sense, then solving it requires more redistribution and less inequality. In this book it has been argued (Chapter 6, pp. 196–9) that poverty cannot be eliminated without more redistribution from the non-poor to the poor and on a relatively substantial scale. This does not mean that poverty and inequality are the same thing, but they are related. A reduction in inequality does not necessarily lead to a reduction in poverty. A redistribution from the rich to the moderately rich, which indeed has been the main characteristic of the redistributive process since the war, might reduce inequality but it would have little or any impact on poverty. Similarly, the elimination of poverty might still leave an unacceptable degree of inequality. Moreover, because poverty in the sense of an enforced lack of socially perceived necessities is not confined to those on the lowest income but extends up the income scale (see Chapter 4, pp. 105–113), the more such redistribution is from the middle- rather than the higher-income groups, the less effective it would be in tackling poverty as well as reducing inequalities.

So, how much support is there for redistribution? Table 7.1 (from the British Election Survey) shows that, in 1979, 55.3 per cent thought that redistribution was a very or fairly important government activity. On the other hand, 28.2 per cent were opposed to redistribution. This indicates less public backing than for getting rid of poverty, which gained 83.5 per cent support. Nevertheless, support had remained roughly static since 1974.

In the *Breadline Britain* survey, answers revealed strong

support for the aim of a more equal society (Table 7.7): 74 per cent thought that the gap between the rich and the poor is too wide, with 21 per cent disagreeing; 76 per cent thought that differences in pay between the highly paid and lowly paid are too great, with 20 per cent disagreeing; 63 per cent thought the government should increase taxation on the rich, while 32 per cent disagreed.

There were sharp differences between income groups, social classes and political affiliation. The rich were much less likely to favour greater equality than the poor: 91 per cent of the poorest households thought the gap between rich and poor was too wide, compared with 53 per cent of the richest. Again 71 per cent of the poor supported higher taxation on the rich, with 25 per cent opposed. The rich themselves were evenly divided, with 48 per cent for higher taxation and 48 per cent against. Similar differences also emerge by occupational group. Working-class households were much more committed to greater equality than the middle class. There was, none the less, majority support across all classes for narrowing the gap between the rich and the poor and between the highly paid and the low-paid, though not for increasing taxation on the rich.

People's political affiliation is also a strong indicator of their attitudes to equality. Both Labour and Alliance supporters are overwhelmingly committed to a more equal society. Conservatives are much less supportive. Even so, among Conservative supporters there is still a slight majority (51 per cent) in favour of narrowing the gap between the rich and the poor, with 39 per cent opposed. A majority (58 per cent) of Conservatives were also in favour of lower wage differentials. In contrast, a majority of Conservatives were opposed to higher taxes on the rich.

There is a strong element of self-interest running through these responses, as in earlier answers. People are motivated by how they perceive themselves to be personally affected. But this is not entirely so. For example, a small majority of the rich and of professional and managerial groups support greater equality, apparently against their own interest. It may be that altruism is an important influence among the better-

Table 7.7 *Attitudes to equality (percentages)*

'I am going to read out a number of statements about Britain today. Please would you tell me whether you agree or disagree with each one.'	All households	Poorest 10%	Richest 10%	AB	C1	C2	D	E
			Net equivalent household income			Social class		
Differences in pay between the highly paid and the lowly paid are too great:								
Agree	76	87	67	59	65	83	83	81
Disagree	20	11	29	37	30	14	13	13
Don't know	4	2	3	4	5	2	4	6
The Government should increase taxation on the rich:								
Agree	63	71	48	40	56	69	71	70
Disagree	32	25	48	54	39	27	23	22
Don't know	5	4	4	5	5	4	6	8
The gap between the rich and the poor in Britain today is too wide:								
Agree	74	91	53	51	64	83	81	83
Disagree	21	7	41	40	28	14	14	13
Don't know	5	2	6	9	9	2	4	5

off. On the other hand, they may not perceive themselves as among the better-off groups who would lose out. As shown in Appendix C, the rich are under-represented in the survey, so we are not sampling the very rich in these answers. They also might well be less inclined to support egalitarian goals if the full policy implications were spelt out. Owner-occupiers with a mortgage, for example, might be less prepared to support the principle of greater equality if it involved a switch in housing subsidies from mortgage tax relief to council tenants. The higher-paid might be less committed to positive attempts to narrow pay relativities, or to a more progressive tax system.

Despite these qualifications, these results show little public backing for inegalitarian values, even among Mrs Thatcher's

Table 7.7 *Continued*

'I am going to read out a number of statements about Britain today. Please could you tell me whether you agree or disagree with each one.'	Political affiliation			None/ Don't know	Sex	
	Conservative	Labour	Lib/ SDP		Male	Female
Differences in pay between the highly paid and the lowly paid are too great:						
Agree	58	85	83	82	75	76
Disagree	37	11	16	13	21	19
Don't know	5	4	1	5	4	4
The Government should increase taxation on the rich:						
Agree	35	84	70	65	66	60
Disagree	58	13	27	25	31	33
Don't know	6	3	3	10	3	7
The gap between the rich and the poor in Britain today is too wide:						
Agree	51	90	80	79	74	74
Disagree	39	7	19	15	21	20
Don't know	10	3	1	6	4	6

supporters. As we have seen in Chapter 1, poverty has risen and inequalities have widened since 1979. This has been the product of soaring unemployment, widening pay differentials, some cuts in benefits and welfare services, and the shift in the burden of taxation away from the rich. It is the poor, not the prosperous, who have borne the burden of the recession and the government's social policies.

The New Right's commitment to inequality

These widening inequalities have not simply been an unfortunate necessity in times of hardship. If this was the case, it might well be asked why measures have not been taken to ensure equal misery for all, with the poor and the rich sharing the burden of the recession.

The government believes that greater inequality is a necessary price for creating the incentives seen as essential for sustained economic recovery. That means both the creation of low-paid jobs and lower rates of taxation, especially on the highly paid. One of the constant themes of current Conservative thinking, backed by right-wing academics such as Patrick Minford, has been that people have been priced out of jobs by excessively high wages, particularly at the bottom end (Minford *et al.*, 1983). In turn, high taxation, especially on the rich, is seen as stifling the effort, entrepreneurship and innovation that are essential to the process of capitalist wealth creation and general prosperity.

These views are by no means new. The arguments for a more unequal society have been implicit in the views of the radical right for many years. Friedman has long stressed the role of income inequalities, risk and uncertainty in promoting the incentives necessary to an efficient society (Friedman, 1962). Lord Robbins has argued that 'the inequality of reward which the market system engenders does not seem to me something which persons of good sense should worry about over-much' (Robbins, 1977, p. 16). Implicit in this thinking is that the role of government in redistribution should be an even more limited one than at present. The right accept the need for some state intervention to tackle poverty, but that this should be confined to meeting subsistence needs only or, as Hayek has argued, providing 'security against severe physical deprivation, the assurance of a given minimum of sustenance for all' (1960, p. 259), below which no one should fall. There should be no question of income transfers to people above the poverty line and only a small degree of redistribution from the non-poor to the poor. Benefit levels should therefore be set at a minimum level, thereby encouraging individuals to make their own additional provision if they so wish. This involves a minimum of interference in market processes, preserves incentives to individual self-help and avoids the excessive redistribution that is seen as a discouragement to enterprise and personal thrift.

Such anti-welfare ideology has been promoted from the fringes of the Conservative party since the war, but until a decade ago such views would have fallen largely on deaf ears within its leadership. No longer. In a speech entitled 'Let the Children Grow Tall' in 1975 in New York, Mrs Thatcher, shortly after becoming leader of the Conservative party, spoke strongly about the wisdom of incentives and equal opportunity and how 'the pursuit of equality is a mirage' (Conservative Central Office, 1975). Many of Mrs Thatcher's ministers are also profoundly opposed to egalitarianism. As seen in Chapter 2 (pp. 15–48), as recently as 1979 Sir Keith Joseph had argued not only that there was little absolute poverty in contemporary Britain but that it should not be defined in relative terms. He went on to argue that redistribution from the rich to the poor would, because of its effect on incentives, simply increase poverty: 'You cannot make the poor richer by making the rich poorer, only by making everybody richer, including the rich' (Joseph and Sumption, 1979, p. 22). In short, reducing inequalities will simply mean lower living standards all round. Others have gone even further. In *Down with the Poor*, a pamphlet published in 1971, Dr Rhodes Boyson had this to say about the welfare state:

> The moral fibre of our people has been weakened. A state which does for its citizens what they can do for themselves is an evil state... In such an irresponsible society no-one cares, no-one saves, no-one bothers, – why should they when the state spends all its energies taking money from the energetic, successful and thrifty to give to the idle, the failures and the feckless? (Boyson, 1971, p. 5)

Of course, Mrs Thatcher has been careful not to be too candid about her record and her real intentions on these issues. She has limited the collection and publication of some of the official statistics required to chart actual trends in these areas. She has also been careful not to present her inegalitarian ideology in too stark a fashion. Instead, she has attempted to give it a more popular ring, presenting it in terms of the meritocratic virtues of self-reliance, thrift, hard work and achievement. In this way she has avoided a potential public backlash. She has often appealed for a return to Victorian values, by which she has meant: 'you were taught to work jolly hard, you were taught to improve yourself, you were taught self-reliance, you were taught to live within your income' (*Daily Telegraph*, 16 April 1983). In the same interview, she went on to stress the importance of the role of charity in helping those in need:

> And many of the improvements that were made *during Victorian times* were made voluntarily, for example, people built hospitals, many of the Church schools were built during that time, and prison reforms came from this tremendous sense of reliance and duty. You don't hear so much about these things these days, but they were good value and they led to tremendous improvements in the standard of living. [Emphasis added]

Beneath the popular rhetoric, however, what is meant is a much reduced role for the state in the provision of social welfare, and a greater emphasis on individual, voluntary and charitable help. Although the government has to date travelled only a very limited way down this road, the measures that have been taken have already combined with the recession to create a more unequal society.

The failure of the Labour party

If Mrs Thatcher can find little comfort in these findings, the Labour party too cannot help but reflect on its failure to have capitalised on these foundations for building public support for a more equal society. Tackling poverty and reducing inequality have been the dominant preoccupation of the Labour party throughout its history. Leading Labour thinkers have repeatedly stressed the centrality of equality to Labour's faith. 'Equality has been the strongest ethical inspiration of virtually every socialist doctrine [and] still remains the most characteristic feature of socialist thought today' (Crosland, 1964, p. 77). Yet in office this fundamental belief has proved to be little more than empty rhetoric. Labour in power in both the 1960s and 1970s did not lead to reductions in inequality.

In the 1960s, this failure is partly explained by Labour being 'blown off course', shelving social objectives to cope with unforeseen and intractable economic difficulties. However, it was also a more fundamental failure of will. From the late 1950s, Labour's public statements and speeches were careful to stress that social spending would have to move in line with but not ahead of economic growth, thereby avoiding the need for higher taxation. In the 1960s, the key task was seen as promoting economic prosperity from which improvements in public services would spring. Labour was engaged in a delicate balancing act designed to win wider public support through an appeal to the middle ground, and the emphasis on social justice was presented as a secondary objective to the primary task of more effective economic management. Such pragmatism was hardly a recipe for a fundamental attack on social and economic inequalities. The poor and those in need were seen as gaining, as they had throughout the 1950s, not by redistribution but by growth. If radical redistributive measures were not even on the agenda in the expectation of economic progress, it is hardly surprising that little was achieved under Labour in the colder economic climate that prevailed in the second half of the 1960s.

Following Wilson's election defeat in 1970, some attempts were made to revive Labour's commitment to social justice. 'A fundamental and irreversible shift in wealth and power in favour of working people and their families' was made a key objective in its 1973 *Programme*, while its 1974 manifesto promised to 'eliminate poverty wherever it exists'. But Labour's record in office from 1974 to 1979 was again at best mixed. It had some promising beginnings with a rapid growth in public expenditure in its first year in office. Some important changes were made in social security policy, notably the linking of benefit increases to earnings rather than prices, the introduction of the new pension scheme and, if reluctantly, the introduction of child benefit. However, faced with the deepest economic recession since the war, social objectives were soon sacrificed. Labour entered the 1979 election remembered as the party that only a few years earlier had launched a programme of harsh public spending cuts.

Of course, there is much room for debate about how much could have been achieved by way of social reform in the prevailing economic circumstances of worldwide recession, mounting industrial stagnation and dramatic inflation. However, the facts are that Labour has never had a coherent strategy for redistribution even in favourable economic conditions, let alone a situation of nil or low growth. Even relatively minor reforms such as chipping away at the regressive nature of tax allowances and reliefs such as mortgage interest relief were ignored.

There is little doubt that Labour's failures to make much impact on tackling inequality raised severe doubts about its credibility as a party committed to radical social change. This in turn fuelled the bitter internal wranglings that beset the party in the aftermath of the 1979 defeat and that helped pave the way for Labour's crushing defeat in 1983. Even during the 1983 election campaign, however, the fundamental question of the need for a fairer and more equal society was not made a central issue. During Mrs Thatcher's first term, inequalities had sharpened, not by accident but by design. Yet, while not unchallenged, Labour did not make the reversal of these trends a central theme of its message. The campaign, instead, was dominated by defence and disarmament, the EEC, unemployment and to a much lesser extent wider issues about the welfare state, though even here the debate was confined to the relatively 'safe' and popular issue of the future of the National Health Service.

The will to act – in principle

Throughout the postwar period, attitudes to the poor have tended to fluctuate according to both the prevailing economic and social climate and the public's 'moral' stance. The birth and development of the welfare state seemed to do little to rid us of the old nineteenth-century distinction between the deserving and the undeserving poor. Certain groups of the poor, such as the unemployed and single parents, have been viewed with much less sympathy than other groups, such as the elderly and the disabled. Hostility towards the unemployed seemed to be especially strong, though far from overwhelming, in the late 1970s, this group being an easy scapegoat for growing economic and social problems.

Since the late 1970s, however, the public mood has shifted. People now show an improved understanding of the causes of poverty, a strong sceptism about the effectiveness of government policy and widespread sympathy for welfare claimants. Although this softening of attitudes is still tinged with some underlying suspicion about the circumstances and attitudes of the poor, the old distinction between the deserving and undeserving poor has become blurred against the background of the deepening recession and the rising number of claimants. The poor, including the unemployed, are now seen as more deserving and less the victims of their own inadequacies.

How far is this change in attitude matched by willingness to support more effective policies? Certainly there is support for the broad goal of reducing poverty and evidence of strong support for a more equal society. In the past, however, other surveys have tended to show some conflict between the goal of helping the poor and the specific policies themselves. It is to this question that we turn in Chapter 9. First, it is necessary to assess the success and failures of welfare policies for the poor.

8

The Collapse of Welfarism
Shifts in policies for the poor

As for Mrs Thatcher talking about the Victorian times, she should
have lived in Victorian times and seen how the poor people were all
repressed and put down. My father, he was out of work and what he
used to do to earn some coppers, he used to get barbed wire, old wire
and you know what we lived on – white puddings. When I look back
I cannot believe I went through and survived through it all.
[A pensioner born at the turn of the century]

In recent years, it has been increasingly suggested that the
postwar welfare consensus has collapsed. This view has been
fuelled by the re-election in 1983 of a government openly
hostile to welfarism. During the election campaign this is
what Mrs Thatcher told a packed meeting of Conservative
party activists at Wembley:

> We are committed to a civilised society where the poor
> and the sick, the disabled and the elderly are properly
> cared for. By the community, by their families, by
> voluntary organisations.

Mrs Thatcher made no mention of the state. Under the
influence of New Right thinking, the leadership of the
Conservative party has become increasingly committed to a
shift in the emphasis of welfare provision away from the state
to the individual. Any significant change in this direction
would have dramatic implications for the lives of the poor.
So how far is Mrs Thatcher likely to go in dismantling the
welfare state and does she have public support?

In Chapter 7, it was argued that the recession and the
rising number of families with direct experience of un-

employment, of financial hardship and of claiming benefits have had a softening impact on attitudes towards the poor and towards claimants. The next chapter looks at attitudes to the welfare state and in particular at how far this general shift in sympathies translates into support for pro-welfare *policies*. But first we look back, briefly, in this chapter at the postwar history of the welfare state.

The foundation of the welfare state

Although there are various conflicting explanations for the birth and development of the welfare state, there is little doubt that the postwar welfare reforms were introduced at least in part as a response to widespread public support for collective state action to secure a fairer society. Such public concern was born both out of the lingering memories of the gruelling hardship and poverty of the 1930s and of the evils of the means test, and out of the experience of war. This was how a 79-year-old pensioner, born in Sunderland, and unemployed for most of the 1930s, described the means test to us:

> Oh that was a dreadful thing. You had people coming to the house. 'You get rid of that.' 'You don't want that.' 'The gramophone – you get rid of that if you want any money', that was the means test, yes. You mustn't have no luxuries and if you got any assistance it wasn't in cash it was in a voucher marked groceries.

And this was how he went on to describe his treatment when unemployed:

> In the 1930s, if you were on the dole, you waited, the time you waited six weeks they put you on the gap, and you got no money. So what did you have to do, you had to go to the parish and you know how much they gave me to live on, 10 shillings. Out of that I had to pay three and tuppence rent for me gas and me phone out of ten

shilling. Well the climax was one day I was walking down the high street, and I collapsed on the pavement. I had to be picked up and taken home and when I got home the doctor came, 'oh', he says, 'it's malnutrition'. I said, 'in other words I'm starving'. It was true, but did I get any more, no. What do you think they wanted to do with me when I went before the committee. She says to me, 'oh well, what we have decided to do, we're going to put you in an institution'. I said, 'what are you talking about'. She says, 'we'll store your furniture'. I said, 'you'll do nothing of the kind'. I said, 'I'm only a young man and that institution you're speaking of, is for old people'.

In addition, the experience of war helped to erode class barriers. Mass evacuation and the air raids exposed the middle classes to the reality of poverty, inequality and the appalling social conditions that still prevailed (Titmuss, 1950). This gave rise to changing attitudes and values, and helped create a new consensus on the role and responsibility of the state in tackling these problems – and through universal rather than selective provision. As John Saville has written:

On the morrow of the electoral victory of the Labour Party in the summer of 1945, nineteenth-century ideas of individualism were widely regarded as outdated as well as socially immoral. The lessons of the grim years of unemployment and wasted resources between the wars had bitten deeply into the minds and hearts of many of the British people, and the anti-fascist war had further strengthened their radicalism. There was at this time a greater consensus of opinion regarding the allocation of resources in the interests of social justice and equality than at any previous time in the twentieth century, or, for that matter, since. (Saville, 1965, p. 199)

Combined with macro-economic demand management aimed at securing full employment, the postwar welfare reforms remained the key weapons in successive governments' anti-poverty policy. In the thirty years after the war, public spending on social welfare – health, education, the personal social services, housing and social security – rose more quickly than national income and public expenditure as a whole. Welfare spending now accounts for about half of all public spending and about one-fifth of GNP. While much of this increase in social spending has been necessary to meet demographic changes, it has also resulted in improved standards. This pattern of growth was associated with both Conservative and Labour governments, giving rise to the term 'Butskellism' to describe the cross-party consensus that underpinned the steady expansion of the welfare state in these years.

This is not to say that helping the poor has been the sole objective of state spending on social welfare. Government intervention through direct state provision of social services had also been justified by classical economists as securing the efficient functioning of the economy. Marxists, on the other hand, have viewed the development of welfarism more cynically either as a response to the requirements of capitalism, acting as a form of social control ensuring the political and social stability essential to its survival, or as a product of working-class pressure in which 'concessions are wrested from an unwilling state' (Gough, 1979, p. 56).

The impact of the welfare years

Whatever the underlying motives, high spending on social welfare has had important redistributional consequences, which overall have improved the living standards and opportunities of the poorest. The net impact of government activity through taxation and social spending is progressive. Those on the lowest original incomes (that is, before government intervention) gain substantially from the tax–benefit system, while those on the highest original incomes are net losers. Overall, the welfare state has redistributed income from the rich to the poor, through the life cycle and between household types – from, for example, the childless to single parents and large families.

Until recently, welfare spending has also operated to counteract the impact of wider social and economic factors that have increasingly served to widen the gap between pre-tax and benefit incomes. Since the war, the share of labour market incomes accruing to the least well off has been falling. In 1976, the poorest 40 per cent of households received 10.2 per cent of labour market incomes compared with 15.6 per cent in 1965, a fall of one-third in fifteen years (Royal Commission on the Distribution of Income and Wealth, 1979, p. 75). This was the result of demographic changes, such as the growing number of the elderly, and changes in employment patterns, such as earlier retirement, less part-time working among the elderly and the increased participation of married women in the labour market. However, these trends towards greater inequality were largely offset by the impact of the welfare state. More and more became dependent on welfare benefits, especially retirement pensions. As a result, the comparative post-tax and benefit incomes of the poor remained more or less constant throughout the 1950s and 1960s (Fiegehen *et al.*, 1977, pp. 19–31). Since 1979, however, cuts in benefit levels and other social policies have weakened the countervailing power of welfarism.

This is not to say that the welfare state is not without major flaws in tackling poverty and reducing inequalities. Relative poverty has not only not fallen since the war, it has started to rise in recent years. In turn, fundamental structural inequalities have remained largely immune to the persistent growth in social spending. The welfare state has offset but not dismantled these basic inequalities.

In part, this reflects the limited objectives underlying the original reforms. The new social security system, for example, was in essence a system of social insurance designed to provide a minimum income in times of special need, such as unemployment, old age and sickness. Its central aim was not a major reduction of income inequalities through redistribution between classes but a redistribution over the life cycle and between work and unemployment, old age and illness. The limited redistributional objective was reinforced by the finance being based on a largely regressive system of national insurance contributions. Although the system has developed in various ways through the introduction of some earnings-related benefits and contributions, non-contributory benefits and means-tested benefits, and an increasing share of the cost being met by taxation, its vertical redistributional impact has remained limited.

Other reforms, especially the setting up of the National Health Service, the introduction of a universal education system and the public housing investment programmes, had more fundamentally egalitarian aims – to ensure that a child's future was no longer determined by where they were born and brought up. It was hoped that such reforms would provide improved access for the poor to decent services and break the link between poverty and ill-health, poor educational achievement and bad housing. However, policies of providing services at free or subsidised prices, paid for by general taxation, have had only limited success in achieving equal access to these services. The link has been weakened but not broken, inequalities have persisted.

Indeed, some elements of welfare spending are not progressive at all. Social security, which accounts for about half of all social welfare spending, is by far the most progressive. Among services in kind, the personal social services benefit the poor to a greater extent than the better-off, while the redistributive impact of spending on health, education and housing is more complex: some elements of these are pro-poor – such as housing benefit; some are broadly neutral – such as nursery and primary education; and others are pro-rich – such as health spending, higher education and general housing subsidies (Le Grand, 1982).

In part, this is to do with the nature of the spending itself. In housing, for example, the replacement of owner-occupier tax concessions with a system of income-related housing subsidies would lead to greater equality. The main explanation, however, lies in the failure to 'counteract the influence of the more fundamental social and economic inequalities that pervade British society' (Le Grand, 1982, p. 139).

Especially important is the failure to make significant reductions in the inequality of money incomes. For those services that are not free, such as housing and higher education, the better-off tend to buy more and so end up receiving more in subsidy. The costs involved in the take-up of services that are free can also bear more heavily on those with lower incomes. The welfare state has, therefore, had only a limited impact on reducing the unequal structure of British society.

As the Oxford Mobility Studies have shown, the poor's chances of improving their relative position compared with those who start at the top are no better now than they were in 1946.

> Since the war, Britain has become a rather richer country. But even though that is true, those who are born at the bottom end, those who are poor, are the ones who are most likely to stay at the bottom end and the chances of staying at the bottom end are no different now compared with those who start at the top end, than they were at the end of the second war. (Professor Halsey in the *Breadline Britain* series, 1983)

The inherent limitations of the welfare state in helping the poor have often been used by writers on the New Right to reinforce their call for the dismantling of key chunks of the welfare state. However, the limited achievements of welfarism are a reason for reforming not dismantling it. There are several ways in which state welfare programmes could in principle be made more progressive. First, the taxation system, which at present is broadly neutral (at least across the top 70 per cent of the income distribution), could be restructured in a more progressive way. Second, the nature of spending could be modified so that it is more biased in favour of the poor. Housing subsidies – especially tax concessions to owner-occupiers, for example – could be redirected so that they are of greater benefit to those on lower incomes. National Health Service resources could be redistributed from richer to poorer areas. Third, income redistribution towards the poor would itself lead to greater equality in the use of certain key public services, such as health care and higher education. The poor are much less likely to make use of the health service, for example, because they have fewer cars and telephones, while manual workers often lose money if they take time off work to see the doctor (Le Grand, 1983).

The growing crisis for welfare spending

Not only has the growth of welfare spending failed to make significant inroads into structural inequalities, the broad consensus that characterised the early days of the welfare state was to prove very fragile and short-lived. As early as 1953, Beveridge was to write: 'the picture of yesterday's hopeful collaboration in curing the evils of want and disease, ignorance and squalor . . . looks like a dream today' (Beveridge, 1953, pp. 360–1). According to another author,

> The story of poverty, inequality and the Welfare State in post-war Britain is one of a retreat from consensus on social justice and equality . . . The period 1950–80 saw a hardening of attitudes towards the poor, less concern for the pursuit of social justice and equality. (MacGregor, 1981, pp. 23–4)

This 'retreat', if retreat it was, was not confined to the public. Throughout the 1950s there were strong voices of dissent from anti-collectivist economists such as Hayek and Friedman and from some Conservative politicians who were opposed to both the mixed economy and state welfare. They favoured the replacement of universal with selective provision for the poor and disadvantaged, a shift away from collectivism towards individualism and greater choice through the encouragement of private provision in health care, education and pensions. Such views, however, were out of tune with the prevailing political orthodoxy, and were insufficiently influential at the time to have much impact.

The precise impact on the poor of a partial or total withdrawal of the state from welfare provision is difficult to evaluate. It would depend especially on what form such withdrawal took and how far it was taken. In general, policies involving one or a combination of reducing levels of benefit, concentrating benefits only on those below a certain income level, and privatising certain services would, depending on the effect of alternative insurance-based services on access to such services for the poor, widen inequalities both of income and of access to services. Concentrating cash assistance on the poor alone would also exacerbate the poverty trap. As seen in Chapter 1, the very limited changes of recent years have reduced the incomes of the poorest, made them more dependent on supplementary benefit, with its built-in 100 per cent marginal tax rate, and contributed to widening inequalities, albeit on a modest scale.

Advocates of such a return to selective income provision for the poor and the abandonment of universal public provision of social services have, of course, argued that the poor – even if they suffered in the short term – would benefit in the long run since the present system discourages incentives and acts as a drag on economic growth. There is no doubt that some trade-off exists between economic growth and greater equality. There must be some level of taxation and public spending that will erode incentives. There is little firm empirical evidence, however, about the level at which this would begin to bite. It is most unlikely that present levels of taxation and public spending, which are lower as a proportion of GNP than in most European countries, impose major constraints on enterprise. Nevertheless, to the extent that such a conflict exists, it is then a political choice whether lower incomes all round is a price worth paying for a more equal society.

Moreover, while anti-collectivist views gained little ground during the two decades after the war, by the mid-1970s they were being more widely voiced and were being taken much more seriously. The favourable climate that had given birth to and sustained the development of the postwar welfare state had begun to grow colder. The immediate source of this new crisis for welfare was the onset of the deepest world slump since the war. The end of economic growth and full employment and the birth of stagflation in the early 1970s created new problems of financing the cost of welfare spending, with the recession and low or zero growth leading simultaneously to rising demands and falling revenue. These problems were further fuelled by growing concern about high rates of taxation, on the one hand, and the effectiveness of welfare policies, on the other. In addition, it was being argued in some quarters that excessive state spending on the social services lay at the root of Britain's poor economic performance (Bacon and Eltis, 1976).

After some expansion in Labour's first year in office, cuts in spending were initiated in 1975/6 and then reinforced under pressure from the International Monetary Fund. This helped authenticate these wider views, and created the circumstances for a revival of market liberalism from the mid-1970s. The debates of the 1950s on universalism versus selectivity, and on individualism versus collectivity, re-emerged, and were replayed in a much more sympathetic climate, leading finally to the election victory of Mrs Thatcher in 1979 on a platform committed to 'rolling back the frontiers of the state'. In the words of the 1979 Conservative party election manifesto, 'The balance of our society has been increasingly tilted in favour of the State. . . This election may be the last chance to reverse that process. . .'. After three decades of steady expansion, the future of the welfare state now looks increasingly insecure. As one author has put it: 'The legitimacy of the welfare state is in serious doubt' (Mishra, 1984, p. xiv).

Welfare under Thatcherism

During Mrs Thatcher's first term in office, the new Conservatism took only limited steps to reduce state involvement in welfare provision. Only in housing did the government make any real strides in attempting to substitute private for public welfare. Here, measures to promote the private market at the expense of state provision included generous discounts to encourage council tenants to buy their homes, the promotion of low-cost home ownership schemes, sharp increases in rents, large cuts in public housing investment and the encouragement of private landlordism. Among other services, tax incentives for occupational health insurance were restored, some local authorities began to privatise some of their services, assisted places schemes were introduced as a further subsidy to independent schools, and responsibility for the first few weeks of sick pay was transferred from national insurance to the employee. With the exception of housing, these changes hardly add up to the kind of radical transformation of welfare provision that many key government figures probably favour.

Partly because of the government's cautious approach in these areas, the level of public spending and taxation, far from falling as the government hoped, rose after May 1979. Real public spending rose by 3 per cent from 1978/9 to 1984/5, and from 40.5 per cent of GDP to an expected 42 per cent. Social spending rose over the same period at a faster rate of some 7.3 per cent. Taxation also rose.

There are two main reasons for the government's failure to achieve its basic target of cutting spending: first, its commitment to increase defence spending, which rose by 30 per cent in real terms; second, a rise in the social security bill of some 30 per cent, accounted for by the rising number of claimants, the casualties of the recession. If social security is excluded, social spending fell in real terms by the order of 10 per cent. Among these areas, housing suffered the deepest cut – of 70 per cent.

As we have seen in Chapter 1, these changes, however limited, reinforced the natural tendency of the recession to accentuate poverty and widen inequalities. While the social security budget rose because of an increase in the number of recipients, individual benefits were cut. One benefit – the earnings-related supplement for the unemployed – was abolished, making the short-term unemployed much worse off and forcing them onto supplementary benefit. Long-term benefits (such as pensions) were raised in line with inflation rather than with earnings, as in previous years. This meant that, by 1983, single pensioners and the disabled were around £1.45 a week worse off, and couples around £2.25 a week, than if that link had been maintained. Child benefit and unemployment benefit were allowed to fall in real terms but were then, as a result of backbench pressure, restored in the April 1983 budget. Even so, benefit cuts over the life of the government amounted to some £1.6 billion. Not only was there a sharp increase in the numbers on benefit, benefit levels were reduced, amounting to a direct cut in the incomes of the poorest. On top of this, cuts in housing reduced opportunities for those in housing stress and sharpened inequalities in the distribution of housing subsidies.

The failure of the first Thatcher administration to achieve its overall objective of cutting public spending gave rise to widespread speculation about future Conservative intentions for the welfare state. In 1982, *The Economist* published extracts from a confidential report from the Central Policy Review Staff on 'options for radical cuts in public spending, many involving the dismantling of huge chunks of the welfare state' (18 September 1982). Ideas considered in the report included the introduction of voucher schemes in education, the ending of indexation for state pensions in order to encourage private provision, and the use of private insurance for the finance of health care. This was followed by the leaked minutes of the Family Policy Group – a cabinet sub-committee of senior ministers – to the *Guardian* in February 1983. These minutes showed that serious consideration was being given to a range of options for reducing state spending on welfare provision (*Guardian*, 17 and 18 February 1983).

The current direction of government policies

In June 1983, the Conservatives were returned with a much larger majority though a slightly smaller share of the vote, renewing speculation about the future of the welfare state.

To some extent it is easy to exaggerate the crisis facing welfare spending. There are certainly some pressures likely to lead to an increase in the cost of maintaining existing provision – in particular some demographic trends, the rising relative cost of some public services and pension commitments. Despite this, the government's own medium-term forecasts suggest that current spending and tax levels can be maintained with little difficulty on projected growth rates (Treasury, 1984). Certainly, the economic climate has become slightly more favourable, with the return of a modest level of growth. If this growth is sustained, reducing public spending as a proportion of GDP will be easier to achieve.

The government, however, has a long-standing pledge to cut the real level of public expenditure and taxation and this will prove much more difficult. It has already cut heavily in areas such as housing and industry, which are the least politically sensitive and where there is less likelihood of public backlash. There is little scope left for further cuts here. It has chipped away at social security. It is unlikely that un-employment will fall enough to allow anything other than marginal savings on social security spending. In addition, the government is committed to at least maintaining spending in areas such as law and order and defence.

If it wishes to cut the real level of spending, therefore, it has two options. First, it could reduce spending in major service areas such as social security, the National Health Service, education and the personal social services. Cuts in two of these areas – social security and the personal social services – would not only help to satisfy the macro-economic objective of cutting public spending but would also meet Mrs Thatcher's ideological belief that the social responsibilities undertaken by the state – such as care of the elderly, the disabled, the under fives and the young unemployed – should be transferred to families and charities, with much greater emphasis on self-help and much less on state protection. Moreover, accounting for over one-third of all public expenditure, the social security budget offers the theoretical potential of large savings. Yet, without a significant fall in unemployment, the options for savings in the social security bill are limited. They would require cuts in the *real* level of benefits.

The Conservative manifesto was careful to give a commitment to protect pensions and other long-term benefits against rising prices. This has led to speculation that unemployment benefit and child benefit would be vulnerable. A cut in unemployment benefit has been advocated by some academics on the right, especially Professor Patrick Minford of the University of Liverpool, as a way of reducing wages and unemployment. Minford (Minford *et al.*, 1983) has argued that high wages, especially at the bottom end, are a key cause of unemployment. In his view, Britain's low international productivity means that jobs can only be created at lower wages but people do not take jobs at low wages because of high benefits. In order to increase the incentive to work, he therefore advocates widening the margin between income in and out of work by a combination of policies designed to increase net income in work and reduce income when out of work. The latter would involve cutting unemployment benefit. Although Professor Minford's views are not widely supported by other academic economists, they certainly command widespread support among some sections of the Conservative party. That unemployment benefit is vulnerable under the present government was indicated in an interview given by Mrs Thatcher immediately after the election in the *Daily Express* of 15 June: 'I would not give an undertaking that unemployment pay would be price protected in the same way as pensions'. In an interview on Channel 4's *Face the Press* on 3 July 1983, the new Chancellor, Mr Nigel Lawson, confirmed that the level of unemployment benefit was under consideration in a new round of spending cuts being looked at by the new cabinet. This simply confirmed the fears of many Tory wets and unleashed a storm of protest.

Another benefit that has looked vulnerable has been child benefit. At a cost of nearly £4 billion a year, cuts in child benefit inevitably look financially attractive to a minister looking for substantial savings. In consequence, there has been speculation that child benefit might be restricted to lower-income families by, for example, phasing it out in favour of a beefed-up means-tested benefit similar to family income supplement.

In the event, despite a new round of public spending cuts announced in the Autumn after the election, child benefit and unemployment benefit have both been protected to date. The social security budget, however, did not emerge unscathed – it was housing benefit that was the victim, suffering a swingeing cut of £230 million. The impact of the cut was devastating, with some 4½ million recipients being affected. Half a million households lost their right to housing benefit completely, while the average loss of benefit worked out at £1.57 a week, with some families losing far more – up to £12.00 or more a week (Goss and Lansley, 1984). Ferociously complicated, the government no doubt hoped it would be able to slip through these cuts unnoticed. As it turned out, however, some shrewd campaigning by groups such as SHAC, the London Housing Aid Centre and the Child Poverty Action Group led to considerable publicity and embarrassment for the government. This did not deter it from its course, however, and, although phased, the cuts were implemented.

The cuts in housing benefit have been felt exclusively by those on low, if not the lowest, incomes. The very poorest have been largely, but not entirely, protected. It is the moderately poor who have suffered most – those on low wages and pensioners with small occupational pensions in particular. The impact has been to reduce still further the incomes of the poorest quarter of the population, a group that the *Breadline Britain* findings outlined in Part I showed was liable to be living below an acceptable living standard.

As an alternative, the government could go for some genuinely radical options, such as those advocated by Professor Minford (1984). His proposals amount to more or less the wholesale abolition of the welfare state, and could cut public spending by one-third. They include the replacement of the National Health Service with private health insurance, the abolition of state schools and the privatisation of education, the privatisation of many local government services, cuts in unemployment benefit and the introduction of a negative income tax to replace existing social security. Such changes would, of course, have dramatic implications for social and economic inequalities and wider opportunities. They are almost certainly a non-starter, and have been described by the former Conservative Foreign Secretary, Francis Pym, as a 'political dreamland' (*Guardian*, 5 May 1984).

The road from welfare

What is clear is that the government is considering how changes could be made to achieve savings. In April 1984, the Social Services Secretary, Norman Fowler, launched what he described as 'the most substantial examination of the social security system since the Beveridge Report 40 years ago'. Inquiries have been launched into supplementary benefit, housing benefit, help for the disabled and help for young people. There is much speculation about what these inquiries really have in store – more cuts (whether substantial or minor) or some fundamental restructuring. Whatever happens, the prospects for welfare services and those who depend most heavily on them look at best uncertain. Before going down any of these roads, however, Mrs Thatcher would be unwise to ignore public opinion, and it is to that we turn in the next chapter.

9

The Defence of Welfarism
Public attitudes to welfare spending

> I think they could bring it up to about £47 a week. That would be more like it. That would get you somewhere. I mean most people are earning quite a bit more than £40 odd a week when they're working. Not only that, but they've got freedom to buy what they want when they want it. We haven't. We have to say please may I. I think we should be allowed enough money to be able to live with dignity. [A single, disabled woman]

The present government has provided the coldest political climate for the welfare state since its foundation. The days of Butskellism are over. But has public opinion moved with that of the government? Has the New Right's dominance at Westminster transformed people's attitudes and thinking?

These questions are important for the future of welfarism. They help to indicate whether, if these views were given more prominence, a government more sympathetic to the poor would be elected. Moreover, they help determine how far the present government will go in pursuing its philosophy. There is little doubt that strong public support for areas such as the National Health Service has acted as a constraint on government policy to date. So to what extent do the public support specific policies towards welfare spending and help for the poor? To assess the current mood, we first take a brief look back.

Attitudes to welfare spending in the latter half of the 1970s

Opinion polls since the war have shown both mixed and shifting opinion. Overall, support for welfare spending has been high but neither universal nor unlimited. The National Health Service, pensions and education have commanded consistently strong public support, but even in these popular areas some people have favoured cutbacks. Other areas of spending, in contrast, such as family allowances/child benefit and unemployment benefit, have received much weaker support.

Table 9.1, based on the British Election Surveys of 1974 and 1979, shows strongly divergent views on the National Health Service, social services and welfare benefits. In 1974, there were clear and substantial majorities in favour of higher spending on the National Health Service (85.6 per cent thought it very or fairly important to increase spending), whereas enthusiasm for spending on social services and

Table 9.1 *Attitudes to social welfare spending (percentages)*

Respondent's attitude to spending on social services:	1974	1979
Social services should be:		
Cut back a lot	13.7	20.8
Cut back a bit	25.2	31.2
Kept as they are	32.9	27.3
Expanded	28.1	20.7
Respondent's attitude to welfare benefits:		
Welfare benefits have:		
Gone much too far	12.3	21.4
A little too far	21.7	28.6
About right	43.1	32.9
Not far enough	17.3	13.2
Not nearly far enough	5.7	3.8
Respondent's attitude to increased spending on the National Health Service:		
Spending on the health service:		
Very important it should	48.3	52.8
Fairly important it should	37.3	36.0
Doesn't matter	6.0	4.5
Fairly important it should not	6.3	4.5
Very important it should not	2.1	2.0

Sources: Whiteley (1981), Table 1; British Election Survey, 1979.

welfare benefits was weaker: only 28.1 per cent thought the former should be expanded, while 23.0 per cent thought welfare benefits 'had not gone far enough'. Nevertheless, there was not a majority in favour of cutting either of them back. The table also provides evidence of some hardening of attitudes towards certain aspects of the welfare state, especially towards welfare benefits, during the second half of the 1970s: support for the National Health Service increased slightly between 1974 and 1979, support for cutbacks in social services also grew, and the view that welfare benefits had 'gone too far' increased noticeably.

How far did this shift reflect some permanent and deep-seated change in opinion? Or did it simply reflect a fluctuation in attitudinal patterns? Pollsters distinguish between issues on which most people hold firm and committed views that have deep roots and rarely change and those that are much more weakly held and that are therefore much more susceptible to the prevailing social and political climate. The evidence of polls over time suggests that certain aspects of the welfare state fall into the former category. Support for the National Health Service, pensions and education has been consistently high, while attitudes towards other benefits has been much more mixed.

If the decline in support for benefits did not reflect a permanent ideological shift in public opinion, there are two other possible explanations for the change. The first is that public antipathy to certain aspects of income support is indeed deep-rooted but had been hidden in the postwar period by support for the National Health Service and pensions. If so, it is possible that under the stimulus of Thatcherism in the latter half of the 1970s this suppressed ideology finally rose to the surface. This view seems to conflict with the evidence presented later in the chapter, which shows a relatively generous attitude towards benefits in 1983. The alternative explanation is that it was a response to the particular social and political circumstances of the time. The late 1970s were a period of retrenchment in public spending occasioned by the economic crises of 1975 and 1976. Few public services were protected in the cuts announced and enacted at that time. This was followed by rising unemployment and successive attempts at wage restraint culminating in the 'winter of discontent' in 1978. The period was also characterised by a new ideological opposition to high public spending as one of the key causes of Britain's long-term economic decline. While such a view had been evolving as part of the new thinking within the Conservative party, it was also influenced by the public spending cuts initiated by the 1974–9 Labour government, which helped to give legitimacy to the idea that state spending was too high. The growing economic crisis also gave rise to a drop in real incomes, an increase in the tax burden and a rise in the cost of welfare. This helped to promote a growing wave of 'scrounger-phobia', reflecting a rising antipathy to social security and to claimants. Fanned by the exaggerated media responses to particular incidents of social security fraud, this mood, on occasions, seemed to reach hysterical proportions (Golding and Middleton, 1982).

Against this background, it is not surprising that public opinion should harden against certain groups of claimants, convenient and helpless scapegoats for the emerging economic and social problems. In turn, these trends must have helped to set the scene for the election campaign of May 1979 and the anti-social-services stance adopted by the Conservatives.

That these changes in opinion towards welfare spending were more of a response to the changing political and economic climate than a reflection of a fundamental shift is supported by another study of opinion changes between 1974 and 1979 (Husbands, 1982, pp. 42–4). This compared the answers to a series of questions from a panel of the same voters in October 1974 and May 1979. It showed that only 41 per cent of voters gave the same response in both years when asked about spending on social services and benefits; 37 per cent gave a more 'left' response in 1974 than in 1979, while 17 per cent gave a more 'left' response in 1979 compared with 1974. This confirms that attitudes on this question are weakly rather than strongly held and led Husbands to conclude that the hardening of attitudes that had occurred over the period was as likely to be associated with the 'particularly reactionary stimuli in the election campaign' as with any permanent shift.

At the time of the 1979 election, therefore, public opinion was probably more sympathetic to anti-collectivist views than at any time since the war. This seems to have been explained by the particular political circumstances of the time – the unpopularity of the Labour party following the 'winter of discontent' and the climax of several years during which wage restraint and rising taxes had held down take-home pay. There can be little doubt that the national mood in the spring of 1979 was especially favourable to the Tories and by implication to propaganda about high public spending and taxation. Even then, this mood was not overwhelming. Despite the growth of antagonism towards claimants and benefits, for example, support for maintaining or expanding spending on social services and welfare benefits was still high and only just short of 50 per cent (Table 9.1). As one observer has concluded, 'welfare spending is still popular amongst the great majority of the electorate . . . the general climate of public opinion in Britain will not accept a fundamental dismantling of the welfare state as distinct from its erosion at the edges' (Whiteley, 1981, p. 473).

Public opinion, however, also tends to be confused and ambiguous. On the question of tax and public spending levels, for example, surveys have shown how people like to have it both ways – favouring both tax cuts and higher spending, especially in some areas. Surveys in the late 1970s showed that the public supported cuts in both overall spending and taxation but also wanted more spent on some services such as the National Health Service, pensions and education. The only item in a list of possible cuts in a Gallup survey in January 1978 to gain a majority was unemployment benefit (Lipsey, 1979). Although opinion polls in 1979 showed large majorities in favour of cutting taxes, when asked to express a direct preference between tax cuts and higher spending, the answers tended to be more favourable to public spending. In October 1979, for example, a Gallup poll found only 20 per cent in favour of cutting taxes and reducing services; 26 per cent were in favour of the status quo, and 44 per cent favoured extending services and increasing taxes.

Current attitudes to welfare spending

Chapter 7 showed how attitudes to the poor found in the *Breadline Britain* survey have shifted since the mid-1970s to a position where far fewer blame the victims and many more blame injustice. There was also evidence of strong backing for a more equal society and little support for the inegalitarian ideology or the widening inequalities of recent years. This is confirmed by shifts in attitude towards spending and specific policies. In October 1983, an identical question to the one asked in 1979 by Gallup showed the proportion favouring extending services had risen to 50 per cent and the proportion favouring cuts in taxes and services had fallen to 17 per cent.

The shift is confirmed in other surveys, which have shown very weak and only minority support for cuts in spending and taxation. A MORI poll in October 1983 found 34 per cent favouring 'cuts in taxes, even if this means a cut in spending on public services', but a clear majority (58 per cent) in favour of 'maintaining spending on public services, even if this means an increase in taxes'.

An identical question in a comprehensive poll of attitudes to local public services conducted by MORI for the London Borough of Greenwich in December 1983 (MORI, 1984) showed 47 per cent in favour of maintaining spending even if this meant higher taxes and 36 per cent favouring cuts in taxes and spending. To test the views of the local electorate on individual local services, respondents were given a list of five basic public services – subsidised council housing, free education for children up to the age of 16, free local hospital care, subsidised public transport, and social security benefits. They were asked which of three options they favoured for each service – more taxes and improved services, the status quo, or lower taxes and poorer services. The answers revealed even greater opposition to cuts in taxation if this meant a poorer service in these individual areas (Table 9.2). Hospital care was the most strongly supported, with 59 per cent favouring spending more to improve the service, even if this meant an increase in taxes, 33 per cent favouring the status quo, and only 1 per cent favouring lower taxes and a poorer service. Education was the next most popular, with 41 per cent favouring an improved servvice and only 2 per cent favouring cuts. In the case of the other three services – council housing, public transport and social security – a majority favoured maintaining the present balance between spending and service but, of the other two options, many more favoured improved services (29 per cent in each case) than supported lower taxes and a poorer service (4–6 per cent for each area).

Labour supporters are, as expected, generally more likely to support improved services in these areas than Alliance supporters, and Alliance supporters are more likely to do so than Conservative supporters. Perhaps surprisingly, however, Conservative supporters are overwhelmingly opposed to spending and tax cuts in these areas: only 3 per cent of Conservatives favoured cuts in education, 10 per cent in council housing, 1 per cent in hospital care, 5 per cent in public transport and 9 per cent in social security. This suggests that there is not even a mandate among Conservative voters for further reductions in public spending on these services, even if this results in lower taxes.

Table 9.2 reveals some interesting patterns in attitudes between classes. On hospital care and education, the middle classes are, if anything, more likely to support an improved service even at the expense of higher taxes than the working classes. On social security and council housing, however, the middle classes are less likely than the working classes to support the higher spending and tax option. These differences are not that sharp, however, and perhaps not as sharp as would be expected on the basis of variations in perceived self-interest. Perception of self-interest depends on how the cost of the service in terms of tax paid is weighed against assessment of personal benefit, where this derives not just from use of the service but also from paid employment in its

Table 9.2   Attitudes to local public services, 1983 (percentages)

'Please could you tell me from this card which of the three options you would favour most for the following services'

	Improve service even if more taxes	Service and taxes as at present	Lower taxes even if poorer services	Don't know
Hospital care	59	33	1	7
Education	41	44	2	13
Social security	29	52	5	14
Council housing	29	51	6	14
Public transport	29	58	4	9

'Please could you tell me from this card which of the three options you would favour most for the following services'

	Improve service/ more taxes			As at present			Lower taxes/ poorer service		
	Conservative	Labour	Lib/SDP	Conservative	Labour	Lib/SDP	Conservative	Labour	Lib/SDP
Hospital care	50	65	74	44	28	23	1	1	1
Education	36	45	47	50	42	42	3	2	1
Social security	18	41	33	60	46	53	9	2	4
Council housing	16	39	26	57	44	60	10	4	4
Public transport	23	36	28	64	53	65	5	3	1

'Please could you tell me from this card which of the three options you would favour most for the following services'

	Improve service/ more taxes — Social class					As at present — Social class					Lower taxes/ poorer service — Social class				
	AB	C1	C2	D	E	AB	C1	C2	D	E	AB	C1	C2	D	E
Hospital care	60	61	61	51	60	32	34	30	39	31	2	1	2	1	1
Education	47	42	46	39	33	38	48	40	48	45	3	1	3	1	3
Social security	22	23	22	33	42	60	54	58	49	42	7	8	6	3	3
Council housing	20	27	28	34	33	53	52	56	48	47	9	9	4	6	5
Public transport	29	28	25	29	31	61	60	63	58	50	7	7	7	11	13

Source: MORI (1984).

provision. In the case of education and health, the middle classes not only make disproportionate use of the services (Le Grand, 1982) but are also heavily employed in them as doctors, teachers, lecturers and administrators. This may explain why the middle classes are especially supportive of an expanded service in these areas. In the case of social security and council housing, in contrast, professional and managerial groups are, with the exception of pensions and child benefit, less likely to benefit from spending. In addition, they are less likely to be employed in these service areas. Despite this, at least one-fifth of professional and managerial workers favoured an improved service and higher taxes in these areas, although this is a noticeably lower proportion than among working-class groups. As we shall see later in Table 9.6 (pp. 266–7) the middle classes are not only supportive of higher pensions from which they are likely to benefit, but a majority also thought that supplementary benefit is too low and a quarter that unemployment benefit is also too low, both benefits in which they have much less of a stake. While self-interest appears to be the dominant factor determining attitudes to the welfare state, altruism is also important. As we saw in Chapter 7, although the middle classes are less concerned about the plight of the poor than are the working classes, they still display widespread sympathy for the position of the poor, which often overrides their immediate class interest.

It is also interesting to compare the attitudes of those 36 per cent of respondents favouring reduced public spending and taxation overall with their attitudes to these individual services. Of those favouring overall cuts, only 3 per cent also favoured cuts in hospitals, 5 per cent in education, 14 per cent in council housing, 6 per cent in public transport and 11 per cent in social security. While supporting the principle of lower public spending and taxes, they are, like ministers, much more reluctant to name the services.

These results therefore suggest little public enthusiasm for cutting public spending, despite this being one of the government's major policy planks.

Attitudes to spending on the poor

In Chapter 3, we examined the items identified by people as essential to a minimum living standard. Not only was there found to be a considerable degree of social consensus about which items were necessities, but these also covered a wide range of aspects of our way of life. However, identifying necessities is one thing. Being prepared to back measures to ensure that people do not fall below this self-determined minimum standard is another. In Chapter 7 it was seen that there is widespread support for more government help for the poor. How far, however, does this translate into dipping into one's own pocket? In order to gain some indication of how strongly people were committed to helping the poor, they were asked whether they would be prepared to pay more in income tax to 'enable everyone to afford the items you have said are necessities'.

First they were asked if they would be prepared to pay 1p more in the pound. Another penny on income tax would cost a standard-rate taxpayer on average earnings about £1.20 a week and would raise about £1,000 million a year. This, however, would have only a minimal impact on raising the incomes of the poor. It would enable an increase in all benefit levels of about 3 per cent, giving, for example, an increase of £1.05 for an unemployed couple and about £0.80 for a lone pensioner. Alternatively it could be used more selectively to, say, extend the long-term rate of supplementary benefit to those unemployed for more than a year and permit a 2 per cent increase in benefits all round. Such a sum would in fact reinstate little more than half of the cuts in the social security budget imposed by Mrs Thatcher's first administration. An increase of this amount was widely supported. As many as three-quarters said they would be prepared to pay one penny more in the pound in income tax, with one-fifth opposed (Table 9.3).

Respondents who were prepared to pay 1p more in the pound were then asked if they would support an increase of 5p in the pound. This would cost a standard-rate taxpayer an average of £6.00 a week and would raise £5,000 million. This

Table 9.3 Preparedness to pay more tax to help those in need, 1983 (percentages)

'If the Government proposed to increase income tax by one penny or by five pence in the pound to enable everyone to afford the items you have said are necessities, on balance would you support or oppose this policy?'

	All households	Net equivalent household income		Social class					Political affiliation				Sex	
		Poorest 10%	Richest 10%	AB	C1	C2	D	E	Conservative	Labour	Lib/SDP	None/Don't know	Male	Female
1p in the £:														
Support	74	71	88	84	73	67	68	68	79	73	77	69	79	70
Oppose	20	20	8	16	22	26	24	24	16	21	19	23	16	23
Don't know	6	9	4	1	5	8	9	9	5	6	3	8	4	7
5p in the £:														
Support	34	36	44	36	36	33	34	33	30	42	40	26	37	32
Oppose	53	48	43	57	50	53	52	53	61	47	46	55	51	54
Don't know	13	16	13	8	14	13	13	14	9	10	15	19	12	13

would finance a big package of benefit increases: a 23 per cent increase in all national insurance benefits; a £2.50 increase in child benefit (a 43 per cent rise); a 10 per cent increase in all supplementary benefit rates, plus the extension of the long-term supplementary rates to the long-run unemployed. By way of example, a long-term unemployed couple with two children would gain about £12.00 a week, and a lone pensioner about £7.50 a week. Such a package would lead to a significant improvement in the lot of most of the poor. Large numbers of households would be lifted off means-tested benefits, with as many as one-third lifted off supplementary benefit. As well as enjoying higher incomes, the problem of the poverty trap would be substantially eased. It is difficult to estimate precisely how these higher incomes would be translated into improved living standards and how many people would thereby be lifted above our socially determined minimum standard of living. Housing opportunities, for example, are not necessarily improved simply by increased income but may also depend on wider policies towards public sector housing. Nevertheless, we have estimated that around one-third to one-half would be lifted above this minimum standard (see Chapter 6). Support for a tax increase of this magnitude was a lot less, with only half of those supporting an increase of 1p also supporting an increase of 5p. There is a clear limit to people's generosity.

How far does willingness to pay vary among different groups? Conservative supporters, while appearing to be more generous than Labour and Liberal/SDP supporters when it comes to paying an extra penny, are less so when it comes to five pence. Men are slightly more willing to pay more than women, and pensioners marginally less willing than non-pensioners. Table 9.3 also shows that the middle class and those with the highest incomes are more willing to pay higher taxes than are the working class and those with the lowest incomes. Thus, 88 per cent of the richest 10% were prepared to pay another penny compared with 71 per cent of the poorest 10%, while 44 per cent of the richest supported an extra five pence compared with the 36 per cent of the poorest. This is of interest because the question is in some sense rather false – any policy to help the poor would primarily depend on those in the top half being prepared to pay more. That this proportion of the rich are prepared to pay is of significance, especially in view of the alleged disincentive effects of high taxation on higher income groups. That those on the lowest incomes are less keen to pay higher taxes is perhaps hardly surprising. Many are already finding it difficult to manage and could not cope with such an increase in taxation.

Since 1979, there has been a marked shift in the pattern of the tax burden away from the better-off. Thus from 1978/9 to 1983/4, the tax burden (including national insurance payments) for a two-child family of five times average earnings fell by 14 per cent; for a similar family on average earnings it increased by 6.5 per cent, while for one on three-quarters of average earnings it rose by 13 per cent (Bull and Wilding, 1983).

The increase in the tax burden of lower relative to higher earners was the result of several factors: the three pence reduction in the standard rate of income tax in 1979; the reduction in top tax rate from 83 per cent to 60 per cent on earned income and from 98 per cent to 75 per cent on investment income; the sharp rise in the threshold for the investment income surcharge; the abolition of the reduced tax band in 1980; and the increase in national insurance contributions for employees. These changes have been aggravated by other factors. Recent years have seen a sharp increase in the number of households subject to the poverty trap, a result in part of the spread of low pay. In 1979, under 79,000 families were in receipt of family income supplement. By 1982, the numbers had increased to 143,000. While increasing numbers are dependent on such means-tested benefits, the severity of the poverty trap has also intensified. This is mainly a result of the sharp increases in the rate at which housing benefit is withdrawn from poor families. Prior to the full introduction of housing benefit in April 1983, rent rebates were withdrawn at a rate of 17p in the £. By November 1984 this rate of withdrawal had nearly doubled to 29p in the £.

There is also evidence that the lower-paid and poorer

households are only too well aware of their growing tax burden and the impact of the poverty trap, even if they do not use the jargon of social scientists. Olga is a hospital domestic assistant earning £88 a week gross. She has three children to look after:

> I wouldn't be any better off if my wages went up because I'll get less family income supplement and my rent will also go up. Sometimes I hardly feel like working because it's not worth it.

Table 9.4 shows that, among all households, as many as 79 per cent agreed that 'there's no incentive for low paid workers to earn extra money because any gain disappears through deductions in benefits and extra taxes'. There were sharp variations by occupational group, with 87 per cent of those in manual occupations agreeing compared with 56 per cent of professional and managerial workers.

The answers to questions on attitudes to spending on the poor appear to show a surprisingly strong willingness for personal financial sacrifice to help them, but can they be taken seriously? After all, past experience has shown how difficult it has been to obtain public acquiescence for higher taxation in order to fund higher public spending. One of the

Table 9.4 *Attitudes to incentives for the low-paid (percentages)*

'There's no incentive for low paid workers to earn extra money because any gain disappears through deductions in benefit and extra taxes':	All house-holds	Net equivalent household income		Social class				
		Poorest 10%	Richest 10%	AB	C1	C2	D	E
Agree	79	81	75	56	73	88	86	84
Disagree	17	10	24	43	24	8	10	9
Don't know	4	9	0	1	3	4	4	7

characteristics of the postwar history of growing expenditure on the welfare state has been the extension of the tax burden beyond the well-off and then beyond middle-income groups to even those on the lowest incomes. While this is partly explained by the lack of progressivity over most of the tax system, it remains the case that the higher taxation required to finance substantial further redistribution of income through higher benefits and public spending on universal services would have to come, not just from the rich but throughout the top half of the income scale, even with a reformed and more progressive tax system. Early in Labour's 1974–9 administration, there was an attempt to expand welfare spending through higher taxation, the term 'the social wage' being coined in an attempt to gain public support. In the later years of the government, however, cumulative trade union pressure to maintain take-home pay combined with pressure from the International Monetary Fund and the recession to lead to a subsequent collapse of that strategy. Klein has summarised these events:

> The 'social wage' was not, in other words, perceived by union members as equivalent to money in their own pockets: they voted, in their wage bargaining, against a policy of redistribution to the elderly and others via the state. (Klein, 1980, p. 28)

The reasons for the collapse of Labour's social contract in the second half of the 1970s are more complex than this, but this does illustrate the difficulties facing a government attempting redistributional policies in the face of limited or zero growth. Moreover, past experience is not the only reason for a note of caution in treating these answers as a fully reliable guide to people's real opinions. When confronted with questions of this kind, interviewees may be reluctant to appear uncharitable or selfish, and it may be easier to say 'yes' than to say 'no'.

Nevertheless, similar questions have been asked before. In a 1974 NOP poll, interviewees were asked whether they would be prepared to pay extra tax 'in order to help people who do not earn so much money as yourself'; only 34 per cent said that they would (Klein, 1974, p. 412). Moreover, the evidence in the previous section suggests that there has been a shift in the public mood on tax and public expenditure, which is now much more supportive of the latter.

Attitudes to social security benefits

The early years of the 1980s, it has been argued, have seen a shift towards greater sympathy for the poor and for certain aspects of welfare spending. Of particular importance, given the evidence of hostility at the end of the 1970s, there also seems to have been a move to greater support for social security. In the *Breadline Britain* survey, respondents were given a list of items of public spending and asked to choose three items for cuts if public spending had to be reduced, and three items for more money should the government decide to raise spending. In an identical question asked by MORI in 1980, social security had headed the cuts roster, with 44 per cent wanting this option compared with just 9 per cent favouring an increase (Table 9.5). By 1983, social security had slipped to fourth place in the cuts ranking, with nearly twice as many (45 per cent) favouring cuts in defence spending as in social security (23 per cent).

This is not all good news for social security recipients, however. Even though social security was much less unpopular in 1983 than three years previously, it was still relatively unpopular compared with other items of public spending including local housing, police, job training for the unemployed, as well as the NHS and education. Its ranking was similar to that found in the Greenwich/MORI survey (see Table 9.2).

There is a difficulty of interpretation about asking people about social security, however, since people's concepts of what this means may vary, and some may see it in a narrow way. Indeed, this low ranking may simply reflect the public's known ambivalence towards certain types of social security recipient. When asked about individual benefits, a more

Table 9.5   *Attitudes to public spending levels (percentages)*

*'If the Government had to reduce
its spending, which three of these
do you think it should cut its
spending on? And if the Government intended to increase its
spending, which three of these do
you think it should increase its
spending on?'*

| | 1980 | | 1983 | |
	Cut	Increase	Cut	Increase
Local housing	14	28	12	29
Social security benefits	44	9	23	19
National Health Service	5	57	2	59
Roads	19	66	17	20
Police	5	34	10	22
Education/schools	5	36	3	55
Grants to local authorities	34	5	25	9
Defence	30	25	45	10
Job training for the unemployed	20	27	13	38
Child benefits	19	18	20	16
Grants for regional development	37	8	39	6
None/no opinion	16	4	19	3

Sources: LWT/MORI survey, 1983; MORI.

generous reaction was found (Table 9.6). Pensions were
heavily supported: 59 per cent thought they were too low, 29
per cent about right and only 1 per cent too high. While this
may have come as no surprise, the same proportion (59 per
cent) thought supplementary benefit – at £59.20 a week after
rent for a family with two children – was too low as well;
another third said it was 'about right', while only 3 per cent
believed it was too high. When put in concrete terms
attitudes are more sympathetic. Equally surprising, 40 per
cent thought that unemployment benefit was too low, 24 per
cent about right and only 9 per cent too high. This suggests
that hostility to unemployment benefit has fallen. This
supports other findings that have shown a weakening in the
antipathy towards the unemployed that existed throughout
the 1960s and 1970s.

Child benefit is the only item to receive lukewarm support, and this is consistent with other survey findings since the war. The persistent lack of enthusiasm for child benefit is partly explained by its universal nature. It is often seen as indiscriminate in impact, going to people lacking in need as well as those deserving help. 'An NOP poll, carried out in 1968, found that 76 per cent agreed with the proposition that family allowances should be given only to those who need them as distinct from everyone with children' (Klein, 1974, p. 411). Lack of support may also reflect a view that since children are the result of conscious parental choice, they should be a burden on those who chose to have them rather than the state. Even so, despite its perceived indiscriminate impact, more (24 per cent) thought it was too low than too high (16 per cent), with 41 per cent thinking it was about right.

Some differences also emerge by income and class. In the case of pensions, support is high across income levels and classes. While pensioners are perceived as especially deserving, this may also reflect an awareness that most of us will benefit one day. In the case of unemployment benefit and child benefit, the differences are pronounced. Nearly twice the proportion of the poor (63 per cent) thought unemployment benefit too low compared with the rich (34 per cent). Only 2 per cent of the poor thought it was too high compared with 11 per cent of the rich. Working-class households are also more generous towards the level of unemployment benefit than middle-class ones. Even so, only a small proportion of the rich and the middle class displayed anti-unemployment benefit feelings, and fewer than in the past. This may indicate that altruism is on the increase, at least towards the unemployed. On the other hand, it may simply be that the middle classes have become increasingly concerned about their own or their family's vulnerability to unemployment. In the *Breadline Britain* survey, the middle classes were certainly as worried about the unemployment prospects of their children as were the working class.

Child benefit, too, is much more popular among the poor than the rich and among manual workers compared with

Table 9.6 Attitudes to benefit levels (percentages)

For each of the items on this list, could you tell me whether you think their level is too high, too low or about right at present?

	All households	Net equivalent household income		Social class				
		Poorest 10%	Richest 10%	AB	C1	C2	D	E
State pensions:								
Too high	1	5	0	0	0	2	2	0
Too low	59	62	65	53	58	59	62	60
About right	29	19	30	34	31	27	27	29
Don't know	11	14	5	13	11	12	10	10
Unemployment benefit:								
Too high	9	2	11	18	10	8	4	7
Too low	40	63	34	26	27	40	53	52
About right	24	19	40	32	29	26	20	17
Don't know	27	16	15	24	35	27	23	24
Child benefit:								
Too high	16	7	16	21	17	14	18	13
Too low	24	40	12	12	16	29	26	34
About right	41	38	53	43	47	44	39	33
Don't know	18	15	19	24	20	13	17	19
Supplementary benefit:[a]								
Too high	3	4	1	3	3	3	3	1
Too low	59	68	52	52	54	67	54	62
About right	33	26	45	33	40	26	39	29
Don't know	6	2	2	12	4	4	3	8

	Political affiliation				Sex		Household type		
	Conservative	Labour	Lib/SDP	None/Don't know	Male	Female	Pensioners	Non-pensioners With children	Non-pensioners Without children
State pensions:									
Too high	1	3	0	0	1	1	0	1	1
Too low	52	66	62	64	63	54	61	56	63
About right	38	20	29	31	27	32	38	28	28
Don't know	9	11	10	15	9	13	1	15	9
Unemployment benefit:									
Too high	14	3	11	9	8	10	9	10	7
Too low	18	62	41	38	46	35	22	46	38
About right	36	12	28	23	26	24	21	24	29
Don't know	32	23	20	30	21	32	49	20	26
Child benefit:									
Too high	23	11	19	15	15	17	27	12	20
Too low	13	34	22	26	26	23	12	32	15
About right	49	38	40	38	37	45	30	48	37
Don't know	16	17	19	21	22	15	31	8	29
Supplementary benefit:[a]									
Too high	3	2	1	4	3	2	3	2	3
Too low	47	73	56	59	57	61	40	65	58
About right	44	24	38	27	35	31	45	28	35
Don't know	6	2	5	11	5	6	11	4	4

[a] Respondents were informed that people who are not working on supplementary benefit received £59.20 a week, excluding rent, for a family with two young children.

professional, managerial and clerical workers. This probably reflects its much greater significance in relation to total household income for poorer families. Even so, a clear majority of professional and managerial workers (55 per cent) thought that the level of child benefit was either too low or about right.

Some interesting variations emerge by sex and household type. Women are less sympathetic to higher pensions and unemployment benefit than are men. Despite the fact that they are the main beneficiaries, women are no more sympathetic to child benefit than men, though fewer are uncertain in their answers. Pensioners are only fractionally more sympathetic to higher pensions than non-pensioners, but they are much less sympathetic to unemployment benefit, child benefit and supplementary benefit. Families are much more likely than the childless to think that child benefit is too low.

Some of the biggest differences occur by political affiliation (Table 9.6). While a majority of supporters of each of the three major parties thought that pensions were too low, a higher proportion of Labour (66 per cent) and Liberal/SDP (62 per cent) supporters thought so than did Conservative (52 per cent). The differences in attitudes to the other benefits, especially unemployment benefit, are much sharper. Thus, 14 per cent of Conservatives, 11 per cent of Liberal/SDP and only 3 per cent of Labour supporters thought unemployment benefit was too high, while more than three times the proportion of Labour supporters (62 per cent) thought it was too low compared with Conservatives (18 per cent), with Liberal/SDP supporters roughly in the middle. A similar pattern emerges with child benefit and supplementary benefit, with Labour supporters much more sympathetic than Liberal/SDP supporters and Conservatives least in favour of increases.

Nevertheless, only a small minority of those polled, even among Conservatives, thought any of the benefits were too high. As we have seen, the survey was conducted at a time of considerable speculation about government plans for benefit levels following cuts in earlier years. These results reveal little support for such cuts if they had been enacted.

The *Breadline Britain* survey therefore indicates both a more generous attitude towards benefits and less ambivalence in the public mind on these issues than were found in most earlier surveys. Earlier surveys have shown a fairly mixed view about welfare services, benefits and their recipients – a high level of satisfaction and support for many welfare services (especially the National Health Service, education and pensions), but at the same time a lack of sympathy for some groups of recipients, a feeling that some claimants are 'scroungers', and opposition to what are perceived as indiscriminate benefits to the undeserving. Although such views have persisted, they now appear less prevalent and less strongly held. The unemployed and unemployment benefit in particular are now viewed with much greater sympathy than in the past.

The low-paid

In the policy debates on tackling poverty, a recurrent theme has been the relative importance of intervention in the labour market, or tackling inequalities at source, compared with wider policies of income maintenance through the tax and social security system. Low pay, of course, is not the only cause of poverty, but it accounts for about one-quarter of those living below the supplementary benefit level and about one-third of those living in poverty on the *Breadline Britain* basis (Table 6.5). In the *Breadline Britain* survey, 76 per cent agreed that differences in pay between the highly and the lowly paid are too great (Table 7.7). Turning to policies for the low-paid two-thirds supported the introduction of a minimum wage (Table 9.7). Such support was also relatively uniform across income levels and social classes. This of itself does not indicate a recognition of the role of low wages as a key source of poverty, but it does suggest substantial sympathy.

In the past, attempts have been made to improve the relative earnings of the low-paid. These have included biasing income policies in favour of the low-paid, and minimum

Table 9.7   *Support for a minimum wage (percentages)*

'The government should introduce a minimum wage for all workers'	All house-holds	Net equivalent household income Poorest 10%	Richest 10%	AB	Social class C1	C2	D	E
Agree	66	71	70	58	65	66	75	66
Disagree	28	23	29	38	31	28	20	27
Don't know	5	6	2	4	4	6	5	7

'The govern-ment should introduce a minimum wage for all workers'	Conser-vative	Political affiliation Labour	Lib/SDP	None/ Don't know	Sex Male	Female
Agree	62	68	80	60	68	65
Disagree	34	23	17	34	30	27
Don't know	3	9	2	6	3	7

wages legislation in certain industries. Neither has been particularly successful in narrowing wage differentials. Indeed, the gap between high and low earnings has hardly changed since the turn of the century.

Tackling low pay itself would not solve the problem of poverty. Indeed, many of the lowest paid are not in poverty: they have few dependants or are one of two earners in the family. Raising the relative pay of those on low earnings would therefore have a relatively limited impact on the totality of poverty, though it would contribute to reducing inequalities. Interventions in the labour market nevertheless, still have an important role to play in anti-poverty policy. Attempts to limit that intervention by the first Thatcher administration have undoubtedly contributed to the deteriorating position of the low-paid since 1979. The Wages Council system designed to set minimum wage levels in low-paying industries was weakened. The number of wages inspectors was cut by one-third, and Wages Councils themselves were encouraged to award low increases. From 1979 to 1982, the gross earnings of the lowest-paid manual workers rose by 42 per cent, while those of the highest-paid white-collar workers rose by 63 per cent. This helps to emphasise that tackling poverty requires a combined approach on earnings, benefits and taxation.

The growing support for welfarism

In Chapter 7 it was found that there was substantial support for the aims of reducing poverty and of redistribution to secure a more equal society. In this chapter, we have looked at how far people are prepared to back the means that could achieve these aims.

Throughout the postwar history of the welfare state, public attitudes to welfare spending have been mixed and fluctuating. The public have been concerned about certain key social problems such as poverty and ill-health, and have generally endorsed the implicit objective of welfare spending to promote greater equality. Generally, however, they have proved to be less supportive when it comes to the policies themselves. Comparison of Tables 7.1 and 9.1, for example, shows that in 1979, despite 87 per cent support for increased government spending to get rid of poverty, small majorities also felt that spending on social services should be cut back and that welfare benefits had gone too far. Similarly, support for certain key benefits such as unemployment and child benefit has often been at best lukewarm.

Although this discriminating attitude has persisted, it is not nearly as pronounced now as in the past. There is not only overwhelming opposition to cuts in public spending on health and education and also on housing, social security and public transport; in addition the public seem willing to pay more in taxes to help those in need. Moreover, a majority feel that not only pensions are too low, but also supplementary benefit. Although there was not a majority who felt that unemployment benefit is too low, it is much more sympathetically viewed than in the past. Only child benefit continues to be viewed with antipathy, and even that is not overwhelming.

This softening of social opinion is probably explained by

the deepening of the recession and the widening experience of unemployment and of claiming benefits. The public now appear to recognise the inadequacy of benefit levels, and to show greater sympathy to benefits, to claimants and to some items of welfare spending that have previously been viewed with some suspicion. Such sympathy, however, is far from powerful enough to give much hope to the poor of an immediate improvement in their relative position. Nor is there much evidence that this shift represents any more of a permanent change than the apparent hardening of attitudes in the late 1970s proved to be. What is clear, however, is that, while Mrs Thatcher may be able to continue to nibble away at the edges of the welfare state without meeting overwhelming public resistance, she will encounter a very hostile public reaction if she tries to follow her convictions and go much further.

Conclusions

10

The Future
What hope for the poor?

> The future to me doesn't hold much hope for me or my family.
> There's no prospects really that I can see of a better job, though I
> might get one if I'm lucky. I don't see any prospect for my children
> 'cos the way things are it looks as though there's gonna be a lot more
> people out of work and – I just don't feel right about it. You know,
> I feel as though I've brought my children into a world that's just
> dying. [Low-paid father of three]

To the poor, the future looks bleak. They see no end to the
problems they have experienced during the 1980s. The
government's much-proclaimed 'economic recovery' seems
to bear no relationship to what they observe: jobs become no
easier to find, benefits remain piteously low. To those, like
Ernie, who lived through the unemployment of the 1930s,
events have an all-too familiar ring:

> I remember the March, the Jarrow Marches, when they
> marched from the north up to London. What's happen-
> ing today is only a repetition. We're back to square one
> aren't we. . . . I'm right pessimistic about the future.
> There doesn't seem to be no way out for people. It's a
> grim prospect for the future. I know it sounds rather
> severe but you can't help but see the way things are
> going.

The recession has made the whole nation poorer, but it is
as a result of the government's policies that the impact of this
declining prosperity has been concentrated on the poor. It is
not just that the government has done little to mitigate the

effects of the recession for the poor; it has positively encouraged the widening of inequality.

Against this background of unemployment, higher even than in the 1930s, and the most hostile political climate for the poor since the war, the findings of this book, somewhat surprisingly, offer a small glimmer of hope for the poor.

The public's definition of unacceptable living standards

The first glimmer of hope comes from the public's view of what constitutes unacceptable living standards for Britain in the 1980s. The survey's findings of the public's perception of necessities are, perhaps, its most important because it is the first time ever that this crucial area has been explored. As reported in Chapter 3, the public take a relative view of needs that is in accord with present-day experience.

In Chapters 4 and 5, we explored how the living standards of the poor compare to this minimum standard set down by society as a whole. The evidence was conclusive: *the poor of today are too poor*. This, it should be stressed, is based not on our personal value judgements (though it is one we share) but on the judgements of the majority of people in Britain, who think that the poor are entitled to more.

The government, however, has consistently refused to take seriously the fact that the poor have unmet needs. Dr Rhodes Boyson, who, as Minister for Social Security, was theoretically in charge of assessing the poor's needs, commented to the House of Commons on the *Breadline Britain* findings reported in the television series:

> The interesting point which the programme suggested is that if someone does not have three things out of 24, he is poor. Those three things could be refrigerators, washing machines and carpets in all living rooms and bedrooms, whereas 50 years ago, or even 25 years ago,

people merely aspired to have such things.
(*Hansard*, 28 June 1984)

Quite apart from giving an inaccurate and misleading account of the survey's findings, Dr Boyson has failed to grasp the essence of 'need'. The observation that the poor of yesteryear managed without goods that were not invented is hardly astute, but what is more it is not relevant. An overwhelming majority of people think that there is more to life than just existing. The key point of the *Breadline Britain* findings is that people today *do* see goods such as refrigerators as necessities for living in Britain today, even though people can clearly survive without such goods.

In Chapter 6, we summarised the survey's findings on deprivation, and developed, for the first time ever, a measure of poverty based on a consensual view of need. We estimated that around 7.5 million people could be said to be 'in poverty' and a further 4.5 million people 'on the margins of poverty'. All the 7.5 million people classed as in poverty found their lives diminished to the extent that they fell below what society at large believes to be a minimum acceptable way of life.

It was not just that they could not afford to go on holiday or that they could not afford a refrigerator – though these would be deprivations by the standards of today – but that their whole way of life was affected. Many could not afford modest items of food, such as a roast joint of meat; many could not afford to clothe themselves according to the minimum standards of today, lacking, for example, a warm water-proof coat; virtually all could not afford the kinds of leisure activities that make life more than just a matter of existing. The personal consequences are a life that is often depressing and nearly always full of worry. This is the reality of 'relative' poverty in Britain in the 1980s.

While this poverty may not be recognised by the present Conservative government, it is based on the public's perceptions. These perceptions offer hope, albeit limited, of a restraining hand on the government's actions. But there is also a glimmer of hope from other public attitudes.

The public's support for policies to help the poor

In May 1979, Mrs Thatcher won the general election committed to a radical change in the role of government. During this century, 'state welfarism gradually triumphed over the market' (Halsey, 1984). Mrs Thatcher set out to overturn this conquest. Ever since the early 1970s, the old Butskellite consensus about the importance of state responsibility in social welfare had looked increasingly vulnerable. As has been seen in Chapter 8, the stage had been set for social and economic changes that would not have been thought possible less than a decade before.

In the event, Mrs Thatcher's first term in office brought only limited changes in policies towards the poor, though, as seen in Chapter 1, these were almost entirely to the detriment of the poor. The government's aims, however, remain the same. In particular, it is desperately searching for ways of cutting welfare spending. The government has launched a series of reviews of the social security system due to report in 1985. While the emphasis is on greater efficiency (an aim that few would dispute), the reviews are in the context of reducing, or (given the rising numbers of elderly) at least constraining, spending. So, are the public prepared to see a cutback in welfare support for the poor?

The evidence presented suggests that any shift away from welfarism would not be welcomed. Indeed, in Chapter 7, we saw that overwhelming majorities support the broad objectives of reducing poverty and inequality. There is clear evidence of a substantial shift in opinion over recent years. People show an improved understanding of the causes of poverty and have substantial sympathy with welfare claimants – the poor are seen as more deserving and less the victims of their own ineptitude. In Chapter 9, we saw that support for welfare spending was also stronger. Moreover, people show a marked willingness to pay for help for those in need (75 per cent supporting a tax rise of 1p in the pound). Such views are widely held by people of different classes, income levels and political affiliations.

This is not to suggest, however, that there is at present

public support for a wholesale attack on poverty. Increasing spending on social security is still well down people's list of priorities. Even in the relatively supportive mood found in the early 1980s, a majority of people did *not* positively support *greater* spending on the key areas of unemployment benefit and child benefit.

However, in the current political climate, the survey's finding that only a small minority of people favour a *reduction* in state spending on the poor is more relevant. There is no widespread public support for a radical onslaught on the welfare state or any widening of inequalities. This is of interest in the light of the Conservative's election victory in June 1983.

On the surface, the findings reported in this study and the Conservative's election victory may appear to be contradictory. People profess overwhelming support for helping the poor and for a more equal society – but re-elected a government that had presided over a sharp increase in poverty and a widening of inequalities. At the very same time that the Conservatives won by a landslide, the majority of people were *not* in sympathy with the general drift of their welfare policies. These contradictions may appear to suggest that people's support for welfarism and the poor is only superficial. There are several reasons for believing that this may not be the case.

First, although Mrs Thatcher increased her parliamentary majority, her share of the vote fell marginally to around 43 per cent. More than half those voting actually voted against the government. The Conservative's overwhelming majority in parliament is the result not of an overwhelming endorsement of 'Thatcherism' but of the split in the opposition, which had resulted from the acute pre-election problems of the Labour party.

Second, the election was fought on much wider issues than the future of welfarism and certainly not specifically on the future for the poor. In particular, the election was dominated not so much by issues as by the personality of Mrs Thatcher and the credibility of the Labour party.

Third, when issues connected with poverty were on the

agenda, they did not necessarily work against the Conservatives. Although unemployment was a dominant issue in the election, the government was not, in the main, seen to be to blame for the sharp rise in unemployment and the Labour party's pledges were not believed (MORI, 1983). Further, as we have seen in Chapter 7, the Conservatives have been careful to hide both the impact of their past policies and their real intentions on welfare policies, even chiding Labour leaders during the election campaign for suggesting that they were planning a rundown of the welfare state.

The government often states, in defence of its policies, that it has been given an overwhelming mandate from the people. As regards the effects of its policies on the poor, this does not seem to be the case. People did not vote on the issue of poverty. To the extent that the issue was even considered, the distinctions between the parties seemed to many to be blurred. And to the extent that people recognised the increased problems for the poor under Mrs Thatcher's first administration and were concerned about it, they may well have been *more* concerned about other issues such as an 'undefended' Britain.

Certainly, the evidence presented suggests that, even among Conservative voters, there is *no* support for any winding down of the welfare state *or* for the kinds of deteriorations in the living standards of the poor that have taken place over the last five years. Indeed, there is now a very public strand of Conservatism that opposes the government on precisely these issues. Sitting on the Conservative benches in Westminster is an 'alternative' government of ex-cabinet ministers. Even before the election, Sir Ian Gilmour set out to restate 'the traditional views of my party' in his latest book *Britain Can Work* (1983). He wished for a return to a form of Conservatism concerned not just with economic doctrine but also with social conditions. In support, he quoted Harold Macmillan:

'It is only so far as poverty is abolished that freedom is increased.' (Gilmour, 1983)

This was echoed by Peter Walker, the last remaining 'wet' in the cabinet, at the Conservative Party Conference in October 1984 when he declared that the 'freedom' of private enterprise was only one aspect of a free society:

> Freedom in the fullest meaning of that word includes the freedom from humiliation and the restraints of poverty.

Francis Pym publicly joined the attack in *The Politics of Consent:*

> It is significant that Margaret Thatcher has seldom visited those areas that have suffered most during the recession and that her election campaign of 1983 involved a studiously selected route through the more prosperous parts of the country. This has increased the sense that the Government cares only about part of the nation and not all of it. (Pym, 1984, p. 14)

The *Breadline Britain* findings provide ammunition for those who wish to place a restraining hand on the government, to encourage a move away from the economic and social policies that have increased poverty. When the television series was transmitted in the summer of 1983, *The Sunday Times* ran a report of some of the main findings. The lessons they drew in an accompanying editorial were for the government:

> One set of people may draw one very simple moral from our reports. Mrs Thatcher's cabinet is, on the whole, a wealthy one. Michael Heseltine, Cecil Parkinson and Peter Walker are reputedly millionaires, while the prime minister herself has never had to worry where the next joint was coming from. That in itself need not disqualify them from an understanding of poverty, since this requires not direct experience, but sympathetic imagination.
> Yet, too often, it is precisely this that the cabinet

collectively has seemed to lack, its rhetoric and increasingly its policies based on all the old, populist prejudices against the poor. Again today, we report more of its plans to cut the state benefits on which the fate of most poor people mostly hangs. Of course, the need to curb public spending is understood, but, in a state budget of £126 billion, does it really have to be at the expense of those who already have so little? (*The Sunday Times*, 28 August 1983)

The future

The groundswell of support for a more 'compassionate' face to the government's policies may prevent the kind of radical changes in social policy favoured by some members of the cabinet. But this, in itself, offers little hope for the poor. Their living standards may still continue to decline, if slowly; at best, the relative deterioration of the last few years may be halted. Even against the backdrop of the anti-welfarism of the 1980s, this would be a very modest achievement.

Part I of this book demonstrated both the inadequacy of the living standards faced by the poor and the enormous scale of the deficiency. In Chapter 6, we estimated that to make any significant impact on the problems of those in poverty a rise in minimum incomes to at least 133 per cent of the current supplementary benefit level was needed. To 'solve' the problem, a rise of nearer 150 per cent was needed. These estimates, we stress again, are rough but they do give an indication of the scale of the problem.

The problem is not only huge, however, it is also desperately serious for many. Among the 7.5 million people living in poverty, there are some 2.5 million people, including nearly 1 million children, whose lives are diminished and demeaned in *every* way so far do they fall below the minimum standards of society today. Every one of these 2.5 million people will have poor and inadequate clothing, an unbalanced and unattractive diet, and long ago they will have cut out leisure activities; most will also face bad housing conditions, miss out on important social activities (such as celebrating Christmas) and have inadequate heating. This is the reality of poverty in Britain in the 1980s.

Effective help for the poor needs much more than halting the decline in their living standards since the late 1970s. What is needed is a sharp improvement in their position. What chance is there, then, for positive changes aimed at this kind of improvement?

One thing is clear. The scale of the problem is such that it would not be possible to 'end' poverty at a stroke or even within the lifetime of a parliament. It would be naive and misleading to suggest that the objective of eliminating poverty was immediately obtainable. The measures that would be required would not, at present, gain public support. While the public are generally sympathetic to the needs of the poor, the extent to which people are prepared to make personal sacrifices is limited. A majority of people are not prepared to support a policy of raising taxes by 5p in the pound to help the poor; and even these sorts of sums, while making a substantial impact on meeting the needs of the poor, would not be enough to 'solve' the problem.

This does not mean, however, that the poor's future need continue to be bleak. The *Breadline Britain* survey has shown that the large majority of people recognise that the circumstances in which the poor live are *unacceptable* in Britain today. Mrs Thatcher may believe that 'people who are living in need are fully and properly provided for', but most people do not view the meagre standards of living suffered by the poor in this way. The government's complacency and indifference are not shared by others. People do accept that the problems of the poor *should* be tackled, and that the *state* has a responsibility to tackle them. These are deep-seated beliefs about the kind of society in which people wish to live – a society in which everyone is *entitled* to a minimum standard of living that is about more than just existing.

However, if the future for the poor is to be substantially improved, support is also needed for the *policies* that will translate the objectives set down in terms of people's minimum living standards into reality. While the public at large do not back the kind and extent of policies needed, there is a substantial body of opinion that would support such policies: over one-third of voters said they *would* support a policy of raising taxes by 5p in the pound, a rise in income tax that is, by any standards, substantial. The question, then, becomes: to what extent can the existing level of support for redistributive policies be built upon? This, in turn, will depend on how people's attitudes to such policies are formed; in particular, on how far they stem from self-interest as opposed to wider ideological values, social pressures and political views.

In recent years, the fashion has been to assume that people act primarily out of 'self-interest' rather than a wider sense of obligation and responsibility. The 'pursuit' of self-interest is central to the government's philosophy, but the concept of the 'primacy' of self-interest has wider currency. For example, Peter Taylor-Gooby has argued: 'Attitudes to welfare are bounded by a calculus of self-interest rather than Titmuss's theme of social integration through the gift relationship' (Taylor-Gooby, 1983b).

The evidence of the *Breadline Britain* survey suggests, by contrast, that people are guided by a mixture of motives. Undoubtedly, self-interest does play an important role: in general, the poor and the working class reveal attitudes that are more pro-poor and pro-welfare than those of the better-off and the middle class. Such patterns are by no means universal, however. The rich and the middle class do show consistently strong support for a range of welfare policies. Clear majorities support egalitarian policies: for example, a significant proportion of the rich favour an increase in tax of as much as 5p in the pound to help the poor. This is not to say that such attitudes are explained solely, or even mainly, in terms of altruism. The middle class are likely to be well aware of how they benefit from the universal aspects of welfarism such as pensions, child benefit, the National Health Service and education. In recent years, the middle class commitment to welfarism may also have been strengthened by the spreading risk of unemployment.

None the less, support for greater equality by higher

income groups is unlikely to be explained by pure self-interest. Altruism, or at least a wider sense of social obligation, does appear to play a role in the formation of attitudes. In general, the findings support an alternative view of human action, put forward by Amartya Sen:

> The operations of a society depend heavily on codes that guide behaviour and the way interests and obligations are perceived. It is hard to explain human behaviour purely in terms of self-interest. (Sen, 1984, p. 25)

These findings are of importance. An appeal to self-interest can be a significant element in winning support for improved anti-poverty measures; in particular, for those that are based on universal principles. In the final analysis, however, tackling the problem of poverty requires a substantial redistribution in society from the top half to the bottom half, and in particular to the bottom 15 per cent. Such policies would certainly conflict with the pure self-interest of most of the better-off. Widespread support for re-distribution thus depends on people's attitudes stemming from a wider set of motivations. The evidence of the survey suggests that this is, to some extent, the case. As such, the survey's findings hold out the possibility that support for redistributive policies could be built not just among the poor but also among those who are not poor, a far larger group of people. This, in turn, is important: redistributive policies are, in our view, likely to be adopted only if they have the broad support of the majority of people.

The difficulties involved should not be underestimated. The evidence of even the very limited attempts at re-distribution under previous Labour governments suggests that resistance by those with a strong vested interest in the present inequalities would be fierce. Bringing about re-distribution would require great political will, far greater than previously demonstrated; and it would require a concerted attempt to win public support for an egalitarian programme. The Labour party, while paying lip-service to the idea of a more equal society, has largely failed to press its case. If it did, it could meet with some success: the survey's evidence suggests that the foundations exist in popular attitudes for building wider support for redistributive strategies.

We have not discussed in this book the precise mechanism for such a redistribution. This, though important, is secondary to establishing to whom money should be redistributed, and on what scale. We have proposed that this can be done on the basis of the public's perception of need. Using this, we have shown that the levels of benefit received by the poor should be increased substantially.

In 1984, the government established a 'review' of the benefits system. The intention was to find ways of making substantial cuts in social security spending. In this book, we have set out to establish an alternative objective by which to judge any changes in benefit – do the changes *reduce* poverty? The aim has been to shift the debate on the future of the social security system away from doctrinaire objectives of reducing public spending towards the unmet needs of the poor.

Without this shift in priorities, the future for the poor will, indeed, be bleak:

> I'm wondering whether it's worthwhile going on living, quite honestly. It's not living, it's existing. [A supplementary benefit claimant, aged 59]

Appendix A   The Likely Accuracy of the Findings

The survey was conducted by Market and Opinion Research International (MORI) on behalf of London Weekend Television's *Breadline Britain* series. (The following account of the technical details of the survey sample has been provided by Brian Gosschalk of MORI.)

The survey sample

Fieldwork took place between 15 and 24 February 1983 among a representative quota sample of 1,174 respondents aged 16 and over interviewed in their homes in eighty sampling points across Great Britain. The sample was designed to over-represent people living in deprived areas, and was then weighted to compensate for this design to produce a representative sample. The sampling points were stratified by region.

If the sample had not been designed to over-represent any particular demographic sub-group, it would have required a sample size considerably larger than around 1,200 in order to have a large enough sub-sample of households likely to be 'in poverty' as defined by the *Breadline Britain* programme makers (see pp. 49–53). Given the budget constraints, it was nor possible to adopt a much larger sample size than that achieved, and it was decided to use the ACORN sampling method to produce a sample of some 200 poor households.

ACORN (A Classification Of Residential Neighbourhoods) is an analysis of the social characteristics of small areas throughout Great Britain. It is based on census enumeration districts (EDs), the smallest unit of the census with 150 households on average. Cluster analysis of EDs, grouping them by forty variables encompassing demographic, house and employment characteristics, allows thirty-six neighbourhood types to be aggregated into eleven broad groups. For the purposes of the *Breadline Britain* survey, the over-sampling was confined to three ACORN groups: urban areas with local authority housing, areas with most overcrowding, and low-income areas with immigrants (ACORN groups F, G and H, in which some 20 per cent of the GB population live). Although ACORN sampling does have various disadvantages, it controls fieldwork tightly – unlike conventional quota sampling, which allows a fair amount of interviewer choice – and can be used for sampling purposes.

This is not the place to debate the relative merits of random versus quota sampling. Suffice to say, we felt the ACORN method appropriate for a survey on poverty, in that it gave a large enough sample of poor households while at the same time providing tight control of the sample (as in random sampling). Thus we could ensure that, for example, respondents on supplementary benefit were drawn from the most deprived as well as relatively 'better off' areas.

Fieldwork was conducted by NOP, a member of the Market Research Society's Interviewer Card Scheme. Ten per cent of all interviews were checked back by field supervisory staff to verify the completed questionnaires, including demographic details. All NOP interviewers undergo a standardised training programme before joining the panel of interviewers, and are personally accompanied, or their work subject to checks, by supervisory staff at regular intervals.

After weighting to adjust for the over-sampling of deprived areas, the sample profile was checked for representativeness of key demographic variables. No further weighting was applied other than to adjust for the ACORN sample.

In terms of statistical reliability, confidence limits can be calculated legitimately only for random samples (that is, where every person in the population has the same chance of selection). In practice, however, the experience of research agencies over many years has shown that random and quota sampling methods produce similar results. This is not so surprising, since quota sampling utilises additional known information about the population in order correctly to specify the structure of the sample. Strictly speaking, the following comments and figures apply to a random sample; however, they can be taken as a guide to the accuracy of the *Breadline Britain* findings.

Table A.1 shows the possible variation that might be anticipated because a sample, rather than the entire population, was interviewed. For example, for a question where 30 per cent of the people

Table A.1   *The reliability of the findings*

Number of interviewees	Approximate sampling tolerances[a] applicable to percentages at or near these levels		
	10% or 90%	30% or 70%	50%
	+ or −	+ or −	+ or −
1,200	2	3	3
500	3	4	4
200	4	6	7
150	5	7	8
100	6	9	10
50	8	13	14

[a]Based on 95 chances in 100.

in a weighted sample of 1,200 respond with a particular answer, the chances are 95 in 100 that this result would not vary more than 3 percentage points, plus or minus, from a complete coverage of the entire population using the same procedures. However, it is not true to conclude that the 'actual' result (95 times out of 100) lies anywhere between 27 per cent and 33 per cent – it is proportionately more likely to be closer to the centre of this band (30 per cent) than to lie at the extremes (27 per cent or 33 per cent). As indicated in Table A.1, the sampling tolerances vary with the size of the sample and the size of the percentage results.

Tolerances are also involved in the comparison of results from different parts of the sample. A difference, in other words, must be of at least a certain size to be considered statistically significant. Table A.2 is a guide to the sampling tolerances applicable to comparisons. These tolerances are based on a 95 per cent level of

Table A.2   *Comparing results for different groups*

Comparing groups of:	Differences required for significance[a] at or near these percentage levels		
	10% or 90%	30% or 70%	50%
	+ or −	+ or −	+ or −
1,000 and 1,000	3	4	4
1,000 and 200	5	7	8
1,000 and 100	6	9	10
200 and 200	6	9	10
100 and 100	8	13	14
50 and 50	12	18	20

[a]Based on 95 chances in 100.

significance; if a less rigorous test of significance was used (say the 90 per cent level), then the percentage differences required for significance would, of course, be smaller. Table A.2 shows that, using the 95 per cent level, the difference between two percentage results of, say, 29 per cent and 33 per cent would almost certainly be a statistically significant difference when based on samples of 1,000 interviews each. However, when these results occurred based on samples of 200 interviews each, the difference would almost certainly not be statistically significant.

The analysis of the findings

The likely accuracy of the findings, and the significance of differences between sub-groups, can be gained from Tables A.1 and A.2. When the findings are presented as referring to the population as a whole, they are based on the whole sample, that is, on nearly 1,200 interviewees. This means, in particular, that the findings on people's attitudes to necessities (reported in Chapter 3) and on the overall level of lack of necessities (reported in Chapter 4) are likely to be a good reflection of reality. The sub-groups of social class, age and household type generally include about 200 interviewees (the most important exception is single-parent families where the number of interviewees is about 50). The income groups used for all households were deciles and contained about 100 interviewees; when income groups for families alone have been examined, the higher-income decile groups have been combined to maintain samples of around 50–100.

The number of interviewees 'in poverty', as defined in the study (that is, the numbers lacking, through shortage of money, three or more necessities), is 206. This is likely to provide a fairly accurate description of the characteristics of those 'in poverty' as a whole. The numbers of interviewees lacking one or two necessities is over 250, again providing a fairly accurate picture of the characteristics of those on the margins of poverty. When sub-groups of those 'in poverty' are examined, the possible error range is greater. In particular, the sub-groups examined in Chapter 5 of those lacking, from shortage of money, three or four necessities, five or six necessities and seven or more necessities are in the range of 60–80 interviewees; as is the sub-group of people in 'intense poverty' examined in Chapter 6. The analysis of households on supplementary benefit is based on 241 interviewees.

Appendix B   The Questionnaire

The questionnaire for the *Breadline Britain* survey was entitled 'Living in Britain'.

Figures in italic indicate percentage responses to questions.
* = less than 0.5 per cent.

SHOWCARD A

Q.1   Here is a list of problems which some people have told us they face. Which, if any, of these are major problems facing you or your immediate family?

Mugging/vandalism *21*
Your own health *14*
The health of someone else in your family *19*
Not having enough money to make ends meet *29*
Poor local schools *6*
Poor public transport *10*
Unemployment *22*
Fear of unemployment *16*
Employment prospects for your children *24*
None of these *17*
Don't know/no opinion *6*

SHOWCARD B

Q.2   The things people can buy and do – their housing, furniture, food, cars, recreation and travel – make up their standard of living. How satisfied or dissatisfied do you feel about your standard of living at present?

Very satisfied *17*
Fairly satisfied *58*
Neither satisfied nor dissatisfied *8*
Fairly dissatisfied *10*
Very dissatisfied *7*
Don't know/no opinion .... *

Q.3   Overall, do you think your present standard of living is higher, lower or about the same as five years ago?

Q.4   And do you think it will be higher, lower or about the same, in five years time?

	(Q3)	*(Q4)*
Higher	26	29
About the same	34	34
Lower	39	28
Don't know	1	9

SHOWCARD C

Q.5a Here is a list of things the Government spends money on. If the Government had to reduce its spending, which *three* of these do you think it should cut its spending on?

Q.5b And if the Government intended to increase its spending, which *three* of these do you think it should increase its spending on?

	(5a) Cut	*(5b)* Increase
Local housing	12	29
Social Security benefits	23	19
National Health Service	2	59
Roads	17	20
Police	10	22
Education/schools	3	55
Grants to local authorities	25	9
Defence	45	10
Job training for the unemployed	13	38
Child benefits	20	16
Grants for regional development	39	6
None/no opinion	19	3

Q.6   I am going to read out a number of statements about Britain today. Please could you tell me whether you agree or disagree with each one.

	Agree	Disagree	Don't know
a) Differences in pay between the highly-paid and the lowly-paid are too great	76	20	4
b) The Government should increase taxation on the rich	63	32	5
c) There's no incentive for low paid workers to earn extra money because any gain disappears though deductions in benefit and extra taxes	79	17	4

d) The gap between the rich and the poor in
   Britain today is too wide 74   21   5

e) Britain's welfare system removes the
   incentive for people to help themselves 57   35   8

f) The government should introduce a
   minimum wage for all workers 66   28   5

ASK ALL WHO AGREE WITH LAST STATEMENT: (OTHERS GO TO Q8)

Q.7 **How much do you think the minimum wage before tax should be for full-time adult workers, excluding school leavers?**

Less than £40 per week	Less than £160 per month	0
£41– £ 50 per week	£160–200 per month	1
£51– £ 60 per week	£201–240 per month	4
£61– £ 70 per week	£241–280 per month	4
£71– £ 80 per week	£281–320 per month	13
£81– £ 90 per week	£321–360 per month	13
£91– £100 per week	£361–400 per month	23
Over £100 per week	Over £400 per month	32
Don't know	Don't know	10

SHOWCARD D

Q.8 **Here is a list of problems which some people say they have experienced in and around their homes. Which, if any, have been serious problems for you with your present home in the past year? (PROBE FOR ANY OTHER HOUSING-TYPE PROBLEMS AND WRITE IN)**

01	Broken windows	7
02	Damp/condensation	24
03	Mice/rats	4
04	Poor heating	20
05	Poor decoration inside	7
06	Lifts not working	1
07	Dirty/unpleasant environment	10
08	Poor decoration outside	10
09	Lack of places for children to play	21
10	Lack of recreational facilities for young people/adults	23
11	Too much noise	9
12	Heavy traffic	16
13	Some other problem(s) (WRITE IN)	9
14	None of these	29

SHUFFLE BOARD AND CARDS   EXCLUDE CARDS ASTERISKED, WHICH RELATE TO CHILDREN

Q.9   On these cards are a number of different items which relate to our standard of living. Please would you indicate by placing the cards in the appropriate box the living standards you feel all adults should have in Britain today. This box (POINTS TO BOX A) is for items which you think are necessary, and which all adults should be able to afford and which they should not have to do without; this box (POINT TO BOX B) is for items which may be desirable, but are not necessary.

GIVE CARDS RELATING TO CHILDREN*

Q.10   Now could you do the same, this time thinking of a family with children

	A Necessary should be able to afford	B Not necessary but may be desirable	Don't know
1 * An outing for children once a week	40	50	11
2 A garden	55	44	*
3 A roast meat joint or its equivalent once a week	67	32	1
4 Meat or fish every other day	63	35	1
5 Heating to warm living areas of the home if it's cold	97	2	*
6 A dressing gown	38	60	1
7 Two pairs of all weather shoes	78	21	*
8 New, not second hand clothes	64	34	1

10	Carpets in living rooms and bedrooms in the home	70	29	*
11	Telephone	43	56	1
12	Refrigerator	77	22	*
13	Indoor toilet (not shared with another household)	96	3	*
14	Bath (not shared with another household)	94	6	*
15	Beds for everyone in the household	94	6	*
16	Damp-free home	96	3	*
17	A car	22	76	1
18	Public transport for one's needs	88	11	*
19	A night out once a fortnight	36	62	1
20	A packet of cigarettes every other day	14	82	4
21	A hobby or leisure activity	64	34	*
22	A holiday away from home for one week a year, not with relatives	63	36	*
23	Celebrations on special occasions such as Christmas	69	30	1
24	Presents for friends or family once a year	63	36	1
25	Friends/family round for a meal once a month	32	66	1
26 *	Children's friends round for tea/a snack once a fortnight	37	53	10
27	A "best outfit" for special occasions	48	50	1
28	A washing machine	67	31	*
29 *	Three meals a day for children	82	8	10
30 *	Toys for children e.g. dolls or models	71	20	9
31	A warm water-proof coat	87	11	*
32 *	Leisure equipment for children e.g. sports equipment or a bicycle	56	35	9
33 *	Enough bedrooms for every child over 10 of different sex to have his/her own bedroom	77	15	8
34	Two hot meals a day	64	35	1
35	Self-contained accommodation	79	20	1

SHOWCARD E

Q.11 Why, in your opinion, are there people who live in need? Here are four opinions – which is the closest to yours?

Because they have been unlucky *13*
Because of laziness and lack of willpower *22*
Because there is much injustice in our society.......... *32*
It's an inevitable part of modern progress *25*
None of these *5*
Don't know *3*

Q.12 Still thinking about people who lack the things you have said are necessities for living in Britain today, do you think that the Government is doing too much, too little or, about the right amount to help these people?

Too much *6*
Too little *57*
About the right amount *33*
Don't know *4*

Q.13 If the Government proposed to increase income tax by one penny (1p) in the pound to enable everyone to afford the items you have said are necessities, on balance would you support or oppose this policy? IF SUPPORT AT Q13, ASK:

Q.14 If the Government proposed to increase income tax by five pence (5p) in the pound to enable everyone to afford the items you have said are necessities, on balance would you support or oppose this policy?

	Q.13		*Q.14*
Support	*74*	*GO TO* Q.14	*34*
Oppose	*20*	⎱ GO TO	*53*
Don't know	*6*	⎰ Q.15	*13*

SHUFFLE CARDS AND BOARD – REMOVE CARDS RELATING TO CHILDREN IF NO CHILDREN LIVING AT HOME

Q.15 Now, could you please put the cards into these four boxes: This box (POINT TO BOX A) is for the items you do have, and couldn't do without; this box (POINT TO BOX B) is for items you have, but could do without; this box (POINT TO BOX C) is for items you don't have but don't want; and this box (POINT TO BOX D) is for items you don't have and can't afford.

	A Have and couldn't do without	B Have and could do without	C Don't have but don't want	D Don't have and can't afford	Not applic- able/ Don't know
Base = 60% for items relating to children					
1 *An outing for children once a week	14	16	8	9	13
2 A garden	51	36	7	4	2
3 A roast meat joint or its equivalent once a week	48	37	6	7	1
4 Meat or fish every other day	47	34	9	8	1
5 Heating to warm living areas of the home it's cold	90	3	*	5	1
6 A dressing gown	33	52	10	3	1
7 Two pairs of all weather shoes	68	19	4	9	*
8 New, not second hand clothes	59	27	6	6	1
9 A television	51	46	1	*	*
10 Carpets in living rooms and bedrooms in the home	71	25	*	2	*
11 Telephone	51	30	6	11	1
12 Refrigerator	78	18	1	2	*

(Continued)

Base = 60% for items relating to children

	A Have and couldn't do without	B Have and could do without	C Don't have but don't want	D Don't have and can't afford	Not applicable/ Don't know
13 Indoor toilet (not shared with another household)	94	2	1	2	*
14 Bath (not shared with another household)	95	2	*	2	*
15 Beds for everyone in the household	94	3	1	1	1
16 Damp-free home	82	4	3	7	3
17 A car	37	23	16	22	1
18 Public transport for one's needs	63	23	7	3	3
19 A night out once a fortnight	19	36	26	17	1
20 A packet of cigarettes every other day	14	24	53	6	3
21 A hobby or leisure activity	50	28	12	7	1
22 A holiday away from home for one week a year, not with relatives	38	31	8	21	1
23 Celebrations on special occasions such as Christmas	61	32	3	4	*
24 Presents for friends or family once a year	58	33	3	5	*
25 Friends/family round for a meal once a week	24	40	20	11	4
26 *Childrens friends round for tea/a snack once a fortnight	10	21	10	5	13
27 A "best outfit" for special occasions	39	41	8	10	1
28 A washing machine	68	18	7	6	1

29	*Three meals a day for children	39	5	2	2	12
30	*Toys for children e.g. dolls or models	30	13	3	2	12
31	*A warm water-proof coat	81	8	3	7	*
32	*Leisure equipment for children e.g. sports equipment or a bicycle	22	16	4	6	12
33	*Enough bedrooms for every child over 10 of different sex to have his/her own bedroom	35	5	4	3	13
34	Two hot meals a day	53	26	17	3	*
35	Self-contained accommodation	87	7	3	3	1

Q.16 A number of people have told us they have had to miss out on meals because of a lack of money. Have there been times during the past year when you did not have enough money to buy food you (and your family) needed?

Yes 13
No 87
Don't know 1

SHOWCARD F

Q.17 For each of the items on this list, could you tell me whether you think their level is too high, too low or about right at present?

	Too high	Too low	About right	Don't know
State pensions	1	59	29	11
Unemployment benefit	9	40	24	27
Child benefit	16	24	41	18
Married man's allowance	4	37	28	31
Mortgage allowance	4	15	35	44

Q.18 People claiming supplementary benefit are people who are not working and who don't have enough to live on because their pension or income is below a certain minimum level. They receive £59.20 per week excluding rent for a family with two young children. Do you think this amount is too high, too low, or about right?

Too high 3
Too low 59
About right 33
Don't know 6

SHOWCARD G

Q.19 I'd now like to ask you some questions about supplementary benefits. I'm going to read out some statements and I'd like you to tell me how strongly you agree or disagree with each one.

	Strongly agree	Tend to agree	Neither agree nor disagree	Tend to disagree	Strongly disagree	Don't know
Most people claiming supplementary benefit are in real need	25	44	8	16	3	4
A lot of people who are entitled to claim supplementary benefit don't claim it	23	51	8	10	2	6
Many people claiming supplementary benefit are on the fiddle	25	37	9	17	6	7

Q.20 Have you or anyone in your family, excluding when a student, ever received supplementary benefits?

Yes *36*
No *63*
Don't know .... *

SHOWCARD H

Q.21 Have there been times during the past year when you were seriously behind in paying for any of the following items?

In arrears

Rent 7
Gas 5
Electricity 7
Goods on hire purchase 3
Mortgage 1
Rates 4
None of these 85

Q.22 And have there been times during the past year when you have had to borrow money from friends or family in order to pay for your day-to-day needs?

Yes 16
No 82
Don't know 2

Q.23 Do you think you could genuinely say you are poor now, all the time, sometimes or never?

All the time 12
Sometimes 28
Never 59
Don't know 1

SHOWCARD I

Q.24a A number of people have told us they have different kinds of personal difficulties these days. Which if any of the items on this card have you worried about or have you experienced in the past month due to lack of money?

Being depressed 18
Relations with your friends 3
Relations with your family 5
Being bored 15
Not having enough money for day-to-day living 17
Feeling looked down upon by other people 4
Feeling a failure 6
Lack of hope for the future 19
Letting down your family 9
None of these 58

Q.24b **Are you personally or is anyone in your immediate family unemployed at the moment or have any of you been unemployed in the past 12 months? RECORD WHO AND WHEN**

Respondent is now unemployed 14
Head of household is now unemployed 8
Other family member is now unemployed 9
Respondent has been in last 12 months 2
Head of household has been in last 12 months 2
Other family member has been in last 12 months 5
None unemployed and none been unemployed in last
12 months 66

Q.25 **Do you have any long-standing illness, disability or infirmity? By long-standing I mean anything that has troubled you over a period of time or that is likely to affect you over a period of time.**

Yes 23
No 77

Q.26 **Generally speaking, do you think of yourself as Conservative, Labour, Liberal, Social Democrat, Nationalist, or what?**

Conservative 30
Labour 29
Liberal 10
SDP/Social Democrat 6
Scottish Nationalist (SNP) 1
Other 1
None/Don't know 23

Q.27 I would like to ask you some questions about your income. It's important for the accuracy of our survey for us to know the amount of money people have coming in each week/month. Could you please tell me the current income from his/her job of the main wage earner, after tax and deductions? (REPEAT FOR ALL WAGE EARNERS IN THE HOUSEHOLD)

WRITE IN

Main wage earner ....

Other wage earner ....

Other wage earner ....

SHOWCARD J

Q.28 Which if any of these do you or does anyone living in this household receive?

A state pension 26
A private pension e.g. from previous
    employer 18
Unemployment benefit 10
Sickness benefit 2
Invalidity benefit 5
Supplementary benefit 15
Family income supplement 1
Child benefit 44
Other state benefit 3
Maintenance payments 1
Income from savings/investments 16
Income from second job 3
(26)
Other income e.g. rent, shares, etc ... 3
None of these 15   – GO TO Q.31

Q.29 How many people in this household receive ...... (READ OUT EACH ITEM MENTIONED AT Q.28)

	None	One	Two	Three+
		Base = 85%		
A state pension	59	14	12	1
A private pension e.g. from previous employer	68	16	2	*

Unemployment benefit 75	9	1	*
Sickness benefit 83	2	*	0
Invalidity benefit 80	5	1	0
Supplementary benefit........70	13	1	1
Family income supplement ...84	1	0	*
Child benefit 41	19	17	8
Other state benefit 82	3	0	*
Maintenance payments 84	1	*	*
Income from savings/invest-ment 70	8	5	2
Income from second job 82	2	1	*
Other income e.g. rent, shares, etc 82	2	1	*

Q.30 In total, and after tax and other deductions, how much do people in this household receive each week from ...... (READ OUT ITEMS MENTIONED AT Q.28)

Amount (WRITE IN)

A state pension ....

A private pension e.g. from previous
    employer ....

Unemployment benefit ....

Sickness benefit ....

Invalidity benefit ....

Supplementary benefit ....

Family income supplement ....

Child benefit ....

Other state benefit ....

Maintenance payments ....

Income from savings/investment ....

Income from second job ....

Other income e.g. rent, shares, etc ....

Q.31 How much do you pay in rent or mortgage payments each week/month? If you don't know the exact figure, what is it approximately? (WRITE IN)

. . . .

Q.32 And what do you pay in rates each month/year? Again if you don't know the exact figures, what is it approximately? (WRITE IN)

. . . .

QUESTIONS 33–35 TO BE ASKED ONLY OF THOSE RECEIVING SUPPLEMENTARY BENEFIT AT Q.28: OTHERS GO TO Q.36

SHOWCARD B AGAIN

Q.33 How satisfied or dissatisfied are you with the service you get from your local DHSS office?

Base = 15%

Very satisfied	3
Fairly satisfied	6
Neither satisfied nor dissatisfied	1
Fairly dissatisfied	1
Very dissatisfied	3
Don't know	*

Q.34 Do you receive payment in the form of a giro cheque through the post every fortnight? IF YES: Does it arrive . . . . . . (READ OUT)

Base = 15%

Regularly on the correct day	4
Late occasionally	1
Often late	*
No, don't receive fortnightly giro cheques	8
Don't know	*

Q.35 When you claim supplementary benefit, how do you feel about it? Would you agree or disagree with these statements:

Base = 15%

	Agree	Disagree	Neither/ D.K.
a) It is a right which I am entitled to ...	13	1	*
b) I would rather not claim it, but have to because I need the money	13	1	*
c) I feel embarrassed about claiming it ..	6	8	*
d) I find it difficult to manage on the amount of benefit I receive	11	3	1
e) I would rather receive more money in supplementary benefit than have improved social services such as hospitals	4	7	2

ASK ALL

Q.36 And finally, I've been asking you all these questions for one of the ITV television companies. They'd be very interested in talking directly to some of the people who have helped in the survey. They do not at this stage want to ask to film you, just to talk to you. Would you be prepared to be contacted by the television company?

Yes 45
No 55

GO TO DEMOGRAPHICS

Appendix C   Income: Concepts and Problems

It is notoriously difficult to establish accurate income data through surveys, and the *Breadline Britain* survey was no exception. Throughout this study, the income concept used is *net equivalent household income* – and at each stage measurement difficulties arose.

The income measure

The most basic problems arose with the measure of 'income' itself. First, there was the question of deciding what constitutes income. The *Breadline Britain* survey collected data only on *cash* income, earned and unearned. A comprehensive measure of the resources that govern people's living standards would have required a far more detailed set of questions and these were excluded for reasons of cost. The significance of these limitations can be assessed from the Townsend study (1979), which compiled a comprehensive measure of resources. Townsend traced the value and distribution of five types of resources: net disposable cash income, the annuity value of assets held, employer welfare benefits in kind, public social services in kind and private income in kind. Of these five types, net disposable cash incomes less income from property and investment formed about three-fifths of the grand total, imputed income from assets another fifth, and the other three resources the remaining fifth. Townsend concludes:

> Although net disposable income, less income from property and investment, is by far the most important component of the resources on which the population depends for its living standards, other resources are also important. (Townsend, 1979, p. 225)

The measure used in this study is not directly comparable to the first of these types, as it includes some measure of income from investment and savings. Nevertheless, Townsend's findings do show that confining the measure of resources to cash income does pose real limitations. Moreover, the distribution of these non-cash resources is unequal. Townsend found that, for every type of resource, the 20 per cent of households with the highest net disposable incomes received the highest money value of other types of resources: 'their advantage in respect of imputed income from assets and employer welfare benefits is striking, though not surprising, but they also had a higher value of social services in kind' (Townsend, 1979, p. 233).

Since the 1960s, when the Townsend survey was conducted, the importance of these non-cash resources to higher-income groups has increased, for example through the spread and range of fringe employment benefits. This means that the simple measure of income taken in this study underestimates the difference in resources between those in the upper half of the income range and those in the lower half. It also means that the distribution of households within each income decile would to some degree change: some households that have been allocated to an income decile on the basis of their cash income would be allocated to a different group if a more complete view of their resources were taken. This is important to bear in mind when the tightness of the fit between cash income and living standards is being considered.

The accuracy of the income data

The second major problem relates to the accuracy of the income data collected.

Some respondents simply refused to answer questions about income. Information was provided by only 74 per cent of households. While this is not a particularly low response rate overall compared with other surveys, non-response is not evenly spread across income groups. Table C.1 compares the socio-economic breakdown of the whole sample and of non-respondents. Among the non-respondents, households from socio-economic groups AB are heavily over-represented, while those from group E are heavily under-represented. Given that income is positively related to socio-economic group, this suggests that the income information is weighted towards lower-income groups, leading to both a downward bias in mean income and an understatement of the extent of inequality.

Those who do answer do not necessarily give accurate information: they are being asked about not just their *own* income but that

Table C.1   *Income non-respondents by socio-economic group (percentages)*

Socio-economic group	Income non-respondents	Whole sample
AB	24	15
C1	20	20
C2	31	28
D	19	19
E	6	19
All groups	100	100

of the *household*; while most people have a rough idea of what benefits they receive and what they earn, they may well not know about their husband's or wife's, mother's and father's, son's and daughter's, or may not be prepared to divulge such information even if they are prepared to give information about their own income. Further, there is a known tendency in surveys for certain forms of income to be understated, such as earnings by the self-employed and by those in part-time employment and income from savings and investment.

The net effect of these various factors is threefold. First, average recorded income is lower than actual income. Second, the extent of inequality is understated. Third, some households may get misplaced in the income ranking. A tentative estimate of the extent of these biases is shown in Table C.2, which compares Family Expenditure Survey income data with the *Breadline Britain* data.

Table C.2   *A comparison of household income distributions*

Income groups	Family Expenditure Survey data[a] as a percentage of the Breadline Britain data
Lowest decile	108
Lower quartile	112
Median	132
Upper quartile	135
Highest decile	124

[a]The latest Family Expenditure Survey figures refer to 1981; these have been updated to February 1983, the date of the *Breadline Britain* survey, by using the average earnings index for all employees, equal to 1.154.

Sources: LWT/MORI, 1983; Department of Employment, 1982.

This confirms that income is understated: the median income, for example, should be about 32 per cent higher than that found in the survey. The extent of inequality is also understated, particularly in the lower half of the distribution. These factors mean that the relationships between income and living standards explored in the book are less significant than they would be with more accuate and reliable income data.

The income unit

Next, it was necessary to decide what 'unit' the income measure was going to cover; that is, whether it is most sensible to take individuals separately, families or households. While a number of the necessities refer to individual rather than household possession, an individual measure of income is not particularly helpful: people who live together pool their resources, to some degree or other. It is more sensible therefore to take either a family or household measure, though this does have its limitations: in particular, the share of the household income received by wives can vary considerably. The more difficult question, however, is to decide how far such pooling extends: if, for example, granny is living with her daughter's family, is it most sensible to talk about the 'family' unit, which would exclude granny, or the 'household' unit, which would include granny. There are no universally accepted rules and different studies have taken different approaches.

In this study, the 'household' unit is used and the respondent has decided who does and who does not class as a member of the household. The income of the household includes the income of every member of the household. While this approach has the advantage of reflecting people's actual living patterns, it does mean that to some extent like is not always being compared with like: for example, if the granny living with her daughter's family in a divided house had been a respondent, she may have classed herself as living on her own but she is likely to be considerably better off in practice than an elderly person living completely on their own with a similar income. Again, such factors mean that the relationship between living standards and income is not as close as it would be if the income units had been more directly comparable.

Equivalence scales

The next problem relates to the differences in the size and composition of these household units. On average, larger households have higher incomes than smaller households, yet they are generally less well-off because there are more people in the household. At the most basic level, the household income needs to be adjusted for the number of people in the household. In reality, however, the questions are more complicated. A husband and wife do not incur twice the expenses of a single person to maintain the same standard of living. In general terms, the problem is how to 'adjust' household income so that the 'adjusted' income of different types of household reflects the same standard of living. The weights used to adjust incomes of different household types to yield the same standard of living are known as 'equivalence scales'. This principle also underlies the supplementary benefit system, and the implicit equivalence scales in supplementary benefit as of November 1982 are shown in Table C.3.

However, just as the supplementary benefit level itself is open to question, so too are these implicit weightings. Some studies have suggested that the equivalence scales do not accurately reflect the relative needs of different types of household; in particular, it is argued that the needs of children are underestimated (see Piachaud, 1979, 1981b). If this is correct (and the weight of evidence is strong), it will to some extent affect the relationship between the income measure and living standards: a couple with children who have the same 'adjusted' income as a couple without children would in practice be worse off because their children are more 'costly' than allowed for in the equivalence rates. Several studies have made estimates of alternative equivalence scales based on expenditure patterns (see, for example, Fiegehen *et al.*, 1977, ch. 7). At their simplest level, such aproaches examine how much additional expenditure is incurred for each additional type of person. However, while these studies have all produced ratios similar to those implicit in the supplementary benefit system, no consensus on a precise alternative has emerged.

In the absence of any consensus, this study uses the equivalence

Table C.3 *The equivalence scales implicit in the supplementary benefit rates*

Single person	0.63
Couple	1.00
Child, aged under 11	0.17
Child, aged 11–15	0.26
Additional person	0.50

scales implicit in the supplementary benefit system. Throughout, the income concept used is *equivalent* household income, which is obtained by dividing the household income by its appropriate equivalence scale. Some attempt to allow for the different needs of children has been made by considering households with children separately from households without children, but even then the equivalence scales for children of different ages have had to be accepted. While, in general, other studies suggest that the effect of adjusting the equivalence scales used on the relationship between household equivalent income and living standards would be relatively small (see Fiegehen *at al.*, 1977) it does mean that this relationship may not be as tight as would be the case if other equivalence scales were used.

Housing costs

The next problem relates to the question of housing costs. The income measure taken is *net* equivalent household income, that is, housing costs have *not* been deducted. Some other studies (for example, Layard *et al.*, 1978) have taken instead *disposable* income; that is, they have deducted housing costs. While the arguments are by no means clear-cut, it seemed somewhat circular to deduct housing costs in this study because a number of the measures of living standards related to housing. This does mean, however, that some people with particularly high housing costs will have lower living standards than others in their income bracket.

Time period

Finally, there is the question of the time period to which the income data refer. Respondents were asked only about their income at that moment of time. It was felt that people's knowledge of their income that week or month was likely to be more accurate than their recollection of their income over the year. However, people's incomes do vary considerably over the course of a year: they may have become unemployed, or have just found work; they may be going through a period of unusually high or low overtime; they may have just retired. All these factors will influence a household's living standard at any moment of time. It means that there will be households who have, at that moment of time, the same net equivalent household income but whose background is very different. This, in turn, will have a considerable effect on their relative living standards. In a more comprehensive study it would be worth collecting information on past as well as current income, but in this context it is worth noting that taking weekly and monthly, rather than annual data, would be expected to loosen the relationship between the income measure used and living standards.

Conclusions

This examination of the income concept used has shown that it is limited in terms of the comprehensiveness of the data collected, in terms of the accuracy of the data and in terms of the intrinsic problems of simplifying the vast range of living patterns into comparable measures. Together, all these factors mean that some people will have been grouped as having the same or similar income who in fact have consideraby different incomes. This is of critical importance when the relationship between income and living standards is considered.

References

Abel-Smith, B. and Townsend, P. (1965), *The Poor and the Poorest* (London: Bell).

Bacon, R. and Eltis, W. (1976), *Britain's Economic Problem* (London: Macmillan).

Berger, P. and Luckmann, T. (1967), *The Social Construction of Reality* (Harmondsworth, Middx: Penguin).

Berthoud, R. (1984), *The Reform of Supplementary Benefit*, 2 vols (London: Policy Studies Institute).

Beveridge, W. (1942), *Social Insurance and Allied Services* (The Beveridge Report), Cmnd 6404 (London: HMSO).

Beveridge, W. (1953), *Power and Influence* (London: Hodder & Stoughton).

Booth, C. (1888), 'Conditions and occupations of the people of East London and Hackney', *Journal of the Royal Statistical Society*, vol. 50, No. 1.

Bosanquet, N. (1984), 'Social policy and the welfare state', in R. Jowell and C. Airey (eds), *British Social Attitudes, 1984 Report* (Farnborough, Hants: Gower).

Boyson, R. (1971), *Down with the Poor* (Churchill Press Limited).

Bradshaw, J. and Harris, T. (1983), *Energy and Social Policy* (London: Routledge & Kegan Paul).

Bull, D. and Wilding, P. (1983), *Thatcherism and the Poor* (London: Child Poverty Action Group).

Central Statistical Office (1984), 'The distribution of income in the United Kingdom, 1981/82', *Economic Trends*, July, No. 369 (London: HMSO).

Conservative Central Office (1975), *Speeches by Mrs Thatcher: Let the Children Grow Tall*.

Cooper, S. (1981), *Fuel Poverty in the United Kingdom* (London: Policy Studies Institute).

Crosland, C. A. R. (1964), *The Future of Socialism* (London: Jonathan Cape Paperback).

Department of Employment (1982), *Family Expenditure Survey, 1981* (London: HMSO).

Desai, M. (1981), 'Is poverty a matter of taste?' (unpublished).

DHSS (1983), 'Families with low incomes, 1981' (unpublished).

Donnison, D. (1981), 'A radical strategy to help the poor?', *New Society*, 29 October.

The Economist Intelligence Unit (1982), *Coping with Unemployment* (London: The Economist Intelligence Unit).

EEC (1977), *The Perception of Poverty in Europe* (Brussels: Commission of the European Communities).

EEC (1981), *Final report of the first programme of pilot schemes and studies to combat poverty* (Brussels: Commission of the European Communities).

Engels, F. (1969), *The Condition of the Working Class in England* (London: Panther).

Fiegehen, G. C., Lansley, S. and Smith, A. D. (1977), *Poverty and Progress in Britain, 1953–1973* (Cambridge: Cambridge University Press).

Friedman, M. (1962), *Capitalism and Freedom* (Chicago, Ill.: University of Chicago Press).

Galbraith, J. K. (1970), *The Affluent Society* (Harmondsworth, Middx: Pelican).

Gilmour, I. (1983), *Britain Can Work* (Oxford: Martin Robertson).

Golding, P. and Middleton, S. (1982), *Images of Welfare* (Oxford: Martin Robertson).

Goss, S. and Lansley, S. (1984), *What Price Housing?*, 3rd edn (London: SHAC).

Gough, I. (1979), *The Political Economy of the Welfare State* (London: Macmillan).

Halsey, A. H. (1984), 'A crisis in the welfare state', *The Listener*, 22 March.

Hayek, F. A. (1960), *The Constitution of Liberty* (London: Routledge & Kegan Paul).

Hemming, R. (1984), *Poverty and Incentives* (Oxford: Oxford University Press).

House of Commons (1984), *Perinatal and Neo-Natal Mortality Report: Follow-up*, Third Report from the Social Services Committee, No. 308 (London: HMSO).

Husbands, C. (1982), 'Labour's greasy poll', *New Socialist*, No. 8, November/December.

Institute of Fiscal Studies (1984), *The Reform of Social Security*, prepared by A. Dilnot, J. Kay and C. Morris (Oxford: Oxford University Press).

Joseph, K. and Sumption J. (1979), *Equality* (London: John Murray).

Kincaid, J. C. (1973), *Poverty and Equality in Britain* (Harmondsworth, Middx: Pelican).

Klein, R. (1974), 'The case for elitism', *Political Quarterly*, vol. 45.

Klein, R. (1980), 'The welfare state, a self-inflicted crisis', *Political Quarterly*, vol. 51, no. 4.

Lansley, S. (1979), *Housing and Public Policy* (London: Croom Helm).

Lansley, S. (1980), 'Changes in inequality and poverty in the UK, 1971–1976', *Oxford Economic Papers*, vol. 32, no. 1.

Layard, R., Piachaud, D. and Stewart, M. (1978), *The Causes of Poverty*, Royal Commission on the Distribution of Income and Wealth, Background Paper No. 5. to Report No. 6 (London: HMSO).

Le Grand, J. (1982), *The Strategy of Equality* (London: Allen & Unwin).

Le Grand, J. (1983), 'Making redistribution work', in H. Glennerster (ed.), *The Future of the Welfare State* (London: Heinemann).

Lipsey, D. (1979), 'The reforms people want', *New Society*, 4 October.

LWT (1983), *Breadline Britain*, a booklet accompanying the television series (London: London Weekend Television).

MacGregor, S. (1981), *The Politics of Poverty* (London: Longman).

Marx, K. (1946), *Karl Marx Selected Works* (Lawrence & Wishart).

Minford, P., Davies, D. H., Peel, M. J. and Spragne. A. S. (1983), *Unemployment: Causes and Cure* (Oxford: Martin Robertson).

Minford, P. (1984), 'State expenditure: a study in waste', *Economic Affairs*, vol. 4, no. 3.

Mishra, R. (1984), *The Welfare State in Crisis* (Brighton, Sussex: Wheatsheaf Books).

MORI (1983), *British Public Opinion, General Election 1983* (London: MORI).

MORI (1984), *Breadline Greenwich* (London: MORI).

Murie, A. (1983), *Housing Inequality and Deprivation* (London: Routledge & Kegan Paul).

National Consumer Council (1984), *Social Security: a consumer review*, Working Paper 5, 'Towards a new social income' (London: National Consumer Council).

Neumark, V. (1983), 'Roll over, Beveridge', *Times Educational Supplement*, 9 September.

Orshansky, M. (1969), 'How poverty is measured', *Monthly Labor Review*, February.

Piachaud, D. (1979), *The Cost of a Child* (London: Child Poverty Action Group).

Piachaud, D. (1981a), 'Peter Townsend and the Holy Grail', *New Society*, 10 September.

Piachaud, D. (1981b), *Children and Poverty* (London: Child Poverty Action Group).

Pym, F. (1984), *The Politics of Consent* (London: Hamish Hamilton).

Robbins, Lord (1977), *Liberty and Equality*, IEA Occasional Paper No. 52.

Rowntree, B. S. (1922), *Poverty: A Study of Town Life* (London: Longmans, Green & Co.).

Rowntree, B. S. (1937), *The Human Needs of Labour*, 2nd edn (London: Longmans).

Rowntree, B. S. and Lavers, G. R. (1951), *Poverty and the Welfare State* (London: Longmans).

Royal Commission on the Distribution of Income and Wealth (1979), *Report No. 7, Fourth Report on the Standing References*, Cmnd 7595 (London: HMSO).

Runciman, W. G. (1972), *Relative Deprivation and Social Justice* (Harmondsworth, Middx: Penguin).

Saville, J. (1965), 'Labour and income distribution', in *The Socialist Register* (London: Merlin Press).

SDP (1982), *Attacking Poverty* (London: Social Democratic Party Policy Department).

Sen, A. K. (1978), *Three Notes on the Concept of Poverty*, (Geneva: International Labour Organisation).

Sen, A. K. (1982), *Poverty and Famines* (Oxford: Oxford University Press).

Sen, A. K. (1984), 'The new economic gospel', *New Society*, 26 July.

Smith, A. (1812), *The Wealth of Nations* (Ward).

Taylor-Gooby, P. (1983a), 'Moralism, self-interest and attitudes to welfare', *Policy and Politics*, Spring.

Taylor-Gooby, P. (1983b), 'Public belt and private braces', *New Society*, 14 April.

Titmuss, R. (1950), *Problems of Social Policy* (London: HMSO and Longmans).

Townsend, P. (1979), *Poverty in the United Kingdom* (Harmondsworth, Middx: Penguin).

Townsend, P. (1981), 'Peter Townsend replies', *New Society*, 17 September.

Townsend, P. (1983), 'A theory of poverty and the role of social policy', in M. Loney (ed.), *Social Policy and Social Welfare* (Bletchley, Bucks: Open University Press).

Townsend, P. (1984), *Fewer Children, More Poverty: An Incomes Plan* (Bristol, University of Bristol).

Townsend, P. and Davidson, N. (1982), *Inequalities in Health, The Black Report* (Harmondsworth, Middx: Penguin).

Townsend, P., Simpson, D. and Tibbs, N. (1984), *Inequalities in Health in the City of Bristol* (Bristol: University of Bristol).

Treasury (1984), *The Next Ten Years, Public Expenditure and Taxation into the 1990s*, Cmnd 9189 (London: HMSO).

van Praag, B., Hagenaars, A. and van Weeren, H. (1980), *Poverty in Europe* (CERPEC, University of Leyden).

van Praag, B., Hagenaars, A. and van Weeren, H. (1981), 'Poverty in Europe' (unpublished).

Walker, D. (1983), 'Cathy comes back for a handout', *The Times*, 25 August.

Waugh, A. (1983), 'On the breadline', *The Spectator*, 5 November.

Wedderburn, D. (1981), 'Review of P. Townsend, Poverty in the United Kingdom', *British Journal of Sociology*, vol. 32, no. 2.

Whiteley, P. (1981). 'Public opinion and the demand for social welfare in Britain', *Journal of Social Policy*, vol. 10, part 4.

The *Breadline Britain* television series is available on video-tape. Details can be obtained from:

> The Community Education Officer,
> London Weekend Television,
> Kent House,
> Upper Ground,
> London, SE1 9LT.

Index